A Life of One's Own

A Life of One's Own

CHILDHOOD AND YOUTH

BY

GERALD BRENAN

CAMBRIDGE UNIVERSITY PRESS

CAMBRIDGE

LONDON · NEW YORK · MELBOURNE

Published by the Syndics of the Cambridge University Press
The Pitt Building, Trumpington Street, Cambridge CB2 1RP
Bentley House, 200 Euston Road, London NW1 2DB
32 East 57th Street, New York, NY 10022, USA
296 Beaconsfield Parade, Middle Park, Melbourne 3206, Australia

First published by Jonathan Cape Ltd 1962
Paperback edition first published by the Cambridge University Press 1979

Printed in the United States of America
First printed in Great Britain by Redwood Burn Ltd, Trowbridge and Esher
Reprinted by Hamilton Printing Company, Rensselaer, New York

ISBN 0 521 29734 6 paperback

TO
DAVID GARNETT

Contents

Illustrations

Preface

Anyone who sits down to write his autobiography should, I think, ask himself why he is doing it. Those three or four hundred pages devoted to his probably quite undistinguished life and doings call for some explanation. It is not enough to say with Sartre that in subjectivity one discovers other people as well as oneself. The fact remains that the autobiographer is asking a large number of men and women whom he does not know to take an interest in his personal affairs.

Yet autobiography is a recognized form of literature. It shows life from an angle that is very different from that of the novel. There is besides a quality about things that have actually been experienced, and are known by the reader to have been experienced, that nothing else can supply. Even though the motive for writing may be mere self-display, such an account, if sufficiently well done, can please and interest.

It was with these thoughts in my mind that I started on the present book. I lacked a subject for a novel and found my own life ready to hand. The plot was given, the characters and the incidents were there —all I had to do was to remember and arrange. When I started I thought that I should not remember much because I had long lost all interest in my early self, but I soon found that memories poured in. And with the memories came the plan that I must follow.

A life is like a long journey in a train. There is the scenery that rolls by outside and there are the incidents that take place in the carriage. I saw at once that I must confine myself mainly to the carriage. That is to say, I must write upon the things that had closely concerned myself and say little of the rest, which in any case I did not remember so clearly Gradually therefore the book grew into an account of the development of the sensibility and character of the child, the boy, the adolescent who, under the pressures and stimulations of his environment, has evolved into my present self. As I wrote on, I was surprised to see how much continuity there was in his nature and how closely the chain of cause and effect could be followed.

With adolescence the story quickens into one of rebellion against and escape from a too narrow and constricting form of life. I turned against pretty well everything that I saw around me. Since I was fighting for myself alone this meant that I became very wrapped up in my thoughts and ideas. Adolescence is the classic age for egoism and I had to lace myself up in mine as in an armour to withstand the pressure on me from the world outside. This affords a certain amount of comedy, but it did not, I fear, make me very likeable. All I can claim is that I had the virtues of my fanaticism and that without it I should never have succeeded in breaking loose from the groove in which I was confined or in developing gradually and after many false starts and failures such literary talent as I had. The struggle to escape and to acquire a life of my own inevitably provides the main theme of this book.

According to Goethe, autobiography is a literary form lying somewhere between biography and the novel. It is controlled by actuality, but is seen from within through memory. That is to say, memory is the ordering and sifting principle, from which it follows that one should refrain from quoting documents or letters because then the angle of approach will be shifted to the very different one of the biographer. I have followed this rule except in the chapters that deal with my experiences in the war, where I felt that the inclusion of a few passages from letters would give a greater vividness and immediacy. But I do not agree with Goethe that any embellishment of one's memories is permissible. On the contrary, I think that the truth is so important that whenever it was possible I have checked the accuracy of my recollections from other sources. The same thing applies to omissions, so that, though this book makes no claim to being a confession, I have been careful not to suppress things that seemed worth recording merely because they threw an unfavourable light on myself.

Finally I would like to say why I have devoted nearly a third of this volume to my childhood. I have done so because I believe this to be the most formative period in anyone's life and that an autobiography which leaves it out condemns itself to superficiality. By the time that a man is twenty all the main features of his character and temperament will have appeared and the rest of his life will merely be spent in making what adjustments he can among them. A book such as this which aims at tracing the growth and formation of a human being will therefore have to devote a fair amount of space to the early years.

CHAPTER I

First Years

I was born, if my birth certificate is right, in Malta on 7 April 1894. My father, though English, was a subaltern in an Irish regiment and my mother, who was eight years older than he, was the daughter of a Belfast linen manufacturer. My birth had been difficult and had taken place just ten months after their marriage.

The accounts I have been given of the little creature that bore my name are not flattering. I had, it seems, a yellow, wrinkled face like a Chinese baby, long, straight, black hair and for many weeks I screamed day and night whenever I was not sleeping. The reason for this, I imagine, was that my mother was too ill to nurse me. Since baby foods had not been invented and nobody seems to have thought of a wet nurse, a she-ass which had recently foaled was procured to give me her milk. Then, as my mother continued to be ill and I fell ill too, my father obtained permission to be transferred to his regimental depot in Northern Ireland. Berths were taken on a P. and O. steamer, my foster-mother and the foal were installed in a place close to my cabin and in this manner we set sail for Plymouth.

My mother has often described to me the horrors of this voyage. We ran into a storm off the coast of Portugal, everyone was very sick and the cabin became filled with cockroaches. Since I could not keep down my milk and lay in a coma, the doctor was sent for. He arrived reeling drunk and breathing out fumes of whisky. 'Madam,' he pronounced in a thick voice after a long, dazed stare at my cot, 'Madam, you're washting your time in shending for me. Our lasht voyage out we had a baby that looked like this. Jusht put it through the porthole.'

However, thanks to my nurse's care, I got through the next few days and we landed at Plymouth. But here a new difficulty arose. The railway officials refused to convey a she-ass in one of their compartments unless a whole carriage was reserved. This at great expense was done and we reached Liverpool and finally Belfast without being separated. My grandmother, to whose house we had gone, was so pleased by the oddity of this journey that she declared that my foster-brother should be brought up in the nursery with me. Whether this was actually attempted I cannot say, but I do know that when, some years later, I had my first riding lessons on him, he proved to be a vicious little brute and took a special delight in bucking me off.

In the fresh country air of my grandmother's house and park I revised my appearance. My hair became fair, my cheeks pink and chubby and my temper improved. Although the diary which my mother kept of my early years—a big black album which I have before me on the table—records many astonishing things, such as the appearance of my first tooth, my precocious love of picture-books and certain witty and epigrammatic sayings, it does not seem likely that I was different from any other small child. But I was destined to see more of the world than most, for in 1897, after a brief stay at Chichester, we took the boat for Cape Town and from there to Durban. My father's battalion had been ordered to go into camp at a small township called Ladysmith, situated on the veldt some 3,000 feet above the sea.

We spent a year and a half at this place—from May 1897 till December 1898—and these months were the happiest of my childhood. For some time, until I was nine or ten, I retained a special feeling for them, comparing the dull life I was leading, the cross faces of governesses and the dark, rainy days, with this sunlit, stationary period. Our house was a very small corrugated-iron bungalow standing a mile or so outside the town, with a boulder-strewn kopje rising immediately behind it and in front, at the foot of a strip of baked garden, a gully which ran into the River Klip. The building was a mere tin box of a place, lost in the red, sun-flattened landscape. It consisted of four diminutive rooms lined with matchboarding and a narrow verandah that ran along the front: behind it were the kitchen and the Kaffir servants' quarters, also of tin, the tent in which my parents slept, and stables for the ponies. A few straggling thorn trees and mimosas gave a pretence of shade, while a mile away across the veldt, its white tents gleaming in the evening light, lay the camp. Every morning its bugles woke us.

We were a party of six. There was first of all my nurse, Annie, with whom I shared a room. She was a large, stoutly built woman who before my birth had been my mother's maid: at this time she must have been about twenty-eight. Nana, as I have always called her, was one of those people of whom there is little to be said except that they are good. Because of some impediment in her mind, she could not communicate: her large, pink and white face and pale blue eyes would beam with a steady benevolence, but nothing was put into words. She expressed herself therefore in her actions and no woman was ever more reliable or more devoted.

The other members of our party besides my parents were my English grandmother—that is, my father's mother—and her only daughter, my Aunt Maude. The distinction between my two grandmothers is capital, so I will make it at once. My Irish grandmother, in whose house I had spent the first two years of my life, dressed and looked like Queen Victoria. She wore a long, black silk dress that rustled as she walked, a white cap on her head and, in the mornings, a silver chatelaine at her waist. Her pleasant, round, plain face and portly figure conveyed age and a homely dignity, in spite of the fact that her hair was still brown. She looked what she was—an old-fashioned country gentlewoman, taken up with the management of a house and estate, its servants, its grooms and its home farm.

My English grandmother was as different from this as possible. She was a Londoner born and bred and lived in a flat off Sloane Square. No doubt because she was much younger than her Irish counterpart, she had unconsciously taken as her model not Queen Victoria but (as she would soon be) Queen Alexandra. In her youth she had been uncommonly pretty in a rather kittenish sort of way, with finely set eyes, delicate features and a good figure and, as she grew older, she set herself to counteract the effects of time by giving more attention to her dress. She always looked elegant, and the number of trunks with which she travelled and the variety of multicoloured garments that came out of them were a subject of astonishment to my mother's soberly apparelled family. But she was not—to put it mildly—a clever woman and was totally lacking in a sense of humour. There would have been little to attract one to her if she had not had a sweet and gentle disposition which was never ruffled by the fact that, like the queen she admired, she was deaf. Although not naturally drawn to children, she showed great patience with me, and I, fascinated by her immobility, by her low whispering voice and by her collapsible ear-trumpet, responded warmly.

Her daughter Maude was a pert, plain, lively girl of twenty. At my Irish grandmother's house she had not made a good impression: they found her 'fast'. She committed the crime of riding a bicycle before it was correct for girls to ride one and of flirting in the wrong way and at the wrong times with the wrong young men. I did not as a small child greatly care for her either: I associated her with marmalade, whose sharp taste I did not like, and felt a grudge against her for not spoiling me. But I recognized her singularity: on my mother's side I had many uncles and aunts, while she was the only one who belonged to my father's. I imagined therefore that everyone had an Aunt Maude, just as everyone had two grandmothers, and that such a relationship was one to be treasured.

Of the four women who surrounded me the one I cared for most, and by a long way, was my mother. I can see her now, seated on the verandah in her white piqué dress with its leg-of-mutton sleeves. On her head is a shady straw hat trimmed with brown ribbons, and in front of her is a table with a silver tea-service. Then beside her appears a delicate-looking, rather priggish little boy with dark eyes, who is dressed in white duck shorts and a cotton blouse. This is myself, for I have transposed upon my original memory another later memory of a photograph.

My mother used to give me lessons every day after tea, before my father got back from the camp. First there was a reading lesson, then came history, geography and scripture. History I learned, as every child should learn it, from a large picture-book. Boadicea in her war chariot, Alfred watching the cakes burning, Edward I lying on a stretcher and ordering his body to be boiled. What a wonderful collection of stories and, unlike other stories, all true! Geography came to me through a less seductive channel, in three fat little books written as propaganda for foreign missions. They were stupid, goody-goody tomes, consisting almost entirely of conversations between lady missionaries and reclaimed children of heathen parentage. But they had illustrations. It was these that I looked at and, miserable though they were, for there was always some angular, stiff-skirted missionary plumped in the foreground, they filled my mind with a longing for travel and foreign countries. Thus, with my mother's encouragement, they helped to instil into me what has been, with literature, the most persistent passion of my life.

I say—with my mother's encouragement. Almost every interest I have ever had has come from her. She was not an intellectual or even a clever woman, but she had an eagerness and curiosity for life with which she infected me. This was particularly the case with my love for foreign countries. As a girl of twenty-four she had done the Grand Tour with a maid and a cousin, travelling through Italy in slow stages as far as Naples and returning by the Rhine. Every available hour of that journey had been spent in sightseeing, as this cousin, who did not like sights, used to complain. After that she had visited Paris and spent a winter in Cairo, where she had met my father. Now, in Ladysmith, all these recollections were poured out on me, filling me with a curiosity about the world and its desirable places.

The geographical zest thus imparted to me invaded everything. It lent its colour to natural history, since behind the animal or plant I sought the jungle or mountain where it was to be found. It likewise threw its mantle over scripture. That was fortunate, because my mother was a very religious woman and every day read me stories and passages from the Bible. The New Testament, for example, bored me: this Jesus seemed to me a very dim sort of person, and the tone in which people spoke of him—like that in which some grown-ups address children—was highly unconvincing. But the people of Genesis and Exodus belonged to my world. Their family histories, their loves and hates and cunning and generosity were something I could enter into and take sides in. Thus I felt drawn to Esau and Reuben and detested Jacob and Joseph, revered Abraham but thought poorly of Lot and Noah. And then did they not all 'dwell' in tents, 'sojourn' in wildernesses and 'depart' on camels? And have such names as Huz and Buz and Mehajael and Tubal-cain and Isaac and Aaron? (Oh, the poetry that stared out from those vibrating double *a*'s!) And witness extraordinary scenes—the burning of the Cities of the Plain, the plagues of frogs and of blood, the crossing of the dry bed of the sea, the dancing round the Golden Calf (my mother said it was a cow), the capture of Jericho? My sense of reality and my love of the marvellous were simultaneously satisfied and I envied my grandmother who I thought must have lived in those times. One day I was heard asking her—and it was not a question that she found amusing—if she had ever known Pharaoh.

Among the Old Testament worthies my favourite by a long way was Moses. The story of his floating down the river in a basket of sedge and being rescued by Pharoah's daughter charmed me. I would like to have floated down a river in a reed basket too. Then there was the magician scene where he defied Rameses, the dramatic flight from Egypt and the interview with God among the dense clouds of Mount Sinai. When I was older this alarming occasion would rise inconsequently in my mind whenever I was sent for to receive a talking-to in my father's smoking-room. It seemed to set the tone for one-sided conversations of this sort. But what confirmed my interest in Moses was the mysterious manner of his death and burial on Mount Nebo. I knew all about this from some verses which my mother used to sing in her high treble voice whenever she wished to keep me quiet. They had been written by a certain Mrs Alexander, wife of the Archbishop of Armagh and author of several well-known hymns, who had been an occasional visitor at my grandmother's house. They began on a rather low and plaintive note:

> *By Nebo's lonely mountain*
> *On this side Jordan's wave,*
> *In a vale in the land of Moab*
> *There lies a lonely grave.*

Then one climbed up to the lines—

> *What though the bald old eagle*
> *On grey Beth-peor's height . . .*

which seemed to me to convey all that there was to be felt on the solitude of mountains, while at the end, if I remember correctly, came the climax with its contrast of long and short vowel sounds, so steeped in nostalgia and melancholy:

> *And no man knows the sepulchre,*
> *And no man saw it e'er.*
> *For the angel of God upturned the sod*
> *And laid the dead man there.*

When one is four and a half poetry is not so much a means of access to an inner world as an incitement to action, so I firmly resolved that when I was grown up I would lead an expedition to discover the site of Moses' grave on Mount Nebo. And meanwhile I had had my first introduction to romantic literature, for the only other poems I knew came from Mother Goose. Although I liked them very much, they were static—that is, content to be themselves. But Mrs Alexander's verse with its sonorous overtones streamed out into the future.

As I recollect it now, an Old Testament air hangs thick and heavy over this sun-drenched age and land. The Kaffir women with their long pendulous breasts, naked except for a bead loin-cloth, were the Amalekites or the Canaanites. I imagined them addicted to dark but fascinating 'abominations' whose precise nature I did not understand: possibly they sacrificed on high places or danced round a cow. The burned-up plain of the veldt, the rock-crowned kopjes that rose above it were the Wilderness, which privately I far preferred to the Promised Land. And were not the cattle standing in the river, the circles of Kaffir kraals, the herdsmen with their long staves, the slow-moving ox-wagons all emblems of the nomadic, pastoral life? One evening, I have been told, after my mother had read to me the story of Jacob's dream, I vanished and was found lying on the edge of the gully with my head on a stone. I wanted, I said, to see the angels ascending and descending on the ladder as Jacob had done. On another occasion I ate a locust, after toasting it in the fire, in imitation of St John the Baptist and can still recall its acrid, pungent taste. And I kept in my playbox a couple of wooden Kaffir dolls, which I told my mother were my *teraphim*.

One may laugh at these absurdities and yet I believe that I learned a great deal from my saturation in the Old Testament stories and customs. They provided another level, remote yet real, onto which I could project my life. Then where better than in the Bible, which is an English book as well as a Hebrew one, can we throw down a root into the primitive experience of mankind? I especially gained by being introduced to it at an early age, since the disagreeably smug and priestly tone of so many of its passages and the religious or political fanaticism of others then passed unnoticed. I took only what I wanted. And that was the picture of nomadic life in the Wilderness, threatened and watched over by an unpredictable Power, who lurked ominously like the desert wind, like the towering rock mountain, like some half-forgotten memory of fear, in the background.

The last member of our family circle of whom I must speak was my father. I remember him as the person who brought into my life a masculine dash and excitement, chiefly in connection with horses. In Malta he had acquired a taste for driving a tandem, but here the roads were too rough for any wheeled traffic but the ox-wagon, so he took up polo and steeplechasing instead. I remember him jumping his horse over a fence that he had put up by our compound, the horse falling, and he lying motionless. He was in bed for several weeks after with concussion.

But, racing and polo apart, horses were indispensable if one wished to get about the country. We had half a dozen Cape ponies and everyone, including my grandmother, had a mount. I rode too. My father would take me in front of him on his saddle and in this way we would visit the town, which offered the inducement of a sweet shop, or ride out over the surrounding veldt. I enjoyed these expeditions immensely. One of my more vivid recollections is of cantering along by the side of the Klip River under some mimosa trees, which made us both stoop low over the horse's neck. As I looked down, the dust flew up under its hooves and the earth raced past. When later on I wished to make this recollection as significant to other people as for some unknown reason it was to myself, I would add, 'You see, in the river there were hippopotamuses.'

My father was not at this time the dominating and frightening figure that he later became to me. Perhaps this was because I did not see a great deal of him, since except on Sundays he did not usually get home from the camp before my bedtime. When I thought of him, it was less, I imagine, as a person than as the head of that very sacred and unique thing—our family. As a first approximation to his character I will say that he was a typical soldier. He liked riding, jumping, playing polo, cutting a figure in a smart uniform and he was fond of good stories and of practical jokes. Yet he was not really a sociable man: he drank little and after dinner used to fall asleep in one of the cane chairs in the mess, which, together with his prickly and irritable disposition, had led a cartoonist who visited the regiment in Malta to draw him as a hedgehog. But when he was awake, he was very awake, talking in a clear, matter-of-fact tone that in the family circle could easily become abrupt and cutting, and laughing when anything amused him in a whole-hearted, staccato way. He was always very much himself, very concrete and definite, and he was completely lacking in imagination.

I suppose that my feelings about him must always have been mixed, because I have been told that from the day of my birth he was jealous of me. (Why is it that we attribute so much to the jealousy of Oedipus and so little to that of his father Laius—to that universal male dread of the first-born which in early times led to their being exposed on mountain tops?) I believe, however, that what I chiefly had against him at this time was that he teased me and played practical jokes on me. Although it is no doubt good for children to be teased a little— for how defenceless are the people who have never been laughed at! —the teaser does not often win the thanks that are due to him. And then, when I tried to answer my father back and went too far, he would suddenly assume the manner of a stern parent. One played a game and found the dice loaded against one.

Whenever my elders have talked to me about my childhood, they have always ended by saying, 'You were the most mischievous child I have ever known.' According to them, I cut the fingers off my mother's gloves, planted the artificial flowers from my grandmother's best hat in the garden, gave the belt of my father's dress uniform to a Kaffir, tried to make a tent of the chintz chair-covers. They never knew what I would do next, and it was of no use scolding me because I had no idea that I was acting wrong. I do not myself remember any of these things, but since this mischievousness, if that is the correct word for it, persisted till it was beaten out of me at school, I set it down here.

What I do remember concerns not my acts but my private experiences. Through the general atmosphere of fog that envelops my early years, some of these stand out with surprising distinctness, though whether this is because they had a special importance for my later life I cannot say. Thus I remember the great cloud of dust that rose over the veldt whenever an ox-cart or a squad of soldiers passed along the road. And I remember watching through the nursery window the long white pencils of the rain falling one by one upon a puddle and turning it into an instantaneous flower. Then comes a somewhat different sort of recollection. Down by the gully, on the furthest limit of our compound, was a place that I felt to be sinister and uncanny. I had once found a hen's egg there, lying white and inert like an unexploded bomb on a bed of red dust. There it lay, smooth and inexplicable, far from the hen-run where the other eggs were laid. When I broke it, it was addled. There were also, among the stones and dry grasses above the bank, a great many grasshoppers. When I caught one and pulled off its legs, I had an unpleasant sensation. For this place, something told me, was evil. I went there, if I interpret my feeling aright, when the craving for evil came over me, when I wanted to think about 'abominations'. But I do not think that I ever 'did' anything, for what was there that I could do? The practical side of evil, the steps I must take to commit some positive act of iniquity, eluded me: my ignorance made me passive. All I could manage was to allow the spirit of the place to sink into me and corrupt me. For it should be remembered that I had as yet no *I* in those days (I still spoke of myself by my Christian name), but was merely a fragment of floating receptivity, struggling to create, with the help of the not-I, its own separate identity and legend. For that an acquaintance with evil was essential.

In contrast to these somewhat morbid recollections, I have others of an entirely different sort. For example, my early childhood was filled with romantic thoughts about girls. When I first arrived at Ladysmith I imagined that—in the phrase my elders used—'my heart was given' to my cousin Helen, a girl a few years older than myself with whom I had played in Ireland. Her photograph, showing a child of five with a straight fringe over the forehead, stood on the drawing-room mantelpiece. Then there crossed my vision an incomparable creature called Marjorie. She was the daughter of our colonel and to reach her house I had to pass over a torrent or river on a single plank. I remember my nurse taking me to tea there and my fear of the swirling water that ran below. Soon after this a party was given on my fourth birthday and Marjorie was invited. I can still recall the excitement with which I looked forward to this moment, when she would see me in all the glory of my new age and of a sugar-coated cake. But the sun that rose on that day rose on a catastrophe. When Marjorie was put at the table beside me I was too shy to speak to her and although my nurse brought us together again after tea, setting us side by side and alone on a heap of dry grass, I was still tongue-tied. After this she vanishes from my memory, though the name Marjorie long remained inscribed on my private scroll of significant names.

Yet it was not so thrilling, not so charged with nostalgic overtones as the name Nancy. The reason for this preference was that my nurse used to sing me a soldiers' song about a girl of that name, which she had picked up, I imagine, at the camp. Although I have never come across it since, I can recollect the first verse:

> *Oh! give my love to Nancy.*
> *She's the girl that I ado-re.*
> *Tell her that I'll never, never*
> *See her any mo-re.*

This song, simply perhaps because it was a song—the only one that I had heard besides the verses of Mrs Alexander and a few hymns—moved me deeply. And so my feelings for it singled out, as the most important word in it, the girl's name. This was the more natural because names, both of people and of places, meant a great deal to me. Out of those in the Old Testament I had conjured up figures of cloudy importance who had walked in the world in ancient times. But names of meetable, fall-in-love-withable girls could be equally affecting, although they belonged to a different category. Thus on the strength of a song I fell in love with this Nancy and with all possible Nancys, wherever they might be found; for since every blue flower must contain some of the essence that is conveyed by the word blue, so every Nancy must ineluctably participate in the original, pathetic, slightly low-down, agonizingly heart-breaking conception which the name in this song contained. This meant that for years I went about the world looking for girls called Nancy and when at length at the age of fourteen I found one, I immediately fell in love with her.

Eros, however, is a god with a double face and here I must set down an experience of a very different sort. My love for little girls was as pure and chaste as Dante's for Beatrice, but I was also troubled by a curiosity about the configuration of grown-up women's bodies and just what it was that distinguished them from men. I saw the Kaffir wives with their long gourd-like breasts and rounded bellies, swaying as they walked under the weight of the baskets they carried on their heads, and wondered what one would find if one looked below their bead aprons. One night I discovered. A scorpion came out of a hole in the wall just above my cot and frightened me. My nurse put me into her bed. When later she got in beside me, I woke and, as soon as I thought her asleep, plunged down under the bedclothes to discover what I wanted to know. On this she stirred and pulled me back again to the top. But I waited and as soon as she was asleep again renewed my quest. I give this apparently trifling incident because, first of all, I remember it extremely clearly and secondly because I believe that this division I had made of sex into two different compartments was to have an effect upon my after life.

I have left till last what I believe to be my happiest memories of these years, because they are not of people but of flowers. The passion I had for them—it still continues in a diluted form today—I owe, like almost everything else that I value in myself, to my mother. She had been a great collector of wild flowers from her youth up and her copy of Bentham's *Flora*, which I now possess, is scribbled over with pencil notes and dates. When I was two she had given me a copy of Anne Pratt, but in Africa this book was useless. To take its place I had a large, illustrated *Child's Life of Christ* that had been presented to me by my nurse. The text did not interest me for the reasons I have already stated, but some of the illustrations did. I liked the scenes of deserts, camels and fishing-boats, but what were much more to the point were the ornamental capitals with which each chapter began. Round these, so small that only a child's eye would have noticed them, were drawn the principal flowers of the Holy Land, and some of these flowers or others very like them were to be found at Ladysmith too.

How surprising are these faces that rise with their symmetrical petals and their fresh, pure colours out of the bare earth! Only familiarity—that poison that slowly spreads through us as we grow older—could dull our minds to them. At four they seemed to me so amazing in their beauty as to take the breath away. I wanted to drink them into myself, to make them part of me. No doubt the contrast to be observed in South Africa between the brilliance of the flora and the dryness and desolation of the landscape is specially striking. When one comes suddenly, among the withered grasses of the veldt, on some bright, gleaming calyx, one cannot repress a thrill of excitement. I remember in particular finding for the first time the Belladonna Lily in bloom. It grew abundantly round our compound and, before it flowered, its great brown bulbs, projecting a little from the earth under their papery coverings and throwing up a jet of tongue-like leaves, had aroused my curiosity. Then one day I went a little further than usual and saw something I could not believe was possible. On the summit of a tall stem, starting out on all sides like trumpets, were a number of huge pink-and-white, lily-shaped flowers. Inside each of these a tinge of green spread outwards into a sky of the purest white and rose, delicately veined and dotted with small red-and-gold markings. A delicious fragrance came out of them.

But *Amaryllis belladonna* was not the only lily of the African fields. Other bulbous plants—gladioli, ixias, nerines, ammocharis—dotted the veldt, thrusting their way up through the baked earth into the sunlight. Then there were the anemones, cousins of those gay, light-hearted annuals that came up after the rains, the everlasting flowers with their papery petals and, on the kopje behind our compound, a riot of scarlet red-hot-poker plants, growing on trunks a foot or two high that expanded into rosettes of sharp-pointed leaves.

Our garden too had its European colonists—zinnias which grew to a great size, French marigolds and two creepers—the blue ipomea or morning glory and the passion flower. There was also a sterile fig tree, which I connected with disagreeable things, and a Pride of India tree (*Melia azedarach*), easy to climb, with fang-like violet flowers that seemed to be spitting out their deep purple pistils, and a faint but delicious scent. I associated all these flowers with girls. I used to pick them one by one and, sitting down under the verandah, would arrange them in a circle, pretending that they were court ladies and that I was a prince. Flowers—aren't they the invariable symbols for girls in every folk poetry?

I will give an example of the very sharp eye I developed for these plants. On the railway station at Ladysmith there grew an oleander. I saw it only once when I was leaving, and then for the briefest moment. But there was a tiny engraving of it in my *Child's Life of Christ* because it was one of the plants that grew in Palestine, and so I memorized the name. Twenty-one years later I was walking down a dry watercourse in Spain. All at once I saw a bush with glossy lanceolate leaves and whorled rose-coloured blossoms. It was an oleander: I recognized it immediately from my recollection of the plant on the Ladysmith railway station, in spite of the fact that I had no idea that it grew wild in Europe.

A suffused yellow light colours these distant scenes as I call them up in my mind: the yellow of perpetual sunlight, of coarse dry grass and rolling plains. But also the yellow of dim and faded photographs. How much do we remember of our early childhood? Directly, I think, almost nothing. All the memories we keep after we are grown up are echoes of earlier rememberings. And into these rememberings have drifted fragments of things that our parents have told us, as well as images from the family photo album. I have been told that when I was small I talked of myself in the third person for longer than most children do, and as I write now it is a little white-clothed boy, only tenuously connected with my present self, that I see. But the child is father to the man and in the recorded experiences of this little boy I see a pattern that is still repeating itself.

In the spring of 1898 we went on a few days' excursion to Harrismith in the Orange Free State. The train climbed slowly up Van Reenan's Pass, which leads through the Drakensberg Mountains to the plateau beyond. Brilliant scarlet creepers hung from the rocks and in the riverbed far below we could see the white bones and huge horns of innumerable dead cattle. It was the year of the rinderpest and the sick animals went to the water to die. This contrast of scarlet flowers with rocks and horns and white rib-bones made a great impression on me. A few days later there was a picnic on an ox-wagon to the Platt Mountains in which some thirty people took part. The oxen moved so slowly that we were able to get down and pick flowers. Then on the way home a thunderstorm came up with a great display of thunder, lightning and black cloud, and we were drenched. With a thrill of self-importance I asked my mother if God was angry with us: I was imagining that we were the Children of Israel on their wanderings and that the Platt Mountains were Sinai.

At the end of the year my father's regiment got orders to sail for India. The Boer War was about to break out, but the War Office did not lightly alter its routine and so the brigade which had reconnoitred and mapped the frontiers of Natal was exchanged for one which did not know the country. We therefore packed up our things and moved down to a hotel at Howick to spend Christmas. My nurse was leaving us: on the boat out she had met and become engaged to a mining engineer who, to my father's disgust, earned as much as a lieutenant-colonel. A man who came down to breakfast unshaved!

I scarcely remember the famous waterfall, three hundred feet high, which brings the tourists to Howick: another memory overlays it— that of a marshy lake surrounded by a belt of white arum lilies. I could pick all I wanted. This botanical excursion was my nurse's parting present. Then we sailed from Durban, my father in a troopship, my mother and myself in a 1,400-ton cargo-boat bound for Colombo.

On our way we called at Beira and at the Seychelle Islands. I remember the coconut palms, their trunks anchoring them like wind-tugged ropes to the ground. I remember the feeling I got of an island lying becalmed in the sea and of its water-bound isolation. Then we disembarked at Colombo and put up at the Galle Face Hotel. Here the great feature was the crows: they were so tame that they flew in at the bedroom window and snatched the biscuits of our early-morning tea off the tray. This was rather a frightening experience for a little boy, since in relation to my size they were as large as vultures and much more lively. When I saw their glossy wings beat the air as they hovered, felt the power of the muscles that drove their necks forward and snapped their beaks, I drew back to the far end of my bed. But when the window was shut and the wings flapped vainly against the blue sky and the raucous caws came thickly through the glass, I felt a sudden disappointment.

I have another memory of walking with my mother on the sandy shore beside the crashing breakers and picking up small white and rose-coloured whorled shells. But something was the matter. I did not want the shells. A deep sadness lay on everything. A day or two later the reason for this became clear, for I ran up a high temperature and was taken to hospital with typhoid. In the ward next to me two men died, but thanks to the devotion of the nurse who had charge of me I pulled through.

As soon as I was strong enough to be moved we went up to the hills. For me this meant a native ayah to look after me and more flowers. Those in the hedgerows had no names and therefore seemed hardly real or possessible, but in the garden there were hydrangeas, periwinkles and plumbago. My Uncle Charlie turned up in very boisterous spirits with a tame cheetah and everyone except myself climbed Adam's Peak. Yet although I did not climb it I have a distinct visual memory of doing so—of a hillside covered with high, waving grass, of a wood in which a leopard slunk away between the tree trunks and of my Uncle Charlie in a red knitted waistcoat and white topee shouting and firing. I must have incorporated an account of the ascent given me by my mother in my own experience.

From Nuwara Eliya we came down to Kandy and I was taken to see the Temple of the Tooth. What interested me here were the sacred tortoises, swimming about in a large stone tank. The idea of animals being sacred, just as John the Baptist and Jesus were sacred, pleased me. At Ladysmith my grandmother had kept a tame chameleon called Joseph and I thought that, as he was rather peculiar, he might well have been sacred too. Then a few days later we were back in Colombo and my father left for India. The hot season was coming on so, instead of accompanying him, my mother and I took berths for England. We sailed in April 1899, a few days after my fifth birthday.

The best part of my childhood was now coming to an end. For many years after this—till I was ten or twelve—I used to look back on the days I had spent in South Africa as a sort of Eden, never again to be matched in happiness and delight. I have the impression that my mental faculties, which had shot ahead in the bracing climate and feminine environment of Ladysmith, now began to slow down and to encounter difficulties. And while I naturally remember a greater number of details about the next five years of my life, these memories have a more prosaic setting.

A last flare-up of early feelings occurred when, on our voyage home, I was taken on deck to see Mount Sinai by moonlight. There it lay, floating on the sea in its many folds, made of a finer and more cloud-like substance than other mountains. A haze enveloped its base and the waters before it glittered in the moonlight like a network of fishes. I made, I suppose, my vows to visit it some day and then, after a little speculation as to the site where the Israelites had crossed the Red Sea (my mother, who in Old Testament matters inclined to the views of Bishop Colenso, favoured the dull if plausible theory that it was through the Brine Lakes, whereas I stood out for the more literal hypothesis), said goodbye for ever to Moses and the Book of Genesis.

CHAPTER II

India and Ireland

On our arrival in England we stayed for a few weeks in London. My mother, with the strong desire she always had to arouse my curiosity and to implant in me a love of the things that interested her, took me to see the sights. It was those associated with long-past ages and with spectacular deaths that made the strongest impression on me—the mummies of the Pharaohs in the British Museum, the spot where Sir Walter Raleigh had been beheaded in the Tower, and the tomb of Edward I in Westminster Abbey. Even more thrilling were the bones of the prehistoric saurians in the South Kensington Museum. They were the creatures who had lived before the Flood and had an even better than Genesis colouring.

June came and we crossed to my grandmother's house in Ireland. Here the children led a segregated life under the eye of nurses, but before I had accustomed myself to this we were off again, sailing in the *City of Corinth* liner for Calcutta. Once more I was shut up with my mother in the small, tense society of an eastward-bound steamer, watching the waves roll endlessly by, watching the dolphins and the flying-fish chase one another and letting my imagination loose like the dove in the Ark whenever we had a sight of land.

Our first stopping place was Malta. We went ashore, and I had the strange experience of being shown the house where I had been born. Here, at one particular moment, I had come into the world and before that, incomprehensible thought, had not existed. At the age of five and a half this fact is much more striking than that other parallel one that some day one will die. Then we passed through the Suez Canal, where the camels walked in single file along the banks, just as they did in the picture-books, and came to the hot, quivering rocks of Aden. The boat was full of lady missionaries, bound for the land where, in the words of the hymn, 'only man is vile', and my mother, who would have half-liked to be a missionary herself, made friends with some of them. One evening, as we were passing Ceylon, one of these ladies took me up on deck after sunset to smell the spice-laden breeze that blew from the shore. So it *was* true, that line in my favourite hymn that went 'What though the spicy breezes—blow soft o'er Ceylon's isle'! Across the darkening water there came an aromatic odour that I had not smelt when, a few months before, I had been living there. I had become a little suspicious of hymns and it surprised me to learn that the words of one of them should be so exact.

At Calcutta my father met us and took us to our quarters in Fort William. I discovered that there was a pony for me to ride and a bearer in a white dress and turban to lead it. There was also a little girl called Dulcie, a colonel's daughter like Marjorie, with whom I played among the brass cannon on the battlements. I was not shy this time, because I was not in love with her.

But one does not, I think, when one is a small English child, enjoy India: one feels it drift remote and very hot across the mind. My recollections of it—temples, Botanic Gardens, bazaars—indicate a state of passivity. Neither the Viceroy's party for children nor the garden party given by a maharajah were what I had hoped they might be. And I had begun to take a dislike to my father, who was now often irritable and bad tempered. He had formed the idea that he and not my mother was the proper person to give me arithmetic lessons, for he was a great believer in the disciplinary effect of mathematics and thought that for this reason they ought to be imparted by a man. Every evening therefore I used to lie on the floor of his study, counting the rushes on the mat, while he sat at his desk and said, 'Now, think well before you answer. What is five added to seven?' When my attention wandered or I gave the wrong answer, his voice would grow sharp and impatient. Then one day, when my bearer had done something that displeased him, he kicked him. I had never seen physical violence before, and I was horrified.

I can sum up my impressions of India in three separate recollections. One is of the peculiar range of smells, which are so different from those of Ceylon or of South Africa. Another is of a banyan tree of vast size growing at the entrance to a village: under it sat men and women of all sorts, some dressed in flowing robes of pink and blue and white and others naked but for a loin-cloth. The ground below was trampled and polished like a threshing-floor. This, I tell myself, is India, though it is possible that my memory derives not from a place but from a painting. My third recollection is more private, for it comprises my earliest mystical experience. We had gone to some gardens a little way down the Hoogli where, if I remember right, the men of the East India Company were buried. In these gardens there was a tunnel of green bamboos. I entered it alone, for it was too low for my parents to negotiate, and advanced down it. Then suddenly I came out into the blinding sunshine and saw the huge expanse of the river dancing in the light and before me a little bamboo jetty with a boat moored to it. I was dazzled not only by the scintillations of the light but by what seemed to me the importance of the experience.

We left Calcutta in March, just as the hot weather was beginning: my father had been offered an adjutancy in England. I well recollect the long, hot train journey to Bombay. Through the windows, which were shaded with curtains of fragrant grass roots and watered every few hours to give coolness, I looked out on a yellow, monotonous country dotted with small, red-berried trees that resembled the mountain ash. In vain I scanned them in the hope of seeing monkeys or a leopard. Then in Bombay there were the Elephanta Caves and, better still, the Towers of Silence, with the vultures waiting on the parapets to devour the corpses of the Parsees when they were deposited within. I embarked with my mother on a P. and O. liner while my father, who was in charge of a draft, took a troopship.

This was the last occasion on which I was to be alone for any length of time with my mother. Into my love for her there had crept a feeling of anxiety that had been absent during the calm and happy African days. This, I imagine, was because her social duties and the demands that my father made on her had allowed her less time to spend with me. Now, every night after dinner, she would return for a moment to the cabin which we shared to give me a good-night kiss, bringing with her a chocolate or a piece of ginger, and I would lie awake in the darkness listening to the rumbling sounds of the ship and to the slip-slopping of the waves and longing for her to appear. Then the door would open, showing the lighted corridor beyond, and I would smell the fragrance of her hair as she stooped over me and feel the smoothness of her fine skin against my lips. In evening dress, with her long, full neck and soft, antelope-like eyes, she was—to her son at least—beautiful.

The Boer War had broken out the previous autumn and Ladysmith had just been relieved after a four months' siege, during which the defenders had been reduced to eating rats. The hero of this siege, Sir George White, was an Ulsterman and a friend of my mother's family. In her enthusiasm she had hung a coloured lithograph of him, in full dress uniform with all his medals, over my bunk and one day she said to me: 'When you're grown up, you must try to be a great man like him.' I gazed at the red wooden face with its white bushy moustaches and wondered if I should ever look as great as that.

On landing we went straight to London, where my grandmother took me into her flat in Cadogan Gardens. My father's new battalion was under orders to leave for South Africa at once. We all went to Waterloo Station to see him off and I remember the surging crowds on the platform, the confusion of noise and train smoke, the faces of the soldiers flattened against the windows and the weeping women. On seeing them the name Nancy came into my mind with a new richness of meaning: all those soldiers going off to die were thinking of her and had her initials tattooed with a pierced heart on their arms as well as a sprig of forget-me-nots embroidered in blue on their pocket-hand-kerchiefs. Then, after a French nursery governess called Julienne had joined us and we had paid a last visit to the fossil saurians in the South Kensington Museum, we crossed to my Irish grandmother's house in County Down.

My days as Vasco da Gama and Ibn Batuta were now over. I was only six, but I could sit back and tell my Oriental and African traveller's tales. And tell them I did—to Mrs Lappin (my nurse's sister), to Julienne, to my cousin Helen and, when these would not listen, to myself. They were stories of escapes from ferocious crocodiles and lions, of thirsty journeys across the veldt where the dying cattle had poisoned the water-holes and of nights spent in tiger-infested jungles. There was also an old, old woman I had met at Port Said who had once known Pharaoh and who, when his mummy had been un-wrapped, had recognized his face. But this story, like Pharaoh himself, already belonged to a vanished age and, when I told it to Lappin, I was at once ashamed of it.

However, these childish boasts aside, my travels had provided me with a strong sense of my own uniqueness and with what one might call a personal legend. My mother did her best to build this up by talk-ing to me about my past—the peculiar things that had happened to me and the strange and wonderful places that I had seen. I was, it seems, a remarkable child, not for what I was in myself, but because of the impressions that remote countries had made on me. Geography, in the semblance of a God, had selected me, marked me, sealed me. It had left, as it were, little pieces of its mysterious substance adhering to me so that, for example, when I pasted a stamp of Djibouti in my album or picked out on the atlas the words Seychelle Islands, I felt an answering echo from something that *was* the Somali coast or the coral islands of the Indian Ocean within me.

This feeling that there was a special quality possessed by those who had seen remote places which distinguished them from the rest of mankind, I also extended to other people. In my mother's family, for example, there was my Uncle Harry, who had been the first person to climb Mount Ararat. He was a gentle, inoffensive, dapper little man, many years older than his wife, going deaf and so slow in his movements that he took an hour and a half to dress every morning. His speech was slow too, full of hums and haws and repetitive expressions, so that no one could quite understand how he had come to be a colonel in command of a line regiment. His ascent of Mount Ararat had been made long before when travelling with his cousin, who was a well-known explorer.

For many years I regarded this uncle with feelings of reverence. I passed over his lowness, his mildness, his inarticulateness, and saw in him simply the man upon whom the mysterious mountain, with its thrice repeated *a*'s, had stamped its image. I longed to ask him to describe his exploit, but did not dare to. When at length, at the age of ten or eleven, I plucked up the courage to do so, I got a disappointing answer.

'Well, let me see, we climbed up—that's it, we climbed up and it was pretty hot. Yes, by Jove, I remember I had to take off my coat. And then, let me see, hm, hm, hm, why, it turned cold. That's it, by Jove, I had to put on my coat again. And on top there was snow, a lot of snow. Ararat's a pretty big mountain, pretty big, you know.'

But at the age of six, among my untravelled cousins and nursery governesses it was chiefly my own heroic wanderings that dazzled me. Looking back, I believe that I can date from this time the beginnings of my peculiar brand of adolescent egoism. This consisted in a belief that my life was in some way unique and remarkable and different from the lives of other people. Also that it had a logic and unity of its own and a future laid out for it which somehow or other it must fulfil. Later on this sense of my having a vocation became very strong and determined everything I did: its successes and failures will provide the main theme for this volume of my autobiography.

My grandmother's house—it was called Larchfield—was a heavy-looking stuccoed building, bright pink in colour and built in what one may term the Irish Early Victorian style. Round it stood a park, planted with clumps of oak trees and rhododendrons, and enclosed, like most Irish parks, by a mile or two of high stone wall. Two drives, leading to different roads, led out of it and within its precincts lay the home farm, stables, gardens and also the small artificial lake that was known rather ignominiously as 'the pond'. Like all these Ulster parks, the place made a splodge of tameness, of Victorian pseudo-feudality in the pleasant Irish countryside, with its white cabins, small irregular fields, turfed banks and foxglove-edged lanes. In the distance, blue as a blue gauze handkerchief, rose the Slieve Croob mountains.

This house and estate had been bought by my grandfather, Ogilvie Graham, some time in the 1850's. He was the younger son of a small country gentleman whose ancestors had come over from Scotland with William of Orange. Going into business, he had done well out of cotton, had then switched to linen and, with the help of a partner called Mulholland, who later became Lord Dunleath, had set up large mills in Belfast. Within a short time he had become one of the wealthiest men in Northern Ireland, High Sheriff first of Down and then of Antrim and on his way to a knighthood. But financial losses followed and when he died in 1897 he was only moderately well off.

My grandmother succeeded to the estate. She was an American, the daughter of an English cotton factor who had settled in Louisiana. As a young girl she had made an unhappy marriage: then my grandfather had met her and fallen in love with her; her husband, who was an alcoholic, had conveniently died and the lovers had got married. They had lived very happily together and had had five children. Of these the eldest son, Ogilvie, took over the business; the second, Charlie, went into the cavalry, while the two younger daughters married and went to live in the south of Ireland. But as they all of them adored their old home and my grandmother loved nothing better than having them round her, they returned to it at frequent intervals. Thus, during my visits there, I generally had some cousins to play with.

My life at Larchfield was of course very different from what it had been when I had lived under the eye of my mother. I was cabined off in the nursery and schoolroom with Julienne and the various nurses and governesses of my cousins. I did not come into meals in the dining-room and except at certain hours the front part of the house, separated from the back by a green baize swing-door, was closed to me. Whenever it was fine I was let loose with my cousins in the pleasure ground, a closed area of lawns and rhododendrons, or went for walks with Julienne down the Crimea Walk to the pond and on to the oak wood. Here there was a mysterious place—the deer park—treeless and boggy: one looked at it through a gate, always kept locked, in the park wall, but could not go in.

The house, however, was a world in itself. It was intersected by long corridors and it had secret regions—Bluebeard's chambers—that one must not enter. The drawing-room was one such place, hung with a glass chandelier and never used except on Sundays or after dinner-parties. The green and blue rooms, though only bedrooms, were others. What is curious is that I did not take the prohibition not to enter these rooms as a law imposed on me by grown-up people, but as issuing from a mysterious property contained in the precincts themselves. The strong sense I had of the *mana* pertaining to places made this seem quite natural to me, so that if I had not been told that there were some that were closed to me, where it was forbidden to penetrate, I should have had to invent them myself.

Most impenetrable of all, though for different reasons, were the servants' quarters in the basement. A little, dark staircase outside the pantry led down to them and when one stood at the top of it and the door was open, one could hear cheerful Irish voices and laughter welling up from the depths. The cook, the kitchen-maids, the house-maids, the laundry woman and the footmen lived in these forbidden regions, and obviously this was the best part of the house, the part which produced most life and fun. As in the stories of the Shea in Irish folk-lore, the really jolly things, the dancing and the fiddling and the joking, went on underground. Thus I came to associate viva-city and gaiety with the people who lived down there, that is with the servants, and at the same time to feel myself cut off by a gulf of class privilege from sharing it with them. This feeling was to have a marked effect on me in later life, so much in our characters being determined by the things that we cannot do precisely because our longing to do them inhibits us.

Of the nurses and governesses who attended on me and my cousins I have little distinct recollection. More vivid are some of the servants. To begin with there was Phoebe, the sewing maid. She occupied a little room that was littered with scraps of cloth and sewing materials and adorned with two rather shockingly naked dressmakers' shapes that stood up like armless and headless Greek statues in either corner. At first I had a prejudice against her on account of her name—it suggested 'fib', a word often used with unpleasant intentions; then I came to like her because she tolerated me. I enjoyed the untidiness of her room, the lazy, burring sound of the sewing-machine starting and stopping, the smell of ironing and not least the seat in the window from which one looked out on that daily ceremony—the old horse walking slowly in a circle in the middle of the courtyard as he pumped the water. When-ever the stable clock struck the hour he stopped and was given a wisp of hay: then after a few minutes' rest he went on. This was a sight I never got tired of for, if I liked anything, I wanted to see it or hear it again and again.

Among the servants, however, the person who made the greatest impression on me was Lappin. She was my late nurse's elder sister, but as unlike her as anyone could possibly be. In appearance—a musty black dress, yellowish blowzy hair, pins stuck all over her blouse, a face in perpetual movement: in character—a sort of pantomime widow, always in a hurry yet never able to resist a bit of gossip, a prodigious chatterbox, an irrepressible fountain of winks and nods and smiles and finger-to-the-lip gestures. Because she was deaf she spoke in a loud whispering voice that carried all over the house and because she was widowed she wore a gold brooch in the form of a heart which contained a lock of hair cut from the head of her late husband, who some time before had been the second footman. Her status in the house was that of my grandmother's maid—a position given her out of kindness, for to any person who employed her she was nothing but a nuisance.

Lappin's claim to my regard came from her adoring all the grandchildren—especially when, like myself, they were mischievous—and considering herself their ally. In their cause she kept up a perpetual feud with the cook and the butler, stealing sugar and butter from their store to make us toffee. When, many years later, in the 1930's, I went to see her, she reverted at once to these early tales, protesting with energy that the rumours spread by the butler were false and that she had never stolen anything for us. She was then living in the south of London with her sister and the favourite amusement of the two old ladies was to stand outside St Margaret's, Westminster, whenever there was a fashionable wedding. She followed with zest all the movements of the Royal Family and could recite by heart the names and ages of the King's uncles and aunts and nephews and nieces. I thus realized that, like myself, she had thought of my grandmother as a symbol for Queen Victoria.

The last of these domestic retainers whom I have to speak of was the butler, Kirk. He was at this time an elderly man with a completely bald head and reddish mutton-chop whiskers. By religion he was a Presbyterian and he had been a long time in the family. I was given, it seems, to creeping into the dining-room before lunch and taking ginger or preserved fruit off the sideboard, and he used to set traps to catch me. Once, I am told, though I have no recollection of this, he filled an Elvas plum with pepper and I ate it but said nothing. On another occasion, which I do remember, he came in by the further door and chased me. Turning round, as I made the corner to the garden steps,

I called out, as the mocking children did to Elisha—'Go up, thou bald pate!' and then, with a thrill of fear, half-expected the bears to come out of the rhododendron bushes and eat me. After this a strange reflection occurred to me. Since no bears came, I decided that the story in the Book of Kings, which had profoundly shocked me when my mother had read it to me, could not be true. The fact that Kirk was not Elisha did not seem to me to matter, because it was on the magic potency of the words, when applied to bald men, that the point of the affair must evidently depend.

Every evening after tea we children were taken into the library where the grown-up members of the family were assembled. There my grandmother would be sitting in her full-bodied, black silk dress, with her white cap on her head. When she kissed me I could smell the faint scent of Parma violets of which all her clothes and possessions bore a trace. She did not, as my English grandmother would have done, take me on her lap or read to me, for she was the matriarch of a large family and had to distribute her time and favours to many people. But under her gruff, homely voice I felt her kindness and benevolence.

Sunday at Larchfield was a day unlike any other. At half-past ten precisely the victoria would crunch up the pebble drive and stop at the pink-coloured porch. My grandmother, dressed in a black silk cloak and wearing a bonnet tied by ribbons round the neck, would climb in; the coachman, Beatty, an old retainer who had been some forty years with the family, would crack his whip and the carriage would move off. It was the rule that one of us children took it in turn to accompany her and when my turn came I would be very happy because I felt that to drive with her was an honour. But I was not so pleased by the church services. The sermons were long and as I sat fidgeting on my seat I would look with impatience on the stiff, bearded figures of the apostles portrayed in the garish stained-glass windows and feel welling up in me an aversion for the whole boring business. As I grew older, my antipathy for these old men with their blowzy beards and their unintelligible epistles increased and turned me more and more against this thing called religion, which seemed to have been invented with the sole idea of spoiling one morning in every week. When later still, at the age of sixteen, I came across that little medieval tale, *Aucassin and Nicolette*, I wholeheartedly echoed Aucassin's protestation that none of the people he wanted to see went to Paradise. None in my case, except my mother.

After lunch came another ceremony, obligatory for everyone who was staying in the house—the walk round the stables and home farm.

My grandmother, dressed in her cloak and bonnet and leaning on a stick, would lead the way—these were the only occasions on which she ever walked out of the house—and my Uncle Ogilvie in his slow, gruff, monotonous voice would keep up a monologue. When we got to the bull, he was still talking about the pigs.

There was one occasion at Larchfield which has left a poetical memory—the annual school feast. When I recall it, the smell of freshly cut hay and the murmur of mowing-machines rise in my mind. The school-children came in their new summer frocks, given them each year by my grandmother, so that the grass in front of the house beside the big candle-flowered horse-chestnut tree was crowded with boys and girls all under the age of twelve. I felt the charm of these fresh little faces (the girls hiding theirs under sun-bonnets) all the more because they were most of them of my own age. What else do I remember? That we ran straight races and sack races and egg-and-spoon races and that the cousin I did not like cried because he failed to get a prize: that of course I wished to speak to the girls and that of course I did not dare to: and that afterwards I helped to distribute bags of sweets all round. Then the sun sank, the happy sun of June 1900, and the dews arose. The school feast was over.

When I look back now on these months I am struck by one thing—the diminished importance to me of my mother. This was not because I lacked opportunities for seeing her. Every morning at seven I would get out of my cot and run down the passage to her room, where I got into bed beside her. Then for an hour she would give me my lessons and read to me. These early lessons and readings, which I greatly enjoyed, continued through the whole of my childhood, until I was thirteen. Yet in spite of them and of my unchanged devotion to her, she had begun to sink a little in my estimation. This, I believe, was because I saw her mixing on an equal footing with her brothers and sisters and cousins. Another side of her character came out—a more worldly and boisterous one—which I did not like. I wanted her to be always pure and simple, always maternal, always bending over me—the blue-robed figure in every picture of the Madonna and Child. Besides I was now caught up in the general life of the house and was less dependent on her. I put on the highest pinnacle therefore the august and benevolent figure of my grandmother.

The time has come for me to say something of my mother's character. She was—but to explain her I must first give a group picture of her brothers and sisters. They were a good-natured, doggy little tribe, expansive and friendly in their relations to the world, inclined to boastfulness in their conversation but at bottom not very sure of themselves. They shared all the tastes of the *nouveau riche* class to which they belonged for sport and for getting on socially. Not one of them ever read a book (the only volumes in the Larchfield library were Burke's *Peerage* and *Landed Gentry* and *The Horse, his Ailments and Complaints*) and not one of them willingly spent a moment alone. My mother, on the other hand, though she did her best to conform to the notions of her family, was imaginative and fond of reading. A lack of self-confidence in her disposition, which made her helpless in sports and games and clumsy in social matters, had driven her along this path. She was the odd and eccentric member of a hearty, boisterous family.

In her governess-ordered youth she had learned to read French and German fluently. Later she learned some Italian. But her desire for knowledge and culture greatly exceeded her capacity for absorbing them. Although sensible and shrewd, she had an extraordinarily ramshackle and muddled mind, while the narrow social code in which she had grown up was an obstacle to her absorbing any ideas that conflicted with it. Since everything connected with her parents and her home life was sacred to her, she never liberated herself from this.

Another side to my mother's aspiring nature was represented by religion. She wanted to be good, to follow as far as in her lay the teachings of the New Testament. This was much more within the range of her capacities, since she had an extremely warm heart, an immediate response to misfortune and suffering and a total lack of selfishness. It is true that she was passionate and therefore given to fits of unreasonable jealousy and hurt feelings, but these passed quickly without leaving behind them any traces. Add that she was totally lacking in pride, vanity and egoism and so honest and truthful that even the possibility of deceiving anyone can never have entered her head, and one will have a fair picture of her moral nature.

There was, however, one flaw which came from her complete acceptance of the way in which she had been brought up. She saw no harm in the great inequalities of wealth which then existed, and when confronted with the shocking poverty of the industrial towns—a poverty exemplified by her father's mill-hands—she took refuge in evasions. The slum dwellers, she would assert—and the slums were always much on her mind—owed their poverty to their own vice and drunkenness. In particular cases she would criticize the selfishness and worldliness of rich people—and especially of that bugbear of the pious, London Society—but in general she was opposed to any change which could affect in even the smallest way the privileges of her own class. And note that this failure of her imagination was due not to her own love of money and position, for she cared little for either of these, but solely to her loyalty towards her own kith and kin.

My mother's first instinct after growing up had been to devote herself to a life of good works. It was a craving that often came over Victorian ladies who were at odds with their surroundings, not unlike that for joining the Communist Party in the 1920's. In every age the sons and daughters of the rich suffer from a greed to enjoy the good things of the poor. She had been led by this to see rather more than was wise of the local clergyman. They fell in love and he made a formal declaration to my grandfather. But the Protestant clergy in Ireland are poor men without any social position. My mother was therefore hurried off on a tour of Italy and the clergyman was replaced by an older man. When she came back, her head full of Italian skies and landscapes, her mind had changed. The charm and variety of the world could no longer be sacrificed to a life of parish work. Her romantic feelings about places, buildings, uniforms grew, and when in 1892 she met a gay young officer in Cairo she felt attracted to him. Then a little later he turned up at his regimental depot in Belfast, saw her in the setting of her family mansion and proposed. The glamour of youth and position—for neither had taken in the other's character—had been mutual.

Marriage led to a great breaking up of illusions. My father turned out to be a man of strange disposition with none of the easygoing, sociable ways of my mother's family. In spite of his Irish name, he was thoroughly English: a fiercely self-centred type inconceivable in any part of that clannish isle. The first days of the honeymoon revealed this. Since my father liked boating, he had decided that they would spend it punting down the Thames from Lechlade to Richmond. But then it rained. My mother did not like boating. The inns were primitive. On the second day, at the Tadpole Inn, the tablecloth set out for supper was not clean. 'Once and for all understand this,' declared my father. 'In future I expect to see a perfectly clean tablecloth at every meal that I sit down to. It will be your business to provide it and, if you don't, I shall want to know why.' The tone in which this remark was made was something my mother had never heard before: she understood the passionate language of quarrels, but not this cold, autocratic rudeness.

Another thing that soon began to trouble her was his exaggerated jealousy. He was suspicious of her friends. In Malta he would not allow her to go to tea with the Colonel's wife unless he was present, in spite of the fact that the Colonel was an old friend of his family. The rule he had made that she must not see people 'behind his back' must be strictly kept.

'Poor girl,' her family exclaimed. 'She has certainly married a difficult man.'

Yet difficulties, it seems, were what, in one part of her nature, my mother wanted. My father's hard, tight, neurotic character and the whip-like phrases he used whenever a black mood came over him fascinated her, dominated her. She often rebelled, she several times planned to leave him, yet she never ceased to the end of her life to love him. But she could not *do* anything with him. Her warm, generous, expansive nature was wasted on such an impervious man. My birth, therefore, was a tremendous thing for her. From the moment that I was old enough to understand, she set herself to pour into me all those impulses towards a deeper and fuller life that she had felt as a girl. What she gave me was much more than love—it was faith in life, an interest and delight in the world about me, combined with an anticipation of further and greater delights to come. No child was ever so charged as I was, and if I have not made a better use of this priming, it is for reasons that will, no doubt, appear later on.

My father came back in November, invalided home with malaria and deafness. He had seen no fighting, only endless marching and counter-marching. He brought me as a present a stamp album and a set of South African stamps: from now on this became my principal hobby, appealing as it did to my love for geography. I was pleased too, in spite of my earlier jealousy, to see him back, for I was afraid of being submerged in the clan-like atmosphere of my mother's family, where I was only one grandchild among many. He represented the more solitary and independent side of my life and gave me in my own eyes a greater consequence.

In the mornings my father would go out snipe shooting with my Uncle Charlie; in the evenings they played billiards, and I was allowed to come in and sit in a corner while they struck the balls. I can see now this room with its green table lit by hanging oil-lamps, over which are suspended deep funnel-shaped shades, white inside, that suggested to me then some unknown, forest-growing flower. A cloud of pipe-smoke and cigar-smoke fills the air, for this was the only room in the house in which smoking was allowed, and a pleasant chik chik comes from the cues. My Uncle Charlie—bald shining head, canary-coloured waistcoat, cheroot in mouth—is marking the score and I am crouched on the settee, pasting in my stamps. They are talking of a man called Winston Churchill, who has just been giving a lecture in Belfast on his escape from the Boer lines. My mother had been to it and had repeated to me the story.

'Awful little bounder,' declares my Uncle Charlie. 'No one could stand him in the regiment.' (My uncle is in the Fourth Hussars.) 'Didn't know one end of a horse from the other.'

'Cannon,' says my father, walking round the table and taking aim again.

'Regular newspaper-wallah type. Had none of the makings of a soldier. Gave away the escape route too by all that speechifying.'

'Seventy-three,' says my father, marking up his score. 'Your turn.'

'Damn, missed it. Can't hit a thing today. By the way, Hugh, did I ever tell you this one?'

And off he goes on one of his tall stories about something that had happened at Bangalore or Potchefstroom. Of how, for example, he had met a tiger on a narrow path, fixed him with his eye, threatened him with his walking-stick and the tiger, overcome by the majesty of the human form, had slunk away. I liked my Uncle Charlie on account of his stories and also because, in my mother's tales of her childhood, he had always figured as naughty, but my father, with his English sense of propriety, disliked his 'bucking'.

We spent Christmas at Larchfield. The hall, a large room decorated with the heads of gnu, bison, antelopes, leopards and so forth which my uncle had shot, was laid out with parcels containing presents. All my uncles and aunts and cousins were assembled and the excitement was great. Immediately after we left for London. This meant for me the South Kensington Museum with its fossil skeletons, but the actual memory that I preserve is different. I am looking out from an upper-story window of the Burlington Hotel in Cork Street. The light is dim and grey and the tall windows of the houses opposite are staring back at me with a grave severity. Straw has been spread over the roadway below because a woman is lying sick in one of these houses and, as the hansom cabs pass over it, the sharp, lively clink of the horses' hooves changes to a soft rustle. Yes, the air is grey, the windows frown because a woman, who has perhaps a little boy like myself, is ill and may die. For this reason the whole street puts on sadness and I, with the sentimentality of children, feel sad too.

My father's poor health had left him in a restless mood. The damp cold of England depressed him, so we left for Jersey. One recollection of our stay here is perhaps worth recording. He used to take me about the island standing on one leg on the back step of his bicycle, and one day we stopped at a cemetery and he showed me a tombstone with my own name written on it. It was that of my great-grandfather, Colonel Edward FitzGerald Brenan. My father liked to make these experiments on me to see what I would do, much as one shows a looking-glass to a kitten. But since the possibility of my own death had never entered into my mind, my reaction cannot have been very interesting.

In February we moved to Paris, where with her usual enthusiasm my mother took me to see the sights while my father shivered with malaria in a hotel bedroom. Then on to Montreux and Clarens, where we rented one floor of a large white house that stood on the edge of the lake.

My parents had decided that, to improve my French, I should go to a day school. This school lay on the far side of the town and the road to it, which was also the main street, was lined by shops of the most fascinating nature. Best among them were those that sold rock crystals of various colours and cups and vases cut out of jasper, agate, cornelian and other semi-precious stones. I gazed at these wonderful objects as Aladdin had gazed at the treasures in the cave and wished that I had the money to buy all of them. But the school did not please me. I had never seen forms, desks, blackboards or the military organization of a classroom before, and then the floor was dirty, the black iron stove did not warm one's feet and the whole place stank of urine. After a day or two therefore I decided that it would be more amusing to spend the morning looking at the shops and to leave the school to get along by itself. This I did. To keep up the pretence that I went to it, I used to return in the company of the other children, exchanging volleys of stones with a girl a year or two older than myself to whom I had taken a dislike. My parents did not discover my deception till we were about to leave.

The snow melted, the crocuses and the blue anemones came out and then we were off. We stopped at Baden Baden where the cherry-blossom lay like a white frost on the villages and the pine trees of the Black Forest guarded the robbers' castles. But the foreign doctors held out no hope of curing my father's deafness and he was in a hurry to return to England. We got back in April and at once set about looking for a house.

CHAPTER III

The Age of Governesses

An event had occurred during our stay in Switzerland which was to have a certain effect upon our family life. My great-great-aunt Simpson had died, leaving some ten thousand pounds to my father, but bequeathing the rest of her estate elsewhere. This old lady, of whom I have only a dim recollection, lived in a small Georgian manor at Fyning, near Petersfield: there was a pleasant lawn and walled garden and a few hundred acres of surrounding land which provided a little shooting. My father had been in the habit of spending part of his holidays with her and had been led to consider himself her heir, which indeed, as her eldest great-nephew, he might claim to be. But then an orphan baby had been sent home from India and Miss Simpson had unwillingly taken it in. My father had gone abroad—worse, had married—and the baby had slipped into his place. Miss Simpson left it not only the greater part of her income, but the family silver and what, if they had been of more value, might have been termed the heirlooms. Although I never heard my father allude to this disappointment, for he was a man who seldom complained of anything except the weather, I believe that he felt it a good deal. He had grown up to think of himself as belonging to the landed gentry and had acquired both their pride of position and their tastes: now he must put himself down among the mere *hidalgos*, eking out his life (till other deaths came to increase his income) on a mere £1,000 a year.

My parents soon found the house they wanted; this was an old rambling place called Bassetts, close to Little Baddow and Chelmsford. They took it for the summer. The trunks that we had not seen since we left Ladysmith arrived and great was my disappointment to find that a collection of tobacco tins which I had packed with plant medicines was not among them. But the house and the country were perfect. On our first arrival in England some weeks before I had been filled with delight at seeing, out of the window of the train, the fields deep in buttercups and the woods as blue under their carpet of wild hyacinths as though a tide of sea-water had flowed into them. The streams and rivers too were islanded with water ranunculus, white as the clouds that sailed overhead in the sky. However, by the time that we were settled in our house, spring had given way to summer—one of those hot dry summers that we see no longer—and the flowers were less plentiful. Those that remained grew mostly along the banks of a canal that ran through fields a short distance away. Here for the first time I made the acquaintance of meadow-sweet, loosestrife, arrowhead, the greater willow herb and other ditch or water-loving plants. I mention these botanical discoveries, as I have previously mentioned others, because, from the age of four to that of eight or eight and a half, they formed, one might say, the landmarks of my aesthetic life, corresponding to the discovery at a later date of new poets and painters. Each plant species that took my fancy became fixed in my mind in all its particulars of form, growth, colour, taste and smell with a sharpness that nothing can give me today. I was especially drawn by their scent. Thus agrimony, a humble roadside flower, came to be a particular favourite of mine and when today I inhale its faint, honeyed perfume and stare into its tiny, five-petalled, slightly irregular yellow face, I catch again for a moment the feeling of those remote times.

It was at Bassetts this summer that I first came to know and love England: its aimless, zigzagging lanes, its clumps of squat blackberry bushes, its dwarfed oaks and short hedgerow elms with their rough leaves, the pebbles that came loose on the surface of the road when carriage wheels dug into it, the film of dust. A dull country, without surprises, but stamped with a character of its own and, above all, intimate. When one got to know it one felt one had been let into a secret. In the drought the grass tufts in the fields grew whiter and whiter, the oak leaves and elm leaves more bluey grey, and then in September the rain fell and there was a huge crop of mushrooms.

One of my more distinct recollections of these months is of a Sunday walk to church. We were dressed up in our best, my father very brisk and positive, swinging his stick and leather gloves, and my mother with that martyrized expression which she always wore when going to communion. Our road lay along a footpath that crossed a cornfield, then over a stile and into a little lane. The dog-roses hung down their flowering sprays, the stitchwort grew tall in the ditches and on the air there lay the heavy smell of early summer. From some distance ahead of us came the sound of church bells ringing, drawing us forward with their sentimental, evangelical chime which told us that everything was peace and perpetual Sunday in a faintly mawkish, faintly unreal world. Then we came up with some village children, the girls very prim in their clean cotton frocks and the boys dragging sulkily after them. My mother, who could not pass children without speaking to them, turned her head to ask who they were. After that —nothing. I do not remember what church we went to, nor what the service was like nor how we came back. This moment alone, as if it had been lived in a different order of time, remains.

My other recollections of this summer are more casual. A horse and a dog-cart in which we paid visits: the markings on an old green gate in which, like Leonardo da Vinci, I read faces: a little girl called Effie who came to play bat and ball with me. Like all the other little girls whom I met during these years, I detested her. Then comes a memory of quite a different sort. My nursery governess, Julienne, had left and now another called Célestine came to take her place. I remember her distinctly—dark, lively, with sparkling eyes and a much vaunted Parisian accent and more interested, I suspect, in grown-up men than in her youthful charge. One afternoon we went for our usual walk to the canal. The deep heavy water, the lush fringe of plants that bordered it made it in that dry weather the natural direction to choose. As we followed the tow-path we came on some water lilies growing close in to the bank, and I wished her to pick them. Célestine sat down and took off her shoes and stockings. Holding onto a tuft of sedge, she tried to reach them, but she was wearing cotton drawers that descended to her knees and her legs sank in. She came out therefore, removed her drawers and, bunching her skirts round her waist, went in again. My memory stops short at this moment with a picture painted in cool Corot-like tones of the scene, but if I may make a guess at my feelings, I would say that I was at first shocked by her boldness and then felt a secret pleasure.

Another example of her exhibitionist leanings followed soon after. One afternoon when my parents were out she took me into her attic bedroom and undressed. After that she proceeded to rub her body over with scent. I remember this as though I had read about it somewhere, for I can neither visualize what she looked like without her clothes nor recall how I felt. The censor has permitted the incident to pass, but suppressed both the details and my reactions to them.

This is the last I remember of Célestine and on looking at my mother's diary I see why. 'After six weeks,' it records, 'Célestine had to be sent away.' She passed out of my memory for some years till one day, when I was sixteen, I thought of her. After that I brought her back to be a regular partner in my daydreams. In my lonely and sexless youth she was almost the only woman I knew to have any erotic connotations.

In October we left for London and took a furnished flat at 7 Sloane Court. A few days later my brother Blair was born. I remember my surprise on learning of this, but not the jealous feelings that I am told that I displayed. For some months, it would seem, I was moody and difficult.

These moods appear to have left traces in the grey and melancholy recollections that I have of London. The windows of our flat faced Chelsea Barracks and I used to sit there and look out, getting a special macabre sensation whenever there was a soldier's funeral. It seemed to me indecent and contrary to the natural order of things that soldiers should die anywhere but on the battlefield. Then there were the afternoon walks—a girl came to take me out—in Battersea Park and round about Pimlico. The great sluggish river with its banks of slimy mud lay sunk and exhausted between the lines of smoking houses and factory chimneys. Looking down at it over the parapet of the bridge, it seemed to me immeasurably sad. Sad too in the foggy November air were the half-stripped trees and the children playing with hoops on the asphalt walks. Sad the chestnut-roasters, the sellers of toy balloons and the organ-grinders. Saddest of all the organ monkeys, shivering in their red flannel waistcoats and holding out pathetic hands for hazel-nuts that never came. But the crowded streets of the Pimlico market struck a rather different note. On these grey afternoons the lamps were lit early and by their light one could see the packed and wrinkled faces of shabbily dressed people passing—endlessly passing. The multitude and the poverty and the anonymity excited me. There were surely too many of these people for everyone of them to have a name. Yet I preferred these dismal streets to the rich ones. Indeed my strongest desire was to see the slums—they still existed just off the Strand in Clare Market—where, so I gathered, scenes of appalling misery and degradation lay open to the eye. I had heard about them from my mother, in whose melodramatic imagination they figured strongly under a coating of reprobation and prudery. The Victorians always had at hand a material representation of Dante's *Inferno* and, because it purged their own repressed inclinations, drew a secret delight and encouragement from it.

In January 1902 we crossed to Dinard in Brittany and rented a house there for three months. Since we were to return to Dinard twice again during my school holidays, I shall put down only one thing about this visit. My mother had the habit of telling me adventure stories of a very thrilling kind. These stories took a serial form, as they do in the *Arabian Nights*, led from one into another and never reached a definite end. One morning at Dinard, as we paced along a quiet street, she led her hero (a boy of course) into a mountain cavern of stupendous size where, just as his light gave out, just as he drew near to the roar of a hidden waterfall, he met a demon of the very worst kind. Not only was this demon invulnerable, able to fly a thousand miles a second through the air, to pass through solid substances and to see in the dark, but he carried a magic wand which had the power of killing instantaneously anyone at whom he pointed it. 'What are you doing in my treasure house?' he demanded in a terrible voice. 'Don't you know it's death to come here?' But before Jack could answer we had reached our gate: the sequel was postponed to next time. But this time never came. That evening I committed some misdemeanour, which led my mother to refuse to continue her tale, and since we left Dinard soon afterwards and were then separated for several months, the story-telling was never resumed. I long puzzled over the possible issue to this adventure and then decided that there was none. I suspected my mother, when she found herself unable to go on, of having made my naughtiness an excuse.

This was not the only occasion on which I was punished by being deprived of something that I looked forward to. My parents had promised to take me to Dinan fair, where, I was told, I should see a wild man of the woods, covered with long hair, who walked on bars of hot iron and swallowed fire. I particularly wished to see this wild man because I believed, on the analogy of cats and dogs and poultry, that the men and women I saw about me were domestic or tame. Somewhere, in some lonely wood or valley, there must still exist examples of the genuine wild species. However, a few days before the fair took place, I was caught taking nougat from the mantelpiece and told that, *because I had stolen*, I could not go. My parents went without me and I was left with a sense of having been treated unjustly. In future, I decided, when I wanted to take sweets, I should do it without scruple.

My parents had now decided to settle definitely in the south of England. While they searched for a house, my brother and I were to stay with my grandmother in the north of Ireland. An English governess was engaged to coach me for school and start me in Latin. She joined us and we set off.

My recollections of this visit to Larchfield show that a change had come over my way of envisaging the world since my last stay there sixteen months before. All sense of mystery about the house and grounds had now gone. I accepted the people around me as a matter of course. Was this due to the absence of my mother and of the strong currents of feeling she always set up in me? Or was I, by some natural development in the functioning of the glands, turning into a positive, extraverted little boy with few poetic or imaginative outlets?

At all events, when I search for some recollections that will enable me to describe the general life of the house, I draw a blank. My grandmother was always the same. My uncles and aunts provided nothing of interest. Secluded in the schoolroom with my plain, calm, sensible governess, a model of the sexless species, I saw little of any of them. To make this society come alive I am obliged to rely on the stories of my mother—that legendary lore which every child sucks in from its parents. What I see then is a map dotted, though more sparsely than in England, with large country houses, between which parties of young and middle-aged people are continually travelling in brakes and carriages. Hospitality is lavish. One arrived for a dance or a dinner and the next day one drove home again.

The great events of the year were the Hunt Ball and the South Down Militia dinner. My grandfather used to drive his family to these in a four-in-hand. After the Militia dinner, which took place in a room draped with orange banners, the men would sit on till they were dead-drunk and most of them under the table. Other occasions were the Belfast races and the Derby, to which my grandfather also took his four-in-hand, and the big pheasant shoots. One of these I remember—a disgusting butchery.

But what of the people who took part in these things? To judge by my mother's stories, many of them were very eccentric. Take old Mr C., who had been my grandfather's best man. He had such a love for horses that he half-imagined that he was a horse himself: every time he spoke he would give a loud neigh. His six sons used to find it a great joke to imitate him, so that when one went to visit him in his large but dilapidated mansion one got the impression that one was in a stable. I do not remember that he was ever observed to pull a carriage, but when he crossed to Fleetwood to see the Grand National, he would insist on being hoisted on board the ship by a crane. Yet this odd man had many friends and a reputation for being a great sports-man. My grandfather, who had no eccentricities himself, was devoted to him.

Another story was that of the Archdales of Castle Archdale in County Fermanagh, who were distant connections of ours. Old Mr

Archdale had such a dislike of ceremonies that he omitted to get married. For years he lived openly with his lady and had a number of children by her, which did not prevent the county in that supposedly prudish century from calling on them. Finally he screwed himself up to the point of going through with the noxious affair and had a last child who inherited the place. I once visited Castle Archdale with my mother: the house stood among heath and bog by a river that plunged suddenly into the earth and some miles further on came up again. There was also a lake studded with wooded islands among which one could take one's choice for a picnic—supposing, that is, that one could find a day on which it was not raining.

When, as I grew up into boyhood, I thought of these strange people, I regretted the ordinariness of my mother's family. They were harmless and good natured, but how uninteresting! Their estate was meticulously kept, but how tame! They had sacrificed their Irish birthright of eccentricity to their zeal for respectability and were now just like everyone else. I would have given anything to have been the impoverished heir to Castle Archdale with its miles and miles of bog and its lakeful of islands and to have had Norman Irish blood instead of Lowland Scot and English coursing like an underground river in my veins. Had I known that, like every Irish clansman, I could claim descent from some epic king or hero, I would have been much better pleased.

But to return to my own life. My excellent governess set me collecting and pressing wild flowers and entering them in an exercise book under their Latin names. I made the discovery that all plants are grouped in families and that these families are divided into genera and species. This brought an intellectual clarification. But the collecting and classifying mania seemed to diminish those poetical feelings of delight which a year earlier the sight of any favourite flower had been able to give. The most I can say for my botanical researches is that they took me out of the dull park with its iron railings and clumps of rhododendrons into the open countryside. Here the fields abandoned to gorse and ragwort conveyed wildness: the lanes bordered with foxgloves led on and on. When one day, getting a lift in a carriage, we reached the shores of a little lough and saw its toy waves lapping on the stones and felt its solitude and silence I got one of those impressions that always remain.

In July my parents wrote that they had found and rented a house in a remote village of the Cotswolds called Miserden. There was a large garden, they said, a stream that flowed in a valley and many wild flowers. There would be a horse for my father and a pony for me and woods, fields, lanes to ride them in. So, a few weeks later, my brother and I set off. At Cheltenham, where we left the train, we found the carrier's brake waiting to take us on the twelve-mile journey.

How well I remember that interminable, three hours' ride! Among the coarse roadside grasses, sprinkled with dust as no road ever is today, a brilliant array of flowers was growing—knapweed, harebells, scabious, campanula, meadow cranesbill. The telegraph poles, holding wiry hands, passed us on, the yellow-hammers flew chirping to one side and a vague, whitish light flooded the empty stone-walled fields and made me think of South Africa. But how long, how extremely long, the journey was! Would we never arrive? Then suddenly we rumbled down a village street and pulled up at the house that for fourteen years was to be our home.

Imagine a long, low, irregular building, box-shaped mansion at one end and gabled cottage at the other. Imagine a garden of three grassy terraces falling to a herbaceous border and to an old brick wall. Imagine two other gardens leading out of it, a paddock separated from it by a ha-ha fence and, bounding everything, a row of dark-leaved horse-chestnut trees. Imagine a vast bushy yew. Then mix in a green-painted verandah, a glass passage, a sunk stone court, a kitchen full of cock-roaches, a stable and coach-house, a wing of uninhabitable rooms, and you will have some sort of picture of the place. It was not hand-some, it was not ugly, but in its rambling, inconsequential way it had character.

My parents had done their best to make the interior comfortable. There was central heating—a new invention that had just come into use; there was a bathroom—my grandmother's house in Ireland had none. For decoration, a medley of African and Oriental things, from Kaffir bead skirts and Zulu shields and knobkerries to Benares brass trays, elephants carved out of teak, Thibetan masks and praying-wheels, four Cingalese drums, a model of a Coromandel fishing boat, three models of Bengal bullock-carts, many large brass vases, many children's toys in plaster of Paris, various hookahs, inkpots, embroi-dered caps, purses, slippers. Ostrich eggs too from Aden were there, saddle-bags and gilded water-bottles from Egypt, rugs and cotton hangings from the bazaars, elephant tusks from Nubia. The whole bedizened East glowed in the dim Cotswold light as though my father's military service had been as rich in loot as the Boxer campaign. But the glamorous nations do not provide wardrobes and cupboards. These had been brought in, of portentous size and solemnity, from

Breton antique shops, together with various oak chests, carved bed-fronts and sculptured figures of peasant art in blackened walnut. Only the drawing-room was English, and its rose-sprinkled chintz sofas, gazelle-legged tables and chairs, paper-thin silver knick-knacks and prints of Lord Leighton's pictures set the tone of refinement which every Edwardian drawing-room was expected to have.

We settled down for the autumn and winter in a quiet way. My bedroom was in the cottage end of the house, with thick whitewashed walls and a diamond-paned latticed window looking out over the garden. The jasmine that hung down from it was so thick that I had to be forbidden to climb in or out by it. The schoolroom was a different sort of place—a dark but cosy den, sunk a little below the level of the ground and commanding the front door and the visitors who came to it. Here in this little room I sat every morning doing my lessons, learning to conjugate *amo, amas, rego, regis*, and to write in a clear, round laborious handwriting. Miss Walker, my governess—plain face, neat dress, mousy hair frizzled daily with curling tongs, equable in temper—was a soothing and steadying influence.

Every afternoon, rain or fine, we went for a walk. One could either climb up through the village and follow one of the two roads that ran along the hilltop, or one could plunge down through the Park gates into the valley. This was the walk I liked best. Down one went three hundred feet through hollow beech woods, past the moat and knoll of a Norman castle, to a gloomy, weed-choked lake. The ghost of a headless lady haunted these trees: the owls had their nests in their trunks and hooted all night. Then, following the stream which bur-bled and meandered along, one could make one's way to a fish-pond known as Heron Water or else to the more open hillsides below Caudle Green. On a few special occasions we would cross the valley and walk on a mile to the Roman road, whose line of solemn, sentinel-like trees was visible on the skyline. I had begun to read Roman history and the thought of the legions who had tramped along its causeway, speaking the ponderous fossilled language I was copying out in my roundhand, was vaguely exciting to me.

But it is the winter evenings in the schoolroom that I remember with the greatest pleasure. The paraffin lamp burned on the table, the snow was heaped up outside, as it always is in the winters of child-hood: the yellow blind had been drawn. When tea was brought in, we toasted our bread at the fire and then, after the cloth had been cleared, Miss Walker read to me. The books she chose were the novels of Mrs Henry Wood, which I especially enjoyed because they showed that there could be a deep undercurrent of melodrama and tragedy in the lives of ordinary families such as our own. Then perhaps we would turn to one of those domestic arts which are the special secret of governesses—such, for example, as the making of many-coloured worsted balls or the gluing together of fir-cones, hazel-nuts and oak twigs onto cardboard squares cut to form picture frames and the painting over of these with thick silver paint. When finished they made excellent Christmas presents—large, bright, and suitably conspicuous and cumbrous. Or else, if not in the mood for creative activities, I would get out my stamp album and sit dreaming over the atlas as I opened the page at Guatemala or Djibouti.

The winter that year was exceptionally cold and after Christmas my mother, whose bureau stood in the large, dark and draughty hall, went down with double pneumonia. Since quiet was necessary and the house was filled with nurses, my governess and I were taken in by some neighbours, Mr and Mrs Hamilton Mills. Of this visit I have one interrupted memory. I am standing in my pyjamas in the middle of a large, well-furnished bedroom and some people come in and begin to cry out. There my recollection ends, but it seems that I have lifted the coals from the fire onto the carpet and that the carpet is smouldering. My usual mischievousness? I do not think so. I recall the sulky, angry feeling I had at the time and suspect that I was trying to set fire to the house as a protest at having been taken away from my mother.

Nor were these feelings entirely allayed by her recovery. During the months that followed I several times got up in the night and wandered about the house, waking only when discovered. Whenever I was estranged from her by what I considered to be an unjust punishment (and I regarded all punishments imposed by her as unjust, because I never intentionally did anything to displease her) I would plan to commit suicide, leaving a pathetic letter behind which would set everyone weeping. I suspect that the anxiety I showed sprang from a feeling that my mother did not sufficiently respond to my love for her, yet, when she did demand sympathy, I hardened myself. Once, for example, when she asked me whether I would approve of my father's marrying again if she died, I answered in my most sensible vein, 'Why not, if it made him happier?' She easily got hurt feelings and for several days after this would not speak to me.

Summer came and with it the season for garden parties. During the past few months my parents had been busy receiving and returning calls, so that by now pretty well everyone within a carriage drive was on their list of acquaintances. The time had therefore arrived for taking a second step and rounding up all these people in some general sort of gathering, which of course, since the cocktail habit had not yet come in, could only be a garden party. Of these sumptuous occasions I remember chiefly the women—huge, shadowy figures, as voluminous as Piero della Francesca matrons, with skirts that swept the ground behind them, corsets that gave them the air of well-tied-up parcels, and hats that resembled platters heaped with flowers, feathers and sometimes fruit. They consumed cake and cucumber sandwiches and cups of tea and played croquet and clock golf in a sedate and leisurely manner, while the men showed their mettle on the tennis court. Then the time for departure came and all these stately slow-stepping creatures passed back through the house and got into their traps and carriages.

August arrived—the August of 1903—and the admirable Miss Walker left. I had reached the fourth declension of Latin nouns and was considered ripe for school. The place selected was Winton House, near Winchester (Hampshire, England, Europe, the Earth, the Milky Way, the Universe—as with cosmological exactitude I and the other little boys used to fill out the address on our notepaper) and its headmaster was a certain Mr Johns, son of the famous clergyman-botanist. Many children from Anglo-Irish families went to it.

CHAPTER IV

Prep School—the Bad Years

When I try to recall my early life at my prep school, the things that come before me most obstinately are the faces of my masters and school-fellows. They float to the surface of my mind, as fresh and as vivid as when I first saw them, and nearly every one of them resembles an animal. I seem to be living in a zoo, each inmate of which is slightly repellent, while taken all together they are terrifying because, like the figures in dreams, I have no control over them. Nor can this impression be entirely subjective, because many of the boys and masters had animal nicknames.

But I had better begin at the beginning and put down my recollections in their proper order. My parents took me to my school and left me there—if I may trust my mother's diary—in a state of excitement and self-confidence. I was tired of my solitary, governess-ruled life, I longed to have other boys as companions and had no doubts that I should get on with them and win their approval. And indeed my first acts appear to show that I felt sure of myself. Within a couple of days of being at school I had put my hand to two characteristic exploits: explored a deep sewer that ran under the main road, and led a party of new boys from my dormitory onto the roof of the house. The first yielded some flint nodules containing blue crystals: the second was discovered and led to my being scolded. Then, a day or two later, I walked off after breakfast and did not return until the evening. 'We call him the Radical Reformer,' my headmaster remarked playfully to my parents, 'because he has no respect for any of the rules.' I imagine that the school had begun to pall on me and that I was trying to repeat the trick that had worked so well at Montreux.

Anyone who took his information about English schools from boys' adventure books might suppose that this brief show of truancy made me popular. But schoolboys, though they love to attribute to themselves all sorts of heroic roles in their daydreams, are in reality the most convention-bound creatures in the world. The right to any show of individuality among them has to be won by a long period of apprenticeship supplemented by skill in the approved kinds of games. Till then their tribal law demands complete uniformity. Now, as it happened, I found myself sinning from the start against the first canon of this law—that which relates to dress. My mother, in her ignorance of school etiquette, had provided me with house shoes that fastened by a strap and button instead of with that more manly kind which have elastic sides. When this was discovered I was surrounded by a hostile mob, staring and pointing at the disgraceful appendages. 'New boy. New boy. He's got buttons on his shoes. He's got buttons on his shoes. He's got buttons on his shoes', the chorus repeated. In a moment my self-confidence, which had never been subjected to a strain of this sort before, vanished.

Thus, by a fatality deriving from a pair of buttoned shoes, I was sent spinning down a slope into the abyss of unpopularity. And this was terrible. In the dense herd life of a schoolboy in a junior form nothing matters except whether he is popular or not, and I was on the bottom rung of the ladder. So abject was my state that I remember wondering to myself at the end of my first term whether the most unpopular boy in the school was a certain Gresley or myself. This Gresley was a pathetic little creature, aged not much above eight, with a baby face, curly hair and a look of having been smeared in butter: on the least provocation he burst into tears. I despised him because, being entirely crushed in my own self-esteem, I had adopted the tribal standards of the other boys; yet out of loneliness I was compelled to consort with him.

The story of every schoolboy's life being simply that of his gradual rise to popularity, I shall not bore the reader by plotting the stages of mine. I will only say that my progress was particularly slow. The usual procedure of boys who, like myself, were not good at games was to link themselves to others more favoured than they were and hope to be carried along with them. But I found this a disheartening business. As a rule I had no difficulty in making friends with a more successful or athletic boy of my own age whenever I happened to be thrown together with him because there were subjects like riding and stamp- and egg-collecting that we shared in common. But then, just as we were beginning to get on, the stigma of my unpopularity would descend. This was a blank, impersonal label, like that of being a Jew in Germany, which attached itself for no particular reason and continued out of habit. It was so much a part of one that one could not dispute it or argue with it. Thus, when my new friend came up against some sudden expression of hostile opinion about me, he would cold-shoulder me and then drop me, while if I struggled against this it would be said that I was sucking-up to him. 'Sucking-up' was a crushing term. We were like the courtiers of Elizabethan times, living all of us by flattery and toad-eating, yet damned as Rosencrantzes if our flattery was noticed.

The sense of being beyond the pale set up a train of morbid states of mind. Thus from my first and second years I preserve a group of memories that all share the same depressing tone. I was still a miserable, deeply unpopular little boy, but among the other miserable, unpopular little boys I had found a few companions. Our pursuits were secretive and macabre. For example, I remember how with another boy (whose face comes down to me as an enormous red pear with a few rat-like teeth projecting from it) I used to creep into an empty lot of building-land that lay next to the railway cutting and which, because it was overgrown with bushes and strictly out of bounds, we called No-man's-land. We had made a tunnel through the dense undergrowth of privet and snowball and along this we used to creep fearfully on our hands and knees. At the end of this tunnel, in a little grassy space, stood a willow tree, gnarled and decaying, and in the hollow of its trunk, under a stone, there lived a toad. We pretended to ourselves that a skull was buried under this tree and that the toad was in some way connected with it. Then occasionally we would dare one another to take it up in our hands. I remember the state of suspense and almost agony I used to be in when I thought that my companion might on a sudden impulse throw it to the ground or squash it under the stone, and I suspect that subconsciously I was tempted to do this myself. Yet had I come on it in my parents' garden I should not have had to resist this sadistic temptation because there I felt secure and happy.

The attraction of this shrubbery came, of course, from its being out of bounds. One escaped when one crept on all fours down its green tunnel and at the same time one entered a disturbing, uncanny precinct. Dead men's bones lay mouldering under the earth, trains rushed by leaving after them a strange silence, a murderer might perhaps be lurking there. One day I came across a dead rat of enormous size lying belly upwards on the ground and was so disgusted that I kept away for a whole term. Rats, toads, dead men's skulls, shrieks of trains and owls, white-sheeted ghosts, the glaring eyes and corpse-like hands of murderers—that is what some little schoolboys' dreams are made of.

Another sinister spot was a small grass-grown mound that stood on the edge of the drive by the front door. We invented a story that our maths master, Mr Wood, known to his pupils as 'The Sheep', had murdered a man and secretly buried him here. Our only reason for this suspicion lay in the fact that The Sheep wore his hair close-cropped and so of course must have spent some part of his life in a convict prison—until, by means of the usual file and two knotted sheets, he had contrived to escape. We worked up this story with such fervour that for a time we actually believed it to be true and determined, as good citizens ought, to expose him. One moonlight night, we swore, when everyone else was sleeping, we would creep out of the fourth-form window, dig up the grassy grave and publish The Sheep's infamy. But when it came to the point either our courage or our faith in our story failed us.

When many years later I began to read books on primitive societies, these early years at my prep school flooded back into my mind. Yes, I knew what it was to be an Arunta of Central Australia or a Dobu Islander of Melanesia or a devil worshipper in an African jungle. In his genteel boarding-school, between the ages of nine and twelve, a modern Englishman goes through a state which is not unlike that in which the more benighted among the primitive races still live.

It must, I think, have been in the Easter term of 1905—that is, when I was nearly twelve—that both my misery and the neurosis that was associated with it reached their critical point. I had taken to reading with all the zest and fury with which one takes to it at that age. Books were my opium and I could hardly bear to have one out of my hand. Boys' adventure stories, especially when they led into remote regions of the world, were my first taste and from them I went on to melodramas written for adults. These sometimes affected me powerfully. During the holidays, a couple of years before, my mother had started to read me *Oliver Twist*, but had been obliged to put it down because it gave me nightmares. Now, lying full length on the divan in the library, I devoured *The Deemster* by Hall Caine. As I read it I imagined that my parents, by some unlucky stroke, had lost all their money, that we should presently sink into a frightening poverty and be obliged to seek lodgings in one of the more dismal quarters of a large town. I even imagined that my father had got into debt, or into some trouble that was worse than debt, and was on the point of being carried off to prison. So real did this imaginary catastrophe become to me that every day I scanned the red, purple-veined face of the headmaster in the expectation that he would call me to his study and tell me that he had just received—a letter. But he never sent for me, nothing happened, and gradually I recovered my equanimity.

When I cast my mind back over these first two and a half years of school life I am amazed at the quantity of misery that this small boy who went by my name had to suffer. The experience of being harried and tormented all day long for no other reason than that he is considered to be a little different from his fellows is something that grown-up people, with all their superior resources of mind and character, are not generally called on to endure. There was the drab squalor of the football field, the agony of the swimming-baths, where one had only to appear to be ducked, the dreariness of the lessons, the harshness of the masters, the kicks and shoves and spitefulness that met one wherever one went. In particular I remember one torture which the older boys were especially fond of trying on the more timid among the younger ones. They would put them in the racket court and kick a football at them. Round and round the ball would go, bouncing off the walls with a hollow, echoing sound and putting me, when it was my turn for this treatment, almost out of my mind with terror. I had lost all self-respect. I had not even the courage to hate my tormentors.

Once at least I must have been ill. I remember lying, shivering all over, on the long settee in the library. It was covered—I can see it now—with a coarse, dingy material woven in a pattern of dark brown lines and fainter cross-lines. Leather buttons held it together and there was a greasy leather fringe along the seam. From about November on, a faint sickly smell, mingling with the dust on the floor and with the taste of 'squashed fly' biscuits, would hang about this place. I connected it with the rats, which every year died poisoned under the boards and rotted in the warmth of the thick, black, hot-water pipes. Workmen came to remove them, taking up the boards as one takes up the roadway over a sewer and revealing an ugly hollow of bricks and beams beneath, but the smell, though it grew gradually fainter, never quite vanished. I realize now that on this occasion I must have had flu. Since the matron never took our temperature unless she could see spots, chills and colds and flus passed unrecognized.

The spot-giving complaints, however, took one at once to the infirmary. Here I went whenever I succumbed to one of the usual children's epidemics. One lay on a bed covered with coarse grey blankets, listening to the rumbling and shrieking of the trains in the cutting outside, and at meal-times ate tepid boiled fish served with equally tepid greens and potatoes; after these came either prunes and custard or that large-grained slimy tapioca which we called cods' eyes. A prematurely stunted skivvy by name Olive, freckle-faced, breastless, with dingy red hair and steel spectacles, aged perhaps twenty, used to read to me every evening from a thick, well-thumbed volume entitled *The Lamplighter*. She belonged to the Salvation Army and I suspect that the book she read to me, though all I can remember of it now is its damp, depressing tone, was a kind of religious tract put into novel form. She greatly feared hell-fire and used to speak of it by some circumlocutory phrase, as people do of cancer. 'It—' she would say, 'It . . . If you die of a sudden and It gets you, you'll burn for ever and ever. Here, have some more gargle.' Her tone made such an impression on me that for a long time after, whenever I heard the word hell-fire, I would have a vision of tapioca, bed-pans and throat gargle, with the white, freckled face of the sky, crossed by wet, leafless trees, pressing against the window.

When I dream, as till I was past forty I used often to do, of this time, I find myself wandering anxiously through cold sunless classrooms, searching for the particular room where I have to be at this hour. Or rather, where I should have been five minutes ago, for the minute hand is already pointing to the first division of the dial and I am that number of minutes late. I have besides not got the book I ought to have—it should be Kennedy's *Elementary Latin Primer*—and what can have happened to my ruler I cannot say. Also my nib is crossed—Phipps minor has seen to that—and my fingers are stained with ink. So that, after hurrying through all those dusty classrooms and running the gauntlet of all those jeering boys, I shall be in triple disgrace: I shall have to listen to the master's bellowing voice as he turns on me: I shall be made to stand up on the form in the sight of everyone and I shall be kept in on the next half-holiday. And then, as likely as not, the dream will change and expand. I am standing in the boot-room passage and a boy who reminds me of a ferret gives me a kick. I am shivering on the edge of the swimming-pool when a cry goes up, 'Throw him in the deep end! Duck him!' A creature whose gums and teeth seem to be breaking out of his mouth like the seeds from a cracked pomegranate, says, 'I'll pay you out.' Hostile faces, hostile gestures, hostile words hem me in like those of the devils in a medieval painting. But they are not devils, only English schoolboys.

Dreams such as this, which once were frequent, provide an evidence that cannot be refuted. The shock of my first years at school was too great. And this brings me to a more general question. There is no misery, I am convinced, to be compared to the misery that is suffered in childhood. Children live very much in the present and have little faculty for hope or faith. Thus, if they are unhappy at their school, they will suffer despairingly, like prisoners who have been given a life sentence, because they cannot imagine it ever ending. This is a thing that parents should take into account before they pack their young son off to a boarding-school.

I now enter with relief upon the middle and more equable period of my prep-school days. The untidy, long-haired, ink-stained, novel-doped little boy whose memories I have inherited is approaching twelve. He was considered clever. He could parse any word in Cicero or Caesar and was well started in Greek, though how this had come about I cannot say. For when I sit here at my table and evoke those far-off school-time hours, I can remember nothing but boredom, drowsiness, hunger and a longing to be anywhere on earth rather than where I was at that moment.

The only subject that interested me at this time was geography, and even in this there was but one branch or department to which I attached much importance—that which concerned itself with oceanic islands. I knew the name and something of the character of every island that was marked on the map of the world that hung on the classroom wall. Some were large, lay close to other lands and were thickly populated. Others, such as Kerguelen or the Cocos Islands or Tristan da Cunha, were small and separated by several thousand miles from the nearest shore. These last were the ones for which I felt the strongest sympathy and attraction—round whose seed-like images on the blue atlas plain my imagination would coil and flow—and any books on the library shelves which I thought might contain an allusion to them were carefully gone through. But a mere visit to one of the islands was not enough to satisfy me. I needed to settle on it. Whenever possible, therefore, some part of prep would be spent in drawing surreptitiously on the back page of my exercise book the favourite of the moment, and since most of the particulars I needed were lacking, I took them freely from my head.

First I drew the island, solitary and uninhabited, and fixed its mountains and its streams. After that I chose a site for my house. A road was built to the port and another road to a more secluded residence. Having accomplished this, the map of the island should have been complete, but a love of planning and general development led me on till I had built harbours, railways, towns and mines and of course settled a thriving population on it. But by this time it had become utterly unfit for me, so that I was forced to migrate to a fresh island, at least two thousand miles distant, and begin the same laborious process over again. For the charm of life on an oceanic island lay precisely in those two thousand miles of water that surrounded it. Two thousand miles from football fields, two thousand miles from Greek conjugations, two thousand miles from old Gabby, our Latin master, and his stink! Till many years after I had grown up I believed that happiness was more easily to be achieved by ridding oneself of the things one did not want than by running after those one lacked.

Oddly enough there was another little boy in my class who had a similar mania to mine. He settled on islands, peninsulas and capes—anywhere, he said, where he could get a footing—in order to bring the blessings of civilization to them. By this he meant—to electrify them. He got his electricity according to circumstances from waterfalls, winds or tides: he set up his plant: he organized the distribution of current and then like myself he moved on somewhere else. Between us we industrialized in the course of a couple of years quite a considerable area of the earth's more scattered surfaces, but possibly because we acted on such very different principles—he out of a conviction of the absolute virtues of electricity, I, in direct contradiction to my most cherished beliefs, under the sheer inescapable pressure of economic law—there was no rivalry between us. Although he would sometimes protest at the unsuitability of my choice when I took one of his newly electrified islands for my hermitage, I never treated his industrial occupations too seriously. And when he moved on from islands and capes to land masses and continents, we turned our backs, as it were, upon one another.

This preoccupation with islands shows that I had some beginnings of a life of my own at this period. I should scarcely have insisted so much upon those two thousand miles unless I had already derived some pleasure from solitude. But in fact the struggle for popularity—which is the one and only passion of all school life, drawing into itself, as the great passions do, almost every other activity and interest—took up (apart from the purely passive addiction to reading) the greater part of my thoughts and energies. To explain the progress I now began to make, I must start with a portrait of one of our masters.

Mr Parker Clark (or Face-ache, as we sometimes called him—not to be confused with Mr Everett Clarke, our history master, commonly known as the Pill) was a young flannel-bagged, Norfolk-jacketed giant who taught us middle-form boys Latin and Greek. He had black curly hair like a negro, a very loud voice and plenty of good nature. Although he was also the sports master, even those boys who were not good at games liked him. He was famous for his original way of conducting his classes. A boy would stand up to construe a passage which he was supposed to have prepared in prep the night before. At the first serious mistake Mr Clark would put on a frown like thunder and start to shout at him. The boy would then mumble and fall into an even worse howler. 'Stand up on your chair,' bellowed Mr Clark, getting up himself and striding about the room. 'Up on your chair. We all want to look at you. Now try again.' Naturally the boy floundered more and more hopelessly. 'You're not high enough. Put a box on his chair.' A box used to keep papers in was put on his chair and he clambered up on top of it. 'Now see if *you* can construe it,' he would say, turning to another boy. 'You can't either, eh? Up on your chair, then.' And before long, unless some cooler head came to the rescue, the whole form would be perched on chairs and boxes upon chairs like so many Simeon Stylites, with Mr Clark pacing to and fro in front of them and bellowing. As he used to explain to us out of class, he was never angry when he shouted: we need not therefore be too afraid unless we saw him turn deadly pale and speak in a whisper: then, however, we must look out. But he was one of those people who are called boyish (even to us he seemed so) and I never saw him seriously annoyed.

Mr Clark had a number of ideas, considered by himself to be of a daring and even revolutionary nature, which for lack no doubt of a better audience he was fond of letting loose upon us. One of these, I remember, referred to the creation of the world in Genesis. Some learned people, he declared, thought that by the 'days' mentioned in this passage were really meant millions of years. And naturally, by the tone in which these words were spoken, we were left to gather that these 'some learned people' were right. This method of interpreting Scripture struck me as throwing a flood of light upon the more perplexing of the Bible stories—those, for example, which describe the sun and moon as standing still while an unimportant battle was fought and the mountains as hopping about in their enthusiasm like sheep—so that from this moment the doubts that had begun to assail the natural fundamentalism of my schoolboy mind were arrested.

It was at about this time too that I first began to feel the fascination of those sweeping statements that begin with the word *Really*. The climate of opinion which a boy or young man then ran into—it is the one which prevails through a large part of the world today—suggested that nothing is what it seems to be, but on the contrary is always something else, and that if one wishes to know what this something else really is (and it is of course entirely different to the natural appearance), one must seek the key or explanation that gives it. An absurd example of this relates to railway-carriage wheels. We had read or been told that compressed paper is one of the hardest materials known to science, and then a boy called Mullins, whom we regarded as an authority on such matters, declared that all railway-carriage wheels were made of it. They might *look* as if they were made of steel, but *really*, as every engineer knew, they were made of boiled-down newspapers. I accepted this as being entirely self-evident—did not every scientific statement bear the same paradoxical pattern?—and continued to believe it until many years after I was grown up, when an engineer to whom I happened to mention it laughed at me. Later—that is, after I had passed the age of fifteen—came the impact of atomic theories, social and economic theories, psychological and philosophical theories and the word Really became the inevitable prefix to every serious conversation.

But to return to Mr Clark, another idea of his that made a great impression on me concerned the rise and fall of empires. Pointing to the atlas and to those large, triumphant blots of red that spread over it, he declared that seven empires had risen and fallen since the world began—here he enumerated the Assyrian, the Persian, the Greek, the Roman and so forth—and that some day the British Empire must fall too. This idea shocked me considerably. For one thing I was an ardent patriot, and then there was the serious effect that such changes would have upon geography. Maps would have to be recoloured, names changed, national and colonial boundaries redrawn. I wanted to think of those great red blots—and of the blue and yellow and green blots too—going on like the mountains and the rivers for ever.

A considerable part of Mr Clark's conversation ran on his public school. It was a small, obscure place—Pillings, if I remember right, was its name—but we gathered from him that it was *really*, in every respect that counted, the best in England. Certainly neither Eton, Harrow nor Winchester came up to it. I got at all events such an idea of its fame and exclusiveness that, meeting in the holidays with a boy who was bound for Eton and wishing to go one better, I remarked casually, 'Well, *I* have my name put down for Pillings.' When I found that he had never even heard of it, I decided that there was no need for me to boast any more—he was too ignorant to be worth impressing.

Mr Clark had brought from his school a creed, somewhat unusual in a games master, that little boys are not saved by proficiency in games alone, but also, in specially judicated cases, by the more elusive qualities of dare-devilry and recklessness. In support of this theory he used to instance the great Clive, who had never done well at bat and ball but was as agile as a cat in climbing steeples. Yet he had conquered India! Now it so happened that I was fond of climbing trees. There was one tree in particular overlooking the cricket field where I used to retire with a book when I was supposed to be watching the match. When I had reached the highest ascendable point, which actually was at the very top, I would settle myself into it and look out. Beneath me and all around rolled a sea of sycamore leaves, each leaf horizontally extended, layer above layer, cutting me off completely from the ground. Above, a few white clouds lay about like comfortable sofas in the sleepy sky, while from the direction of the playing field the thud of cricket bats striking on balls made a lazy cushioned sound. Until the school bell rang I was almost as free from interruption as if I had been on my oceanic island.

One afternoon, when I was sitting up there, I dropped my book. As chance would have it, Mr Clark, got up in his white flannels and gaudy Pillings blazer, was just then passing underneath. He called me down in his stentorian voice and sent me back to the match, but I noticed that from this time on he treated me with special kindness. Whether thoughts of Clive and the great empire builders of the past had anything to do with this I cannot say, but since he was the most popular master in the school his support helped to remove the more athletic boys' prejudices against me.

At the same time other factors were beginning, though still slowly and uncertainly, to turn the scales in my favour. Even for schoolboys, time passes. The little hunted animal I had been, to whom flight and taking sanctuary had become a second nature, was beginning to change into a more sedate and self-possessed creature. In all schools there is a current which, however often one slips back, carries one inevitably towards the top. The boys above leave, new boys queue up behind and, by the mere passage of time, prestige and popularity are acquired. The last year of my life at Winton House was to be as happy as my first two or three years had been miserable.

CHAPTER V

Prep School—Rise to Popularity

From my earliest days at school I had been regarded by my masters as clever. 'Clever but inattentive', ran my reports. 'Careless, dreamy and absent-minded.' 'Could be at the top of the class if he tried.' All through my school life my preceptors believed that I was intelligent, whereas the truth is that I was moderately bright sometimes and dull at others. Such intelligence as I possess has always been of an intuitive kind, short-winded, easily confused, hampered by a bad memory and in no way to be relied upon.

During my first school years, therefore, I was always in trouble. Regularly every Saturday I would be sent for to Mr Johns's study to receive the swishing that fell to those who got more than twenty black conduct marks. I took these punishments philosophically: the cane did not hurt my feelings, because it was administered without malevolence. It might even help in reducing my unpopularity. However, by the end of 1905 these clashes with authority were becoming a thing of the past and before long scholastic triumphs had begun to scatter their laurels and to make up in some degree for my other inadequacies.

I starred first in geography. It became one of the features of exam week to look at the notice board and see my name at the head of the school list, marked either 99 or (full marks) 100. Then I crept to the top in French, Scripture and History. In Latin and Greek—the main subjects—I was less proficient, while in maths I was near the bottom of my class. I detested algebra, arithmetic and geometry.

Just in front of me, but divided by a gulf, was Barrington-Ward. A small, dark boy, silent and watchful as a woodland animal (we called him 'Dormouse'), he sailed easily ahead in Latin and Greek, although he was a year younger than anyone in the class. The Barrington-Wards —there had been several of them—were always cleverer than anyone else. Then he got a scholarship at Westminster—I think it must have been at the end of the 1907 summer term—and I became the head boy in the school. This meant a safe position, happiness and all the popularity I needed.

I should be ungrateful, however, if I did not make it clear that I owed this ascent to the schoolboy Olympus in great measure to Mr Parker Clark. During the summer holidays of 1905—a few months after he had discovered me hiding in the tree—he married and settled with his wife in a little villa on the Basingstoke Road. Since they had a spare room and not much money they wished to take in a boy as a boarder. Probably because they felt that I needed encouragement they chose me. Thus I found myself exchanging the dreariness and inhumanity of the school classrooms and library for the friendliness of a private house. In one term my school reports went over from bad to very good. My backwardness and my bad-conduct marks had been due solely to my feeling of insecurity.

Yet my recollections of the two years I spent with the Clarks are not, as might be supposed, of an entirely pleasant kind. There still hung about me traces of that pre-adolescent guilt or morbidity which breaks out in children who are not secure or happy. This showed itself as an element of disgust or horror hidden under what, to other people, would have seemed perfectly ordinary things. Take, for example, the road I used to follow to and from school. It was a typical suburban road that, after crossing the railway cutting in a casual sort of way, ran down a hill between vacant building lots and private, shrubbery-screened villas. In summer it seemed an innocent enough place, with its flowering privet hedges on one side and its wilderness of long grass and weeds on the other, yet this innocence was tainted for me by several things. One was a feeling I suddenly developed about the sufferings of hawk-moths. The lamplighter, an old, crooked, dirtily dressed man who had a broken thumb, caught them and put them into match-boxes which later he fished out of his pockets and gave to me; and when I opened these boxes, in which they lay tightly packed like mummies in their cases, I could see their antennae trembling a little and hear their feet scraping on the bottom. This was horrible. I took a dislike to this old man who was my accomplice in atrocities and one night dreamed that he was a gravedigger, burying bodies. But I could not for all that give up my collector's craving for rare specimens.

Autumn followed summer and there came days on which a state of inevitable, increasing evil hung over this road. Spiders' webs draped themselves like mildew over the bushes, a late tortoise-shell butterfly crawled about in torpor, there was a smell of mould from the fallen leaves that lay piled up in the gutters. Then came the first frosts, when the Jerusalem artichokes turned black in a night and the whole vegetable garden seemed to be writhing in agony. And when at length spring arrived, it was not with flowers but with a plague of frogs which got squashed under the car wheels and left flat, green patterns on the road surface.

But it was after nightfall that the thermometer of morbidity rose highest. The road had now become a string of lamp-lit pools, fringed by shadows. Out of these a stealthy figure could at any moment appear—Jack the Ripper—moving in great hops like a kangaroo because he had springs under his boots to pounce on the unsuspecting parlour-maid. Then one summer evening, in the long grass of a vacant lot, I saw a man lying on top of a woman and moving his body over hers in a curious manner. Was he strangling her? Ought I to inform the police? Or—?

Once in the Clarks' house the sense of sinister things lurking just out of sight vanished, but a mild repugnance took its place. I had never been in a small villa before. Like most children I was extremely sensitive to taste and smell as well as very conscious of the class emanations of my environment. Thus the shoddiness of the cheap furniture repelled me, the smell of new linoleum in the passages, the smell of slops when the maid emptied the pails and especially the black, snuffling snout of the bulldog—an animal which symbolized for me the lower middle classes and which had once made a mess in the dining-room. How different was this ugly box of a place to our own old, rambling, comfortable house which fitted every mood like a glove and where everything seemed to have come together casually through the processes of Nature!

However, in the centre of this red brick villa lived Mrs Clark. In her early twenties, plump in the right places, extremely pretty, she had on her face that look of dreamy contentment which newly married young women, expanding in the soft air of sex, sometimes have. Not only her mouth but her whole body seemed to be smiling and these smiles corresponded to a tone—protecting, insinuating, incriminating, loverly—which burgeoned out in the usually gruff speech of Mr Parker Clark. Every day I ate my eggs and bacon and porridge to the accompaniment of a lovers' dialogue. Now this was new to me. In our house in Gloucestershire, as in my grandmother's house in Ireland, there had never been anything of the sort. Sex—the word was not in our dictionary: among people who had been properly brought up it did not exist. Evidently, therefore, some sort of distinction must be made. The background for sex was not grey Cotswold walls, flowered chintz chair-covers, blue bowls of potpourri, stone-tiled kitchens, but Bulldogs, Bicycle sheds, Gas fires, Slop pails, Cooking smells, Cheap hard furniture. In other words it was an occupation for the lower middle classes (by which I meant, for those who did not dress for dinner) and so not altogether, in fact not at all, or only at certain moments, and those rather dubious moments too, proper and respectable.

A number of disconnected pictures flit through my mind when I think of my life at this villa—Mr Parker Clark in his green Norfolk jacket leaning back against the mantelpiece with his hands fumbling in the pockets of his trousers: Mrs Clark in a pink flannel dressing-gown passing hurriedly across the landing: Mr Parker Clark again, this time in the bathroom, looking like Hercules after he had taken off his lion-skin cloak. They spoke, no doubt, they said important and memorable things, but I do not remember what they were. The only episode of which I retain any recollection is that which relates to jam tarts.

Lunch was just over but the plates not yet cleared away when Mrs Clark, who was alone in the house with me, left the room. On the table there were two jam tarts and, without stopping to think, I put one of them in my mouth. Hardly had I done so when Mrs Clark came in again. She saw me gulping, she saw the empty space on the plate and she connected the two things. 'Have you taken a tart?' she asked. 'No,' I replied, shaking my head, 'oh, no.' 'There were certainly two tarts on that plate when I went out of the room and now there is only one. You must have taken it.' 'Indeed, Mrs Clark, I did not.' 'Then why has your mouth got jam on it?' 'I don't know. I didn't take it.' 'You're telling lies. I don't mind a bit your taking the tart, but you shouldn't lie about it. Come, own up.' 'But I swear I didn't take it, Mrs Clark. I swear I didn't.'

She went on insisting I should confess, I continued to deny, and even her husband when he came home could not make me admit to having done it. She was much more annoyed than he was and it shows, I think, unusual sense in a schoolmaster that he should have let the matter drop without reading me a moral lecture. He was an easy-going man, happiest when he was coaching boys on the football field or otherwise employing his loud, stentorian voice, and perhaps too he thought more highly of Clive than of George Washington. I, however, felt a deep shame over this incident which I imagined had disgraced me for ever in the eyes of Mrs Clark, and made a resolution never again to tell a lie unless I could do so without the risk of its being found out.

Now that I was in the top form I began to see a good deal more of our headmaster, Mr Johns. 'Jumbo', as we called him, was a large, ugly man with a purplish-red face, a coarse nose, huge red ears and beautiful eyes. In his youth he had been affected by the aesthetic movement of the eighties and because of this he wore his black, glossy hair a little longer than was usual, spoke in a drawl that, when he wanted to be funny, turned to a lisp and, when he shook hands, held out a weak, almost dripping paw for the other person to press. He was very clever at dealing with parents, mixing wit with flattery in his carefully chosen allusions to little Tommy and at the same time, by the bland, airy insouciance of his manner, conveying a sense of the indescribable social privileges that were attached to an education at his establishment. Yet, though he lived by others' snobbery, he was not, except in a general way, a snob himself: his life was too closely bound up with his school to leave him much time for other interests. All the great zest and enjoyment he drew from being a headmaster found scope in it. Indeed, as one watched him passing from chair to chair at a cricket match, practising his *bons mots* on parents, his jokes and ear-tweaks on smirking boys, one realized that he got as much of the aesthete's pleasure out of running his own school as a younger man might have done from carrying a lily down Bond Street or Arthur Balfour from being the leader of the Tories. If, seen from our angle, his bearing proclaimed an Oriental hedonism, tempered by a good deal of punning, there were also bursts of sultriness; and when, after one of these, one entered his study in the evening, one would find him playing the 'cello in a darkened room with half-closed eyes. Those beautiful velvety eyes with their clear whites that seemed so sad at having to live in such a face!

Some years before I arrived at the school there had been a scandal. Mr Johns's partner, Mr X, had been discovered in a compromising situation with a boy and had had to leave. This was something which it took a good deal of social manner to live down, for although I am certain that Mr Johns was always more careful in his actions as well as, in all probability, more timid and indefinite in his feelings, it was only too obvious that his tastes lay in the same direction. This ugly, refined, autocratic, humorous man gave the whole of his emotive side to boys and made the school where he assembled them the centre of his life. That was why for those of us who were over twelve or thirteen (he did not interest himself in the younger ones) he was such a good schoolmaster.

It was amusing to see him at meal-times in the crowded dining-room, sitting upright in his big chair at the head of the principal table and surrounded by the jabbering, gobbling, giggling schoolboys. He

looked like Haroun-al-Raschid taking his ease among his sixty con-
cubines. Suddenly he would bang his hand on the table and the whole
room would fall into silence. 'Perks minor, was that you who made
that unseemly noise? Be so good as either to refrain or to leave
the room.' He was a pasha all over, unpredictable in his moods, now
flushing with anger, now gentle, but most often relaxing into a
pun.

Another occasion on which to see him was on our Sunday morning
visits to church. The whole school would turn out, dressed in Eton
jackets, striped trousers and top hats and form into a crocodile. In
this manner we would wend our way down to the town. Beside us
walked Mr Johns, big ears, purple face, Homburg hat, short Niagara
moustache, swishing a Malacca cane: lisping occasional jokes to the
boys nearest him, but also on the look-out for breaches of discipline.
Other men might have been ashamed to be seen in such a ludicrous
situation, but he in his grand way was proud of us.

To the younger boys Jumbo was always a somewhat alarming
figure. One could not predict his moods. On Saturdays he swished one
—he was very fond of caning—and on Sundays he read aloud Sherlock
Holmes and distributed sweets. The same offence on different days
would lead either to a tweak of the ear and a pun, or to a thunderous
brow and five strokes of the cane. However, this was what we liked
about him. It is a great mistake to suppose that small boys demand of
their rulers impartiality and justice: like the politically undeveloped
races, they prefer a benevolent autocracy given to bursts of passion
because they understand that better. The only things they must have
are generosity and humour.

As I have said, it was only when one reached the top form that one
got to know Mr Johns well. That was because he took the seniors in
Greek. When the hour marked on the notice-board came, we would
troop up the passage that led to his private house and knock on his
study door. Then we would settle ourselves into sofas and armchairs
and construe Homer or Xenophon. If he was in a good mood puns
would fly about and sweets be distributed, but if he frowned one had
to be careful. Yet he was not a good teacher. He made no attempt
whatever to arouse our interest in what we were reading. Either he
made jokes about the Homeric epithets or else he set us searching for
odd figures of speech, as though they were the principal objects of
interest in literature. What I remember from these hours is chiefly
therefore a rag-bag of onomatopoeias, oxymorons, hypallages, ana-
coluthons, hysteron-proterons and so forth—all of course quite

pointless. Like James Joyce, he seemed to love words in order to make fun of them.

But it was on mothing expeditions that one got to know him most intimately. Mr Johns was a great entomologist and most of the school collected moths and butterflies. On fine summer evenings therefore (motors were fast coming in) he would take two or three of the older boys out in his car. The procedure was this: we would pull up at an oak wood, smear treacle on the trees and then, after a short wait, during which we had cocoa and buns by the car head-lights, collect the moths that had gathered. It was only his special favourites that he invited on these occasions, but as I was the friend of a very good-looking boy called Burnside, who was his fancy of the year, I was nearly always included. One July night we went as far as the New Forest, stopped in a glade by some great oak trees and on our way home had dinner in a hotel at Southampton. This—the long moonlight drive followed by the restaurant meal—was for me a new and wonderful experience. Lying back in the smooth darkness of the car, watching the antennae of light that stroked the edges of the road, smelling the brilliantine from le beau Burnside's hair as he leaned upon my shoulder seemed to hold out promises of new pleasures awaiting me when I grew up.

I was now at the head of the school and one of a small, close but also rather quarrelsome group of friends. The two that I was most bound up with were Cooke and Mackenzie, my rivals in class. Then came Burnside, captain of the cricket eleven, for whom I had conceived a romantic attachment because he reminded me of Charles I. He was a rather staid boy, with such fine curly black hair and such a milk-and-roses complexion that to feel entirely pleased with himself he had only to look in the glass. Other boys in widening circles followed, among whom I will only cite Patterson, captain of the football eleven. A plain youth with an honest dog face, ashamed of being in a low form, he took a certain liking to me and one day explained to me, with a solo demonstration, the secrets of sex and the peculiar and, I thought, repellent way in which children are made. Was it possible, I asked myself, that my parents and all those other dignified grown-ups one saw at cricket matches had at some time or other been obliged to go through this ungainly performance?

Mackenzie was a dark-haired, dot-eyed boy, very small in size, who suggested to me a mouse or a monkey or still more an ant nibbling at something. Being of exactly my own age, he had come up with me through the circles of misery and unpopularity, but always several places ahead because he was better at games. Now, however, on more mature inspection, his stock began to fall. This was because he was discovered to be a 'copy cat'. Lacking imagination and invention, he would listen to what other boys said and then repeat it in his little mincing way as his own. What was almost equally serious, in spite of his excellent memory he was poor at Latin and Greek but good at maths. The temper of the top form being classical, this was another reason for looking down on him.

One Christmas holidays, just before I was twelve, I had gone to stay with Mackenzie. He lived at Hastings with two maiden aunts, for his parents were dead. Through the kindness of these aunts we had a wonderful time, racing about the town on trams with our pockets full of caramels and every evening eating lobster mayonnaise followed by Devonshire cream and fruit salad. But the aunts didn't dress for dinner—in fact they didn't dine at all, but instead had high tea. Deeply shocked in my social susceptibilities—for in these matters it was I who was the copy cat—I told my mother that I could never go to stay there again. When some time later I quarrelled with Mackenzie, I was tempted to pass on this dreadful secret about his aunts' habits to one of the other boys, but luckily was restrained by my sense of schoolboy propriety. For, the ethics of tale-telling apart, no subject is so taboo at prep schools as that of parents. I have known boys boast of having committed indecent acts with their sisters who would have died of shame rather than admit that their fathers were stockbrokers or major-generals. One knew nothing about one's school friends' home life until one went to stay with them, and what one saw then could never be mentioned again, even to them.

Cooke, the other of my particular friends, was a much more genial boy than Mackenzie. Younger than myself, high-spirited and intelligent, he had the face of a laughing, sensual cupid under his curly, brown hair. He had a fine mezzo-soprano voice and there was something bubbling and gurgling about his whole temperament which alternately attracted and repelled me. When I went to stay with him at Hampstead I realized that his almost Italian gaiety was connected with his having a happy home life. His father was a barrister and to show their Cockney *joie de vivre* the whole family would throw themselves into the Highgate Ponds every Christmas morning and come out laughing.

This Triple Alliance—Cooke, Mackenzie and myself—was broken by a cruel event that took place just before the end of my last term. Cooke and Mackenzie were caught in some sexual misdemeanour and the whole school, which was very strait-laced in these matters, turned against them. They were put into Coventry. I acted in a despicable way. Although privately I was puzzled rather than shocked by what my friends had done, as soon as I was with the other boys a spurious indignation poured into me from the reservoirs of herd emotion outside and I became one of the leaders of the mob that jeered at them. This led to my having a fight with Cooke in which we ended by rolling over and over on the ground, our noses bleeding, in a furious rage. Everyone applauded: I was a hero. But remorse soon set in. I had suffered too much in the past from the mob mentality not to know how these two were feeling, and a deep shame and self-disgust came over me as I thought of the part that I had played. I resolved never to act in this way again.

And now the summer term of 1908 came to an end and my days at Winton House were over. My name had been put down for Harrow, where my mother's brothers had been educated, but there was as yet no vacancy. Where then should I go? My parents desired Winchester, whereas Mr Johns pressed the claims of Radley, which he declared to be a very special school, second only in the gentleman-building qualities to Eton. For it was for this that our parents paid such high fees. In the end I went up for examinations at both Winchester and Radley and in each case gained one of those minor scholarships known as exhibitions. But since the result of the Radley exam came through first, it was there that I went.

CHAPTER VI

Holidays

Like all schoolboys I was one person at school and another in the holidays. At school a little herd animal, living in the outer compartments of my mind, straining to win the good opinion of my fellows: at home a human child, safe and emotionally dependent upon my family. Two such parallel lives require two separate accounts so I will go back a few years and describe as best I can the periods I spent with my parents.

Both my father and my mother believed in my having as much liberty as possible. So long as I was in time for meals or arranged to take a snack with me I could do pretty well what I liked. I grew up therefore to be an independent, outdoor-loving boy, going for walks or for rides on my pony by myself, collecting all the various things that boys collect and in the summer spending happy afternoons by the stream, where I built dams for model water-wheels which the village carpenter made me and lifted stones to catch crayfish without any risk of being scolded if I got dirty and wet. I especially loved riding, and my father, who at this time was pleased with me, would spoil his day's hunting to take me out with him to follow Captain Elwes's hounds or the Cotswold. When it snowed we went tobogganing and when it froze there would be much talk of ordering skates, although, on its thawing immediately after, the order would be cancelled and the matter postponed to next year.

The person round whom our house revolved was my father. He was now deaf, and to hear used a little silver trumpet shaped like a snail's shell. Since he was a very quick, alert man, lithe and abrupt in his movements, he would swivel it about from one person to another with great adroitness. This lent a special air of intensity to all conversations with him: one could not—at least we could not—speak casually or carelessly into such an instrument, especially when one's eye was caught by his yellow bristling moustache beside it. For that moustache seemed to be saying: 'I give you just ten seconds to put your views in. I can't listen for longer.' However in general company, where he had very good manners, his attentiveness was what most impressed people. Since his voice never acquired the deaf person's monotone and his quickness enabled him to take in so much, strangers easily forgot that he did not hear almost as well as everyone else.

However, he suffered under his disability. By nature an impatient, irritable man, deafness laid on him a load he was scarcely fitted to bear. It also cut him off very much from the world. He read little and every communication that reached him from outside had to be couched in a definite, telegram-like form. The finer shades, the over-tones given by things overheard, eluded him. This was in part, of course, because he wanted it. He hated hesitation—through an ear-trumpet a hesitating voice is agony—and in the family insisted that everything should be in clear-cut, yes-and-no terms. The consequence of this was that he became more and more imprisoned in himself and in his really immense and overbearing male egoism. For in the house no one else counted. His mood, perpetually varying, became the family weather. At one moment he would be genial and kind, at the next, for no reason at all, dangerous and unapproachable. We—my mother and myself—were like peasants living on the slopes of a volcano: every morning we would look up to see if the sky was clear or whether smoke and lava might be expected to come rolling down upon us.

The explanation offered by my mother for this phenomenon was a thing called 'the liver'. My father's nature was in itself good and kind, but when 'the liver' assailed him, a black cloud came over it. Prog-nostication on the state of this organ became therefore an important business in our life: it turned us, my mother particularly, into Roman augurs. Now the moment when its condition could best be detected was at breakfast. My father got up at eight and after doing some dumb-bell exercises and drinking a tumbler of fruit salts, went to the bath-room. If my mother was still in it, he would rattle on the door and she would come out hurriedly, wrapped in a faded flannel dressing-gown, without perhaps having had time to dry herself. At this hour the smallest interruption to his toilet put him out. Then he would shave, often cutting himself in the process, and dabbing on the cut a piece of white cotton-wool which remained there till dinner-time. (For years I used to look with awe on these white blobs, regarding it as a proof of his inherently ferocious nature that he had to begin the morning by wounding himself.) After that he would dress, muttering to himself in a low voice as he did so, and ending with a tussle with gaiters and riding-boots. Still he was not ready to come down: he had to say his prayers and then—though here I am perhaps anticipating by a few years—to sit in meditation for five minutes with a book in front of him.

At length the critical, haruspicious moment arrived. At precisely twenty-five minutes past nine he would come downstairs, tap on the barometer that hung in the hall and then, blowing his nose loudly on a silk bandanna handkerchief, would enter the dining-room and, without a word to anyone, go to the sideboard and pour out a cup of coffee. My mother, who had long finished her breakfast, would be in her place knitting and as he came in she would turn an anxious gaze towards him, waiting for the omen. For the coffee was the test. If it tasted right on his palate, he would say with a beaming face, 'The coffee is excellent this morning. Congratulate Frankton.' Then we would know that we were in for a good day and my mother would lean across to him with a happy expression and make some remark about the letters she had received. But if it tasted bad, he would snap out, 'This stuff is filth,' and on really catastrophic occasions would stride to the bell cord and pull it out of the socket. 'Send for the cook,' he would command in a taut, angry voice, but as he did not really want the cook sent for—for he only meant to frighten my mother— he would allow her to dismiss the parlour-maid who answered the bell with a weak explanation and accept the promise that she would speak to the cook afterwards. The odd thing was that the coffee was always the same, that is, always bad, because my parents having got the idea that only the French can make it, the pot was filled with a mixture that was one-third chicory.

Deafness, 'liver' and ego eruptions apart, my parents were getting on badly. Was my father, now a man of thirty-three or -four, tired of living with a woman who was eight years older than himself? It would be hard to answer this conclusively, for he was always tired of everything. No house, no occupation, no person could suit him for more than a very short time. He was chronically dissatisfied and unsettled. A flat-minded Byron, perpetually bored and perpetually at war with himself, he found my mother a convenient person on whom to vent his sense of grievance. However, it must be admitted that there were things about her which under any circumstances would have irritated him. He disliked her enthusiasm, the jaunty, optimistic note that too often came into her speech, her lack of dignity, that something scattered and resilient in her mind which prevented her from either standing up to him firmly or yielding completely. His task, as he conceived it, was to reduce her to order, to discipline her, to bring her down to his own matter-of-fact and positive level. As others saw it, to make her entirely subservient to him. Yet during the pauses that varied the lifelong warfare he waged against her, there would come over him moments of remorse, recognitions of that endless goodness and unselfishness of hers which welled up out of her great love of life. She, when given a chance to be happy, was happy; he was not. Perhaps one may sum up their mutual situation by saying that they were two incompatibles—she a Christian of the second century, he a Stoic with a sense of guilt. Yet because love is so often founded on incompatibility, she never ceased to be in love with him while he, after his own fashion, was fond of her. If it was not a very vigorous fashion, that is because there was no place in his nature for deep feelings towards other people. His own problems kept him absorbed in himself.

During these years that I am describing—that is to say, while I was still painfully climbing the ladder to popularity at my prep school— my parents' dissensions were going through a particularly violent phase. One reason for this, I imagine, was that my father, who was still a young man, had nothing to do. To the end of his life he was to suffer from boredom because he had no occupation and could not bear to restrict his freedom by taking work of some sort, but at this time the predicament was especially onerous because it was new. Then his deafness increased his natural impatience. As he grew older he developed a philosophy which taught him, in some measure, to adapt himself to circumstances and to restrain or damp down his more violent impulses, but in these years, whenever he felt like rampaging, he did so.

The great scenes always began in the same way. My father, in his black mood, assailed like Prometheus in his liver, would look round for someone on whom to vent his irritation. This someone was always my mother. Bursting with a sense of injured impotence, craving to rend and destroy, he would find his opportunity in one of those appeasing remarks that, with incurable tactlessness, she invariably made when she saw trouble coming. Without looking up, he would snub her and then, throwing down the *Morning Post* which he had been reading, he would turn on her in the rude and contemptuous tone that came so natural to him. The tone of the Victorian gentleman addressing his wife, which even the Married Woman's Property Act had done little to mitigate. She, obedient wife that she was, would take this meekly, only muttering to me apologetically under her breath that this morning he had 'a little touch of the liver'. But meekness was a spur to my father. He wanted to hurt, to injure, yet he was afraid of going too far, because he did not like scenes. One would therefore see him hesitate. Usually, with that quick metallic step of his, his heels striking sharply on the ground, he would stride out of the room to his sanctum, where the latest communication from his stockbroker would provide a soothing influence. Manipulating stocks and shares—*his* stocks and shares—gave him an intimate satisfaction. But sometimes the longing to break out would prove too strong and he would play the fatal card—that is, make an insinuation on some member of my mother's family. Now the fat was in the fire. Losing her self-control completely, my mother would flare up, while he, frightened by what he had done, would either hurry noisily from the room or else begin, in a hard, injured tone, a verbal justification. Such was the classic pattern—the attack and retreat being much more prolonged and argued out in later years, but at this time abrupt and violent.

One of these scenes—it took place in January 1904, when I was not yet ten—I recall with painful vividness. My parents were standing facing one another in the dining-room. What they were saying to one another I do not know: all I remember is that my father made an angry gesture and that my mother fell at his feet on the smooth parquet floor as though he had struck her. To me it was exactly as if he had done so and a feeling of the greatest horror came over me. Today, however, I understand the matter more clearly. My father, sadistic though he often was in his feelings towards his wife, was incapable of physical violence and it was my mother, with her melo-dramatic masochism, who had misinterpreted his gesture. A more cynical person might discover in this scene one of those symbolic dramas into which so many married persons project their love life.

When I was older a quarrel between my parents usually ended with-in a day or two in a reconciliation, after which my mother, whose side I would have taken, though not so strongly as she had wished (for I always tried to act as mediator), would turn somewhat against me. But in the years that I am now describing, my father's moods—exacer-bated perhaps by the after effects of malaria—were more consistently black and when, after the scene I have just described, I came back for the Easter holidays, my mother greeted me with the words, 'Since you were here last, your father has not spoken a single word to me.' He had got into a silent, bitter frame of mind and had frozen in it. Then one morning a thaw came, and he melted.

It would be natural to suppose that these quarrels between my parents made a deep impression on me. The dark, cold rooms, my father's violence and my mother's distress stand out vividly in my memory. I have no doubt that they did something to increase the insecurity and misery of my life at school. Yet I must be careful not to exaggerate. My father was at this time nearly always kind and friendly to me. This was partly because, when he was at odds with my mother, he had to be pleasant with everyone else. He could not bear to have the whole house against him. But it was also the case that he liked schoolboys and, till I showed signs of growing up the wrong way, he made me his companion. Thus he taught me to sit my pony and to take fences, to play billiards and snooker, to help him at his photography and in his carpenter's shop. Later he taught me to shoot. I was, I think, genuinely attached to him even though I was never entirely at ease in his company. For how was it possible to be? There were so many small things that irritated him that one had to be perpetually on one's guard if one wished to avoid a snub. And then, since one of his greatest pleasures was the sensation he got from wielding power, even the most insignificant instructions tended to take the form of orders. A few words delivered in a tone of this sort would destroy whole hours of pleasant companionship.

The other member of our household of whom I must speak was my grandmother—that is, my father's mother. Although she had a flat in London, she spent Christmas and most of the summer with us. My mother, who was not allowed to have her own family to the house for more than a couple of days at a time, did not grudge having her to stay because she was so quiet and unobtrusive. Wrapped in her deafness (to make her hear one had to shout into a black collapsible trumpet, or else into a long flexible tube that gave her the air of a snake-charmer) she passed sedately and with a faint rustle of silk about the house or sat embroidering cushion covers on the drawing-room sofa. From time to time she would make some remark of an innocuous kind. Thus every evening after the first of September came round she would say in her thin transparent voice (I thought of it as a skeleton leaf) that the days were drawing in—this would give occasion for a sigh—and then after Christmas had passed, but in a slightly firmer tone, that the spring fashions that year were unbecoming. When not addressing us she would whisper gently to herself as she moved her needle—an innocent, sibilant monologue that usually began with a 'Helen says' or 'Hugh says' and would then go on to repeat some remark that had been made to her half an hour before. She took in little, she was as vegetative as a fern in a pot, but there was a charm in her gentle, un-ruffled appearance and dignified manners that made one love her.

My grandmother's London life was largely conducted for her by her strong-minded and eccentric elder sister, my great-aunt Addie, of whom I shall have much to say later on. One of their principal shared interests lay in the feuds and cabals that divided their club in Dover Street. Another was in clothes, over which they disagreed sharply, while the third, where they were entirely of one mind, was antivivisection. When my grandmother arrived at our house, she left the club and its intrigues behind her with a sigh of relief, but brought with her her two other preoccupations.

The most interesting of these from my point of view was antivivisection, for with it went a hatred of blood sports and a great love of animals. I was fond of animals too though neither of my parents cared for them. My father, it is true, had a high regard for horses because he rode them, and he likewise approved of dogs because one could give them orders. 'I should like to keep a dog,' he once remarked to my sister-in-law, 'for my own purposes.' His reason for not doing so was that he feared it would poach in one of his neighbours' woods and so cause that neighbour to write him a letter which would require an apology. But my mother had no such motives for tolerating them. Afraid of horses and of large dogs and uneasy with smaller animals, she would declare, when the subject came up, that it was 'unnatural' to give to pets what was due only to human beings. All her protective feelings went to children.

My grandmother, in spite of her gentle air, had a fund of obstinacy and from time to time she would make an open stand in defence of her principles. I remember one occasion of this sort, when my father, dressed in his hunting clothes, was eating his eggs and bacon with the *Morning Post* erected like a screen in front of him. The coffee omens that morning had been unfavourable and my mother and I were waiting in trepidation for him to push back his chair and ride off.

'Hugh,' exclaimed my grandmother suddenly, tapping his paper barrier with her trumpet. 'Hugh!'

He lowered the corner of the sheet and looked up.

'You should stay at home, Hugh. You ought not to go hunting. It's a cruel sport.'

My father without a word raised his paper again and went on eating.

'You're a cruel man, Hugh,' persisted my grandmother, tapping again on the paper. 'You ought not to take pleasure in killing. I say, you're a cruel man.'

As my father continued to pay no attention, my mother came to his defence with one of the usual arguments. Although she herself could not bear to see an animal killed, she believed in blood sports because they were part of the life she had been brought up to. But the old lady, having once made her protest, had no more to say.

Another of her characteristics was a love of nature. It was rather a theoretical love, because she was a born Londoner who thought of the country chiefly as a place to which one retired for short periods for the sake of one's health. It was the idea of nature that she enjoyed rather than the actuality. So while we all shared her indignation when great woodland trees were cut down, we were surprised at the strength of her protest when my mother announced her plan for turning an old rockery, overgrown with couch-grass and ground elder, into a rock garden for alpine plants.

'You should leave it as it is, Helen,' she declared. 'It is much prettier as it is.'

'But it's a mass of weeds, Grannie. When I've got them up I shall put in such lovely new flowers.'

'You have all the rest of the garden for your flowers. Weeds have their right to live too.'

This argument made a great impression on me. I liked flowers and was anxious to see the new alpines, whose pictures I had been shown in the catalogue, yet my grandmother's declaration of the rights of weeds struck a responsive chord in my mind. My experiences at school had taught me the need for tolerating the unpopular.

Besides the members of our family, there were the servants. Our cook, Frankton, was a lean, bony woman who, before coming to us, had been cook-housekeeper to an unmarried clergyman. A parson of the old style, people said, who had ridden to hounds twice a week, made his parish visits in a frock-coat and gained the reputation of being a *bon viveur*. During her thirty years of service with him Frankton had got a good deal set in her ways, wearing a sort of washed-out bonnet on the top of her head and priding herself upon having never travelled on a train or seen the sea. Besides this, she carried a perpetual smile on her rather acrid face, read the Bible every night after supper and made the hardest and most indigestible cakes and puddings in Gloucestershire. Her only other dishes were roasts and boiled vege-tables.

My father, who had the digestion of an ostrich, never noticed these limitations in her cooking. Food to him was food—that is, something to be put into the mouth at meal-times and swallowed—although on suitable occasions, when my brother or I were present, he would indulge in a rather forced joviality over strawberries or ice-cream. Nor was my mother much more exacting, for although she professed a great respect for 'good, wholesome food' and the need that growing boys had of it, she scarcely ate at all herself. If the dishes that were set on the table escaped criticism, she was satisfied. Yet she must have had some obscure inkling that there was an anti-Frankton case, for every now and then, when the subject came up in her mind, she would proceed in her own characteristic way to silence her scruples.

'I do think,' she would suddenly declare, speaking in her most forthright tone, 'that we are awfully lucky in having Frankton as our cook. She gets on so well with the two maids. And then, you know, she was old Mr de Sarcy-Evans's cook for a very long time and he was famous through the whole county for doing himself well. People— and I mean people who know—recommended her specially to me for that reason. But of course it's the old English style of cooking that she understands, not the French. One can't expect everything.'

When some years later I inquired of a person who had known Mr de Sarcy-Evans how he could have been such a *bon viveur* if he had Frankton to cook for him, I was told that he sustained himself principally on port and claret.

Of the other servants who flitted through these years, I recall only the parlour-maid, Bosbury. She was a tall, stoutish woman of about forty who conveyed to me, I cannot say why, a feeling connected with bluebottles and beetles and other pugnacious forms of insect life. A juster simile, however, would change her musty black serge to khaki and draft her as sergeant-major into a tough women's army, for she possessed a determined voice and air, a firm step and a bold, martial carriage. Her talents were many. She had a considerable fund of country lore and once cured me of some warts I had on my hand by burying a piece of meat in the garden and muttering a spell over it. She was also very knowing on the subject of dreams, omens, tea-leaves in cups (she called them 'tittles'), fading coals in fires, the art of sieving or 'riddling' ashes and other methods of divining the future. She once told me that she always knew by these means when there was going to be a funeral. But the principal talent of this masculine woman lay in arranging flowers. Whenever there was to be a dinner party (a rare occasion in our family) she would shut herself up in the dining-room as soon as the tea things had been cleared away and begin her preparations. Once, opening the door, I caught her putting in a rose here, taking out a tulip there and stepping back to look at the effect.

'And it's not only the colours, Master Gerald,' she said, 'that have to match. It's the ideas. Them's what bothers me.'

In fact she kept in her pantry a little paper book on the language of flowers.

It was this artistic talent of Bosbury's that led to her undoing. One evening when some neighbours of ours were coming to dinner, she draped the whole table, from the silver candlesticks to a hook on the ceiling, with ropes of feathery asparagus among which there peeped out little elfin faces of forget-me-not and borage. On the cloth itself, decapitated begonias. My father, who hated any departure from the conventions, especially when it suggested eccentricity, was so infuriated that he tore down the aerial decorations and instead of letting my mother, who could say the most difficult things without causing hurt feelings, 'speak to her', gave his own orders for the future himself. A few days after this Bosbury was found dead-drunk in the pantry. It appears that she kept in her room a bottle of spirits and that she had had lapses of this sort before. She was given notice. And though my parents, who were neither of them unkind in these matters, kept in touch with her, intending to have her back 'when she had learned her lesson', she never returned. Instead she went to hospital and died suddenly. Then it turned out that no one knew anything about her or where she came from, except that she had always declared that she had no relations.

The family and the servants made up the inner circle of our life: beyond it there were the neighbours. In those days all those who claimed to be gentry lived in houses of a certain size and, unless they were clergy, kept an indoor staff of at least three to maintain them in their proper state of social importance. The cottage-dwelling gentry, compensating for their relative poverty by a display of antique furniture, brass warming-pans and nooky quaintness, did not come into existence till after the war, when income tax and higher rents descended on them. Thus in our remote and bleak district the only visitable people were the squires, the clergy and a few odd families who, like ourselves, occupied what had once been dower houses. The farmhouses, which were later bought up at fantastic prices by city people, avid of medieval picturesqueness, were still left to struggling tenant farmers. Country life therefore was much more monotonous than it is today and for most of the year centred round sport. My father hunted twice a week during the season and would be invited to shoot on at least two other days. When nothing else offered he could go pigeon shooting, or ferreting with one of the Park keepers.

For me the prospect was less attractive, or at least would have been if I had not been perfectly accustomed to amusing myself. All our neighbours were middle-aged people, many of them verging on the elderly, and only one of them had boys of my own age. As for girls, they did not exist. Occasionally from some far-off vicarage a little girl called Gladys would be brought to play with me, but she was an abomination. Nothing could be got out of her but smirks and giggles. I dreamed of pale-faced, dark-eyed girls dressed in loose cotton frocks with long, brown, sweet-smelling hair, but I did not meet them.

Our nearest neighbours were the people at the Park. They were an ill-assorted couple—he a furtive, slovenly man only interested in his woods and gamekeepers, and she a city-dressed woman with all the airs and graces of an Edwardian *grande dame*. Her exaggeratedly refined manners and affected, drawling conversation upset my mother, making her feel even more simple and homely than she was, though really, I think, Mrs Leatham was merely a timid and socially insecure woman acting a romantic part to herself. They had a son in the Army and also a daughter, Eleanor, who was a great beauty, perfect enough in feature, figure and complexion to have been a model for Praxiteles, but so dumb and expressionless that the young men asked down to meet her never came again. For this reason her mother was always complaining of her and her father had taken a dislike to her, so that under her covering of ice the poor girl had grown up resentful and lonely. Taking me out for a walk one day—she being eighteen and I barely nine—she taught me to say 'Damn your eyes', 'Blast you' and 'Go to Hell' much as one teaches a parrot to say 'Poor Polly'. 'Go on,' she would urge me, 'say them again, say them louder.' A few years later this girl married a Guardsman, Lord V., and escaped from her family.

The Leathams were little liked in the neighbourhood, partly on account of the airs that Mrs Leatham gave herself and partly because there was something mean and ferrety about her husband's disposition. He dressed badly, affected a rough stable accent and had the mania of excusing himself from shaking hands because, he would declare, his were dirty. He disgusted my mother by telling her that the best way to get rid of rats was to catch some, soak them in petrol and set fire to them; then let them go. Shifty and sordid, he lived for his game and his vermin, though for some reason he never went shooting himself. But what leaped to the eyes when one saw him with his wife was the failure of their marriage. This was too deep for quarrels, too far gone even for comment. Each went their own way, exaggerating in their manners the qualities that the other lacked—he each year a little coarser, she more lavishly dressed and more *grande dame*—until there was no ground left on which they could meet.

The rector, Mr Earée, was a more original figure. With his large, handsome head—always capped by a black biretta—grey, waxed moustaches and short, immensely stout body, he was a person who could not help attracting attention. In most people stoutness when combined with shortness is a blemish. He, however, had made of his belly an organ of dignity and pride, and as he walked down the road with his hands clasped behind him and the huge black protuberance swelling bulb-like in front, he created an area of respect and importance around him. And in fact he had some claim to these. He was an eloquent preacher who for many years had been chaplain to the British Embassy at Berlin and he was the greatest authority in the world on postage-stamp forgeries. His two-volume work on the subject was the bible of all serious philatelists.

As it may be imagined, I found this a strong recommendation. Even stronger, however, was the store of encyclopaedic knowledge that he seemed to possess on almost every subject. To grown people he might be—and in fact was—a bore, but I found his conversation more stimulating than that of anyone I had met up till then. He knew, for example, how opium is extracted from the garden poppy, how the queen bee conducts her nuptial flight, how certain Mexican ants milk aphids like cows and cultivate crops of edible fungi. Picking up a fallen horse-chestnut, he would discourse in his snuffling, professorial voice on the application of the word horse to a tree which had nothing in common with those animals. I listened enthralled, for I have always had a taste for odd and useless information. The climax of our talks came one evening in his shoddy, cheaply furnished study. We were sitting by the table, lit by a badly trimmed oil-lamp, bottles and jars and stuffed birds standing dismally around us on the shelves, while from the next room his three stout daughters could be heard bustling about among the smells of cooking. From biology (he had been showing me his microscope) the conversation had drifted on to physics, and suddenly he entered upon a great synthesis. The Universe, he declared, was made up of material atoms and vibrations. The first and slowest of these vibrations were those of sound; then came those of heat, then those of light and after them with increasing speed and fineness those to which we gave the name of electricity. Some people, he went on, *some people* considered that beyond these lay the vibrations that we knew as Thought and beyond them, more rapid and subtle than all, far finer and more transcendent, was ... Here he stopped, but I understood at once that he was alluding to God. Greatly excited, I ran home and repeated his words to my mother and my grandmother.

They were impressed, and my grandmother, who, I was beginning to realize, was a believer in divine immanence, inclined to Oriental faiths and doubtful of the validity of Church Christianity, asked me to repeat what he had said over again. Science, it seemed, was coming to the support of her view that God is everywhere, and she liked the connection with Thought. She had always believed (this was the philosophic basis of her respect for animals and plants) that Thought was everywhere too.

The only other neighbours whom I need describe at present were Mr and Mrs Hamilton Mills. They were an elderly, childless couple who lived in a house known as Sudgrove Manor, distant about half a mile from our village. Mr Mills, though he had inherited from his father a house with a thousand acres of woods and pasture and a comfortable income, was not a country type. Trained as a solicitor, he had ended as company director to a large brewery and to other industrial concerns in Stroud. He dressed therefore in dark, pepper-and-salt trouser suits, wore a stiff, grey Homburg hat and presented an appearance of financial and city-bred affluence and respectability. In character he was a shrewd but kindly man, fond of his comforts and much enjoying a good story or a joke. My father, with his common sense and his rather elementary humour, attracted him and till he died late in the 1920's Mr Mills was his best and indeed almost his only friend.

Mrs Mills was a pleasant woman too—indeed she was even pleasanter than her husband. Tall, solidly built, with a large oblong face, she looked as if she had been cut out of a single block of yellowish wood and left unfinished. As she moved about the croquet lawn, stiff and well-corseted, she seemed the personification of a chess queen. But if her monumental build made her imposing, her smiles took away all reason for timidity. She was extremely good-natured. This amiable serenity of her temper attracted my mother, who was one of those women, lacking in self-confidence themselves, who like to choose some older, stronger person of their own sex to lean upon. The two therefore became close friends.

The Millses, through their friendship with my parents, were to have in all kinds of small ways a distinct influence on my life. In times of strain they counselled calm and moderation. Yet I always felt a certain awe of them. Mr Mills in particular seemed to have no understanding of young people and the quizzing way in which he would look at me through his pince-nez, as though he were wondering what sort of a thing a small boy such as myself could be, would disconcert me. He and Mrs Mills, admirable though they were, seemed to me to be grown-ups twice over.

The era of cars was now coming in and we had not been long in our Cotswold house before my father bought one. It was a five-seater Wolseley, without a windscreen, and it ran on carriage wheels shod with solid rubber tyres. As it could not climb any of the hills that separated us from the towns, we only used it for short runs on the summit. One set out on a five-mile expedition without any certainty that one would arrive at one's destination.

Other and better cars followed. My father became such an enthusiast that at one time we had three of them, including a Panhard in which six people sat facing one another as in a bus. As all this was expensive, he gave up keeping horses, hiring one for a short time in the winter to give himself a few months' hunting, and selling my pony. He had a natural taste for machinery and as the cars were always breaking down, he would be kept busy for days at a time lying flat on his back on the ground and swearing to himself as the oil dripped on to him. Then, as they became more reliable, the era of long motor trips began. Packed tight as sardines in a small open car, sending up behind us thick clouds of dust, choked in it ourselves whenever we passed or were overtaken by another of our species, we would set off on sightseeing visits to towns, castles, mansions, churches—anything within a hundred miles' radius. The climax of these trips was a tour of the châteaux of the Loire, during which my mother, my father and one of my mother's cousins quarrelled all the way.

Motoring apart, I usually spent some part of every holiday away from home. Till my Irish grandmother died, my mother would take me on short visits to Larchfield, stopping on the way back at her sister's house near Dublin. Then there were visits to school-friends and visits to London. Here I would stay at my English grandmother's flat in Cadogan Gardens, sleeping on the drawing-room sofa and waking to hear the drays and hansoms trotting past.

These early hours before anyone but the servants were awake are what I remember best of these occasions. Lace curtains kept out most of the greyish-yellow light and the densely packed and draped and encumbered rooms were as mute and still as an aquarium. Lying curled up on my sofa between the cool, clean sheets, I would feel a peculiar, anticipatory happiness as I listened to the sounds that came in from outside and tried vaguely, like an inmate of Plato's cave, to guess where they came from. Soon, when eight o'clock struck, I would know, for then I would get up and look out through the window, but for the present I found it a greater luxury to lie still and speculate about them. Besides there were other things to occupy my attention. Those satin-covered chairs, that marqueterie cabinet, that draped piano, whose notes were never heard because no one in the house could play it, seemed to be filled with a dense and poetic life that came from their having so profoundly fulfilled their own natures. Plunged in their conviction of their own unchangeable identity and fixed in a sort of courtesy towards one another which showed itself in their mutual positions—chair by escritoire, pouffe by divan, velvet curtains by airy lace—they stood grouped in the grey, yellowish light with a solemnity that had no need of language. A river of sounds outside, a lake of silence and pure being within—that for me was my grandmother's flat in London.

But suddenly my contemplative mood would be interrupted by my Aunt Maude's pert and lively voice calling me. I would dress and we would sit down to breakfast.

The great treat that my grandmother held out to me was a visit to Drury Lane or to some other theatre where a musical comedy was being given. This was made doubly exciting by the fact that we drove there and back through the lighted streets in a hansom, yet somehow the evening always ended in a vague disappointment which I did not admit even to myself. For while my grandmother revelled in the dresses and the scenery and my Aunt Maude enjoyed the saucy jokes, I had to make the best I could of some rather gushing songs and of a row of chorus girls who, for reasons I did not even try to understand, kept pulling up their petticoats. Then we came back a little sadly to a tray of hot lemonade and ginger biscuits and I listened to the dining-room clock, followed by all the clocks and chimes in London, striking twelve. This was the culminating moment of the evening. I felt that I was crossing the frontier of a new and mysterious country—a sort of scarcely inhabited lunar region—and wished that I could be allowed to stay up all night.

I was just fourteen when a change in the family arrangements set in. We took to spending the Easter holidays at Dinard in Brittany where my father could play golf while my brother and I—he was now a lively little boy with a gift for imitation—practised our French. These visits I enjoyed enormously. Out of them grew a love of France and of everything French which has continued to this day. Looking back, I can see that I owe this very rewarding penchant to my mother. It was she who saw to it that I learned to speak and read French with fluency and at the same time implanted in me her admiration for everything

connected with that land. Once, when I was eleven, she had taken me
to Paris and we had had a breathless, crowded week, sightseeing by
day and in the evening visiting the theatre—not so much to *see* Sarah
Bernhardt, who played most of her part in *La Dame aux Camélias* reclining on a sofa, as to listen to her unforgettable voice. In the world my
mother came from a love of France and of French things was very
unusual, so I feel that I owe her a special debt of gratitude on this
account.

The house we took this year—it was now 1908—was called the Villa
de la Baie. It rose straight out of the waters of the Rade: the waves
washed the rocks beneath its foundations and, looking out from its
balconies, we would see opposite us the walls and solitary church spire
of St Malo, the grave, steep-roofed tower of Saint Servan and the island
on which Chateaubriand was buried. Across the water of the estuary
the *vedettes*, as the motor ferryboats were called, plied regularly to and
fro.

This indented coast-line enchanted me. At each low tide the sea
would be fringed by shelving beds of sand and studded with rocky
islets, over which the waves broke continually in fountains of white
spray. Mesmerized by the movement, I would sit in a trance watching
the tossing up and scattering of the crystalline particles. Or else, tired
of inactivity, I would explore the rock pools with their coloured algae
and sea anemones or, armed with a hook, draw the long razor-shells
out of their burrows. Then, while we were shopping or having lunch,
the tide would turn, the water pour back with accumulated force
from where it had been heaped up outside and all these glittering and
gleaming regions would be buried. The hyacinth blue of the sea rose,
rose with a sense of increasing power and life until it had covered
everything except the grass of the headlands.

The town too provided much to please and entertain. Everything
down to the dogs was different and I noticed that even the simplest
things said or heard in French had an interest and importance that
they would not have had in English. Then, subtly interwoven with
the exciting odours of the sea, there were certain delicious smells—
those of roasting coffee and of hot bread that came wafting out of
open doors, and others, of *madeleines* and *babas au rhum*, that hung about
the *pâtisseries*. To these pleasures I must add the taste of certain home-
made caramels, sold in a little grocer's shop and better than any
caramels one can buy today.

However, the great moment of this visit has yet to be described.
Going into my bedroom one night after dinner I discovered the full

moon pouring in through the double windows and filling the little box-like space with its light. It seemed to be distending and pushing apart the walls with its brightness, to be filling the room, the bed, the cupboard to bursting. I stood gazing at it for a moment. Then, stepping out onto the balcony, I looked down on the long glittering path it had laid on the water and heard the waves splashing softly far below. All at once a feeling I find it difficult to describe came over me—a sense of some enormous force and beauty existing around me: a presence, a state that promised unspeakable delight and happiness if only I could join myself to it. But I could not so join myself. I was my ordinary self, carried suddenly into an over-charged, over-resplendent world. For a time I stood there, overcome by the sheer transcendency of the spectacle, then gradually the impression faded and I went away.

This was the first of a series of special moments when the natural world appeared to me with a power and authority that seemed overwhelming. I have recorded it because these moments were to acquire a great importance for me later on. But on this occasion I was taken by surprise: nothing in my experience had prepared me for such a revelation, and so it remained without effect upon my life.

A few months after this visit to Dinard I left my prep school and went to Radley, but before embarking on an account of my life there I will relate an episode that occurred a little later, during the Christmas holidays. My parents had realized that the isolation of my home life was bad for me and that I should grow up into a strange sort of youth if I never met any girls. They therefore—at least this was the reason my mother gave me, though I later learned that my father had others of his own—took a furnished house for the winter in Cheltenham. I have pleasant memories of this visit. Cheltenham, like Dinard, is a civilized town laid out with the aim of affording pleasure. There was a roller-skating rink which I attended every afternoon, bookshops which had already begun to attract my spare shillings, and a haberdasher who sported a fine array of green and purple socks, decorated with clocks embroidered in other colours. And when these failed there was always the gay, tree-shaded Promenade, where one could imagine oneself in a foreign town, and the Cadena Café, with its excellent coffee and sweet cakes.

Every evening after tea I went to a children's dancing class. These were painful occasions when I had to display my clumsiness in front of other people. However, it seemed to be accepted that boys do not really have to dance and before long I had learned to hobble round in some sort of fashion. Then the day arrived when I should be put to the test. A dance for the young people of the town had been organized at the Montpellier Rooms.

I still have the dance card I carried on that occasion. The first three dances bear forgotten names, and then the word Nancy breaks out and is repeated in an increasingly illegible hand to the end of the programme. And this corresponds to my memory. I met her, felt a sort of mist gather about us and isolate us as we galloped round the room and never let her go till the band played *Auld Lang Syne*.

Nancy G. belonged to a very English type of girl whom I have always found attractive. Her hair was brown, her eyes hazel, her nose turned up a little and her teeth stuck out—but not too much—between rather full lips. This gave her an eager expression that in an older person might have been called rabbity, but which at thirteen—that age when girls so often have the air of gazelles—suited her to perfection. She seemed a tangible embodiment of that open, amorous, rather plebeian type of girl which ever since my childhood days the nostalgic name of Nancy had evoked in me. We parted that night after some very warm kisses, to meet at her mother's house on the following day.

Nancy had a younger brother and sister, so after tea we decided to play hide-and-seek. Nancy and myself went off to hide, which we did by shutting ourselves in a small cupboard, while the unfortunate younger children were obliged to keep on searching. This became a settled routine. At the end of every evening, drunk with kisses, I would cycle home, feeling that no one had ever been so much in love as I.

But the day was not yet over. I had first to go through the ordeal of dinner with its stifling humdrum of family conversation: even my mother's remarks now irritated me by their insignificance. Then, free at last, I would slip out into the garden and lean against a tree. There was the moon—but how different to that savage God who had poured into my bedroom at Dinard! This was the soothing, nightingale-voiced orb which arranges the *mise-en-scène* for lovers. Taking my bicycle from the shed I would ride to the square in front of Nancy's house and try to imagine behind what lighted window she was sitting. When later I told her of this, she would appear in her nightdress and signal to me.

My passion for Nancy did not long survive my return to school. As soon as her badly written, childish letters began to arrive, I felt a disappointment that I could not conceal from myself. Then when I saw her in the Easter holidays, she seemed to have altered. The spell was broken and many years had to pass before I experienced the intoxication of love again.

CHAPTER VII

Radley

A friend of mine, Mr Louis Wilkinson, who went to Radley some ten years before I did, has kindly sent me his impressions of it. 'It was', he says, 'a school entirely untouched by the Arnold ethos—a sort of annexe of Eton, a poor relation of it. Many of the boys who set the tone at Radley had elder brothers there. This meant that the keynote was laxity and attendance at games optional. The one thing that mattered was good form. Almost all the boys were from county families and there was little bullying.'

This was no doubt the picture that Mr Johns had in his mind when he recommended Radley. But unfortunately for me, the character of the place had changed before I reached it. Reforms had swept away the amenity, a nagging discipline had tightened up the laxity and the 'poor relation of Eton' was as much like a penal establishment as any other public school in the land. One went there to be knocked into shape and stupefied, and if, by the end of his schooling, a boy had not set in the prescribed pattern, he left without confidence in himself or in the rest of the world.

It is true that in the choice made for me of house-master and course of studies I was particularly unfortunate. Since I was to go into the Army—and four generations of my paternal ancestors, by taking the Queen's commission, had decided this for me—I was naturally placed upon the Army or, as it was more properly called, the Modern Side. This meant that I had to give up Latin and Greek, which I was beginning to like, and to take instead science and maths, which I hated. It also meant that I met in my class precisely that sort of boy whom I was least fitted to get on with. In addition to this my father, in his wish to correct my lack of interest in games, had deliberately chosen for me the leading games house or 'social', which at this time was in charge of a man who was a popular writer on golf and who disliked both boys and schoolmastering.

My mother, though equally set on the Army, which in her eyes was the one romantic profession, had wanted me to enter it through

Oxford. Her eldest nephew, then at Harrow, was about to do this and whatever was thought right for her brothers' children, she automatically thought right for me. Besides—though this argument was less important to her than the snob one—she believed that my bent for the classics and for reading generally were things to be encouraged. To this my father had replied that it was time that the dreaminess he had observed in my character should be checked, that only a strict discipline could do this, and that in any case Latin and Greek were useless acquisitions, not to be compared as mental exercises with mathematics. He himself in his school-days had had a taste for algebra and he still got a certain satisfaction from adding up shillings and pounds. A final argument—that he could not afford Oxford—clinched the matter.

From my first week at Radley, therefore, I realized that I was back in the same abyss of misery and unpopularity from which I had escaped after such a long apprenticeship at my preparatory school. And how much harder it was to be there a second time! My whole nature, now grown accustomed to success and happiness, resented it. All the despair of the new boy who knows that he cannot play games came over me when I reflected that I was here on a four years' sentence. However, I found that I had been spared one thing. Because I was a scholar, I had the right of sharing a study with another boy. By this privilege I escaped the fate of those lower-form wretches who had no place to call their own but their desk in Hall. When I looked in at this den by the brick doorway and saw them, heard them—

> *Diverse lingue, orribili favelle,*
> *parole de dolore, accenti d'ira,*
> *voci alte e fioche, e suon de man con elle*

—I saw that I had been let off the worst.

I had another piece of luck in my form-master, Mr Wilson Green. He was a quiet, precise little man, very natty in his dress, a flower always in his buttonhole, his gown draped in immaculate lines, who never addressed us except in a tone of elaborate politeness. Sometimes, when our stupidity provoked him, this politeness would become ironic—a manner of speech he favoured because he regarded it as French. He took his duties as a schoolmaster seriously, showing great patience with the backward boys and scarcely ever resorting to punishments, but as he did not attend school matches, he failed to win either the respect or the liking of his class. The subjects he taught were French and English literature and, since I was strong on both of these, I became one of his favourites. I cannot say that he had any influence on me, because there was something mild and reasonable about his whole disposition—in politics he inclined to a sort of Garden City socialism—which failed to arouse my enthusiasm. When, for example, we read in class essays by Hazlitt, Lamb, Stevenson and De Quincey, he would single out for praise the first three whereas I would have given them all for *The Opium-eater*. But he made my life at Radley far less harsh than it would otherwise have been by taking me out on bicycling expeditions and talking to me as though my opinions were worth listening to. I owe his memory therefore a debt of gratitude.

My second form-master—for after a year I moved into a fresh class—was Mr Bryans. He was an elderly man—white moustaches, trembling hands, irritable, fussy and fidgety—but a figure of standing in the school because he was a senior house-master. He lived with his mother, read aloud with a sort of nervous gusto the leading articles in *The Times*, whose style of composition he admired, and in the summer holidays went fishing in Scotland.

Mr Bryans was a man of solitary disposition who still kept a secret fund of enthusiasm for the subjects (history and French) which he taught, but long years of schoolmastering had embittered him. He hated the sloppiness, silliness, laziness and downright stupidity of boys. For this reason he could scarcely ever bring himself to speak to us except in a sarcastic tone. Now and then, it is true, beaming down in a genial after-breakfast mood through his well-polished glasses, he would start speaking in a voice that bubbled with enthusiasm on, say, the character of Bismarck, or else perhaps on certain strange mistakes of a historical sort that Thackeray had made in *Henry Esmond*, when— Odds bodikins, Dash my wig and buttons—he would catch sight of Clark major looking out of the window, and at once the emotion would fade from his voice, the glitter in his eyes would die away and the heavy sarcasm would return. For ridicule was his great weapon. Like all tyrants—and his over-susceptibility made him one—he knew how at the same time to relieve his irritation and to draw the class over which he ruled to his side by turning it against one of its members. And since he quickly discovered that I was the most unpopular boy, he generally, indeed almost invariably, turned it against me.

Very soon, I think, my presence in his class began to be a sort of obsession with him. To begin with I was the favourite pupil of his arch-enemy, Mr Wilson Green, who one day, as he probably foresaw, would succeed him in his house-mastership. Then I was untidy, absent-minded, careless. And then—but how can anyone ever know the precise things in his nature that cause him to be disliked by others? What is certain is that he deliberately and persistently persecuted me, keeping me in on very slender excuses on Saturday afternoons, especially when, the weather being fine, he suspected that Mr Wilson Green had invited me out on a bicycling expedition.

'Just mark my words,' he would exclaim on these occasions after, for example, I had mislaid my pencil or written my composition in the wrong exercise book. 'Just mark my words, all of you. That boy will live to be hanged.'

A strange attraction often draws together the persecutor and the persecuted. Although my pride struggled against it, I could not entirely resist liking Mr Bryans and wishing I could please him. 'I'm not what you think I am,' I longed to cry out. And he, though he wanted to crush me, mortify me, terrorize me, kept in some corner of his nature a soft spot for his victim. This was not because I was his best pupil—on the contrary, my proficiency in the subjects he taught was simply one more ground for his irritation—but because I enjoyed Scott. Every year he set a prize for the best holiday essay on a novel by his favourite novelist, and I generally won it. When he announced the result he would throw me a curious, half-whimsical glance through his glasses and for a week there would be peace between us.

I was unpopular in my class, I was unpopular in my house. I had no friends in either and could count on my fingers the boys who spoke to me in a friendly way. This continued to be the case until I left Radley. During my first three years there I was liable at any moment to be kicked, hit, mobbed, thrown in the bushes, as well as called by every sort of abusive name. The games prefects took such opportunities as they could find for beating me. But my reaction to this treatment was entirely different from what it had been at Winton House. Then I had accepted the judgement of the school and had tried to worm my way into popularity. But now, after a term or two of hesitation, my pride rallied to my support and refused to allow me to make any compromise with my oppressors. At first I tried taking boxing lessons—without success, since my shoulder muscles were weak. I could not even throw a cricket ball. Then I withdrew into myself, became silent and sullen and built up with the help of books and Nature a private world of my own in which I could find another kind of happiness.

At many periods of my life I have felt myself to be acting alternately the roles of my mother and my father. Of almost any particular trait in my character I can say that it belongs either to the one or to the other of these two. Now at Winton House I had been my mother. Like her I had learned to submit until submission gave recognition, had accepted without demur the values of the other side and had finally got under the guard of the enemy by developing, as she had done, a buffoonish tone. So that in the end my eccentricities, such as liking books and flowers and playing games badly, had come to be regarded as amusing and I had ended by acquiring friends. But at Radley I assumed the role of my other parent. That is to say, I drew on the stoical philosophy I had observed in him, fortified myself in my pride and dignity and returned hatred for hatred. Only my interior life, which for the first time began to be very important to me, was my own—or at least completely free from the influence of my parents.

One of the things on which Radley most prided itself was the stress it laid on religion. The school had been founded in 1847 as an offshoot of the Tractarian Movement and although with the progressive coarsening of the times it had become muscularly Protestant and philistine in its general character, it still preserved in its chapel services some traces of its former High Church flavour. I, being a boy, found these services tedious, although there were passages in them such as the *Benedicite* and the psalm that begins 'The heavens declare the glory of God' that I enjoyed. And I used sometimes to go of my own accord to the voluntary service of compline which was taken by a master whose High Church sentiments were sincere, because I was affected by its language. But the official attitude to religion revolted me because I could see in it little else but hypocrisy. Were there, I asked myself, as many as two masters in the school for whom Christianity meant anything more than a sanction for the prison rules and cult of organized games by which we were kept down? And when the Bishop of London visited us, as he often did, to deliver one of his crude sermons, I was so repelled by his personality that I felt that I could not bear to believe anything that he believed. If he had said that Gloucester Cathedral was beautiful, I should have changed my opinion and thought it ugly. Thus, when I came to take my confirmation, I felt nothing, believed nothing.

This impression, that the whole moral and religious teaching of the school authorities was false and hypocritical, was confirmed when I stumbled upon the practice of what they called self-abuse. I had made the discovery by accident, for the natural prudishness of my disposition and my disgust at the dirty language and sex talk that I heard around me had put me against any deliberate experimentation with my body, but when I did discover it I was enraptured by the quantity of pure ethereal pleasure it afforded me. I would go out into the woods and there among the crushed bluebells and broken stalks of sappy woodland plants would give myself up to this delicious dying and fading away and to the pure and innocent fantasies that accompanied it. But the problem then arose of how to keep some check on those practices. When I gave way to them too often I found that it produced a certain deadness in my reactions to Nature and poetry. As these were what I valued most in my life, I entered on a serious struggle to acquire self-control.

In doing this I had the school authorities on my side. They were vociferous—a good deal too vociferous—in their warnings and admonitions. Not only were we told in sermon after sermon that our purity was our most precious possession (one preacher, I remember, spoke of the violation of it as a 'deliberate defiance of God') but that it was something, like the sense of honour or decency, that no one with any pretension to being a gentleman could afford to lose. For example my house-master, that famous authority on golf, a hard-bitten, leather-faced man who looked like an orang-outang, gave us a special talk on the subject in which he spoke as follows.

'I want you boys to try always to be clean in your thoughts and habits. Remember, whenever you are tempted, that uncleanliness is the sign of a cad. You know what a cad is—he is the sort of person who does things in secret which he wouldn't do in the open. He is the opposite to a sportsman. In this house we try to turn out sportsmen and pukka sahibs who in after life will be a credit to the school. Remember that whenever you feel any temptation to do underhand things.'

Then, as the Radley authorities probably realized that these arguments were not likely to impress us, they circulated a pamphlet that, though unsigned, purported to have been written by a doctor, in which it was stated that self-abuse led to terrible diseases and that those who practised it often ended in the lunatic asylum. There was, in short, no lie that they were not ready to tell in order to prevent us from doing something which, until they were married, they had practised regularly and as a matter of course themselves. The gaff was blown on all this hypocritical talk when the master who trained the Radley eight would advise them to let off steam (he used a coarser word) a few days before the race, so that they might not be too fresh. Winning a race for the college took precedence over everything.

This struggle, exacerbated by the warnings of the terrible pamphlet, led to my one and only religious crisis. During the spring term of 1910

I went to the sanatorium with flu. On getting up one afternoon to make water, I found that my urine was coloured a bright red. At once it flashed through my mind that I had contracted the terrible disease of which the pamphlet spoke as being the final consequence of onanistic practices. And this disease was syphilis. It is true that I had heard that syphilis was only caught from prostitutes, but sexual excesses can be solitary as well as shared and it seemed reasonable to suppose that one could get it without feminine intervention. Certainly the veiled but allusive language of the pamphlet seemed to support this. In deep agony, therefore, for I conceived syphilis to be a disease like leprosy in which one's nose and lips rotted and dropped off and boils came out on one's body, I buried my face on the pillow and began to pray.

First I prayed for myself and then, feeling this to be selfish, I prayed for my family. Parents, grandmother, uncles, aunts, cousins, second cousins, once and twice removed—I prayed separately and with great energy for each of them. Might they live to be old, might they be happy all their lives, might they never be afflicted by the calamity that had befallen me! Now, as it happened, there was in the next room a boy who was very ill with meningitis. On the following day he died and I lay in my bed in terror, examining my body for swellings and expecting that his death, in some way that I could not have explained, would hasten on mine. I tried to pray again, but the springs of my faith had dried up and I could only mutter a short and simple petition for myself. Then on the third day my temperature dropped to normal and I felt well. The awful symptom had not repeated itself. Immediately my terrors left me and became as if they had never been. I left the sanatorium in a rage of disgust at all this false and hypocritical propaganda, and I never prayed again.

At about this time I passed into the top form on the Modern Side and this gave me the right of entry into the Wilson Library. Here I had the opportunity for delving into English literature. As it happened, however, the book that fascinated me most was not of this sort. The library possessed a copy of Elisée Reclus' *Universal Geography*—a vast work in nineteen thick volumes. Ensconced in a window-bay that overlooked the lawn of the old house and its row of lime trees, I let my imagination feed upon the descriptions, the illustrations and most of all the plans and maps it offered of remote and thinly inhabited countries. England might be beautiful, but it was the regions of the world where life was noble and simple because it was attended by hardships and dangers that most attracted me.

1 Helen Brenan, the author's mother

2 Gerald Brenan aged about two, before sailing for South Africa

3 Brenan on his pony at Fort William, Calcutta, in February 1900

4 Blair Brenan, the author's brother,   5 Gerald Brenan aged 19
aged 17

6 Aunt Maude, who was considered 'fast', in the author's father's car
at Miserden House

Reclus was a French Protestant from the Gironde who left his father's religion to become an anarchist. His attitude to geography, though severely scientific and objective, had therefore a strong anthropological bias. He felt more interest in the obscure tribe with its primitive customs and religion than in the civilized nation. In purely geographical matters too he was drawn to the remote and exceptional and would devote as much space to the lonely island, the scarcely known volcano or the horseshoe bend of a river as to the important city or the well-settled tract of corn-land. And the island, the volcano and the river would be illustrated with a large-scale map.

My mania for map drawing had not ceased with my removal to Radley. It had become a branch of my love for making plans. Once, during my last years at Winton House, I had filled several notebooks with the schedule of a tour of the world which would last, with continuous travelling, some thirty years. Now I began to restrict my interests and, after a brief flirtation with Central America, fixed on the Near East, Arabia and Persia and that region of deserts that lies beyond the Pamirs·as the part of the world that had most to offer me. The maps I drew were therefore of desert oases, of rivers draining away into the sand and of imaginary Oriental cities.

This map drawing took place during the classes of maths. Mr Pugh, our maths master, found it impossible to teach me anything, so he shut his eyes to my scribbling. I covered pages with cartographical displays which were often of the most extravagant and, one might say, rococo kind. And when I got tired of map making I would try my hand at copying Arabic writing or (because I meant to keep a diary in it) Runic. Anything rather than struggle through the abstract wastes of logarithms and trigonometry. But now that I am back in Mr Pugh's classroom—a little dingy box with barred windows, squeezed between the quad and the long passage—I feel that I must pause for a moment and give a sketch of his character.

He was a man of about forty, rather short, with a red, round face like a clock and a thatch of snowy white hair above it. At the first glance one could see that there was something singular about him, something unattached and rootless, and in fact, though perhaps he did not know it, he was a homosexual. The form which this inclination took showed itself in the curious game he played with his class. In the pauses that he allowed every now and then for rest, he would let drop a pun or *double entendre* of a mildly bawdy kind which would be aimed at provoking a stronger reply from the audience. At once a hum of conversation would rise from the older boys on the back benches, out of which as often as not some rude phrase, condensed like a transparent aura around its monosyllable, would make itself heard. This was what Mr Pugh was angling for. Beaming all over his rubicund face, shaking the long sleeves of his gown and rocking a little from side to side, he would say with mock urgency, 'Hush, boys, hush. No more of that, please. Hush, now.' But still, since his tone showed that he did not expect to be taken seriously, the noise and smutty talk would continue to grow. Smirking, beaming and rubbing his hands together, Mr Pugh would stand facing us, uttering a succession of Hushes when any rude word reached him and doing a sort of wriggling dance with his sleeves and his feet to express the delight he felt at his bashfulness being overcome. Then when the noise had gone far enough, fearing perhaps what some chance passer-by might hear, he would turn his back, rub vigorously on the blackboard with the duster and, facing the class again, say, 'Now then, boys. Enough nonsense. We must pull ourselves together.' And he would begin writing figures on the board once more.

Mr Pugh showed that weakness, that complaisance with his class which elderly men, tantalized by vague and hopeless lusts, sometimes show in the company of girls. He lowered the tone of the conversation as much as he dared, put out appeals for collusion and, if these were not taken up, blew his nose and tittered in a bashful way. But should a boy reply in the same tone, he would snigger delightedly and go on sniggering till he remembered his responsibilities as a master. Yet it was only the collective presence of his class that affected him in this manner. Upon the rare occasions when he went out alone with a boy or invited him to his room—where, rumour had it, he sometimes offered him a glass of whisky—he would be reserved and silent. For this reason he made no friends. One would meet him wandering about the grounds with his hands behind his back, benign and shadily clerical, or walking into Abingdon on some unknown errand, but without a companion. Yet he was liked by his class, partly because he was good-natured and never punished or spoke sharply to anyone, but also because he was a brilliant teacher. If anyone could have taught me to enjoy dynamics or quadratic equations, he would have done so.

Some years after I left Radley I met Mr Pugh again at a pub in the West End. His face lit up when he saw me and the good-looking youth who accompanied me—we were both in uniform—and he invited us to join him in a drink. At once there began to seep into his conversation those mildly suggestive allusions, those little wriggling heads of forbidden ideas, followed by retreating, apologetic chuckles, which I remembered so well from the past. As he talked he kept his eyes fixed on me with the riveted look of the shy clinging to the person they know, though really he was addressing my companion. But how dull and insipid he was! It gave me a shock to think that this man whom I had built up in my mind as a Rabelaisian figure, puncturing the dense atmosphere of the school with his buffoonery, was at heart as conventional and respectable as the rest. Then, as we talked, the animation faded from his face and he sank into glumness. Finishing his glass, he put it down and with a wave of the hand went out.

After Reclus' *Geography* the reading I was most given to was poetry. My liking for this began when I was a little over fifteen. The first poem to affect me was *Annabel Lee* by Poe. For weeks it completely filled my mind, partly, I think, because it reminded me of *Clementine*, that mock pathetic song in which the miners of California parodied a Spanish ballad, *Dónde vas tú, caballero,* whose tune they could not get out of their heads. As a small boy I had been moved by its pathos and annoyed at the ironic way in which the verses were made to end. Now in *Annabel Lee* I found not only the same monotony of rhythm, but a pathos that, though equally great, stopped just short of absurdity.

The next poet whose acquaintance I made was Shelley. He became for perhaps two years the most potent figure in my life. The tale of his sufferings at school and of his quarrel with his father, which I read first in a little hagiographic work by H. S. Salt and then in two big, richly detailed volumes by Edward Dowden, bore an obvious resemblance to my own case. I saw in him one of those heroes of whom the young stand in need—a pure and Christ-like figure who gave an example in his own life, a rebel against the heartless stupidity of the world, and, not least, a youth who had died before the coarseness of middle age could grow over him. Besides, his poetry was a poetry of liberation and escape. The whole of Nature with its clouds and rustling leaves, its winds and waves and waterfalls, seemed to be on the move in his verses. The very rhythms, light and variable and tripping, bore one along, yet here and there one came to wonderful stationary glades where flowers perpetually gleamed and soft airs blew. And always behind his verse one felt the blast that drove the poet forward on his flight—the cruelty and the stupidity of men, the intermittency of the poetic insight, the failure of the Good to achieve its lasting reign.

I do not often open Shelley today because I miss in his poetry a sense of the experience of life, but at sixteen or seventeen he was exactly what I needed. Reading him, I felt that the defeats I suffered daily were really victories and that the attitude of revolt I had adopted was justified. For the world, he seemed to say, was divided into two sorts of people—the slaves and the free. The slaves were the majority, those people imprisoned in the crust of their own blindness and stupidity, whereas the free were those who had an inner life, who loved Nature and poetry. To be free was the only ambition any serious person could have and the surprising thing was that so few had it. After reading Shelley I became something of a prig, but at least I never doubted or looked back.

Of the many other writers whom I read at this time I must mention William Morris. Lying in the long grass close to the lime-tree avenue, protected by a hawthorn bush from straying prefects, I read one after the other his prose romances. Their sham medieval idiom—stiff, I then thought, as a tapestry—their heavy, summery sensuality, their descriptions of imaginary travel seemed to accord with the lush, drowsy landscape of the Thames valley. However, these romances did not satisfy me for long. That winter I ousted them for H. G. Wells's novels, *Kipps*, *Tono-Bungay* and *Mr Polly*. They gave me a more realistic but equally exciting picture of England because the life of the lower middle classes was new to me. Then I moved on to Thomas Hardy, Emily Brontë and George Borrow. They helped to reconcile me to the English scene, which school and home life were making so unattractive, and thus served as an antidote to Reclus, from whom I had gathered that foreign countries alone offered something to the imagination.

The private world which I built up as a refuge against the misery and emptiness of school life contained two elements—books and Nature. My discovery of Nature grew out of my determination to avoid playing games. I found that by appearing as useless as possible on the football field I got relegated to a small group of muffs who were so despised by the games prefects that they did not bother to call their roll. If I could slip off, therefore, without being seen I was moderately safe. I generally succeeded in doing this and then, so long as I kept to the fields, I could go where I wanted.

These daily evasions gave me a childish pleasure. I enjoyed, as a hare might do, the thrill to be got from keeping out of sight and circumventing danger. To increase it, I took to trespassing in Bagley wood, which was heavily guarded by gamekeepers, and to exploring the areas along the river where I risked meeting masters or prefects. In winter, when the floods were out, this waterlogged country was dreary, but I did not mind that too much because when I entered it I was free.

For longer excursions there were the two weekly half-holidays, but they were generally taken up by a school or house match. A roll-call was held and shirking was difficult. In the end, however, I found a means of dodging these occasions by joining the Natural History Society, a moribund institution that comprised some half a dozen boys, and finally becoming curator of its museum. On the strength of this I could usually get a pass to go somewhere or other and so miss the match. At the same time I made a friend. The only other active member of the Society was a boy some two years older than myself called Thornton. He was a remarkably ugly youth, short and squat, with a broad Mongolian face and flap-like ears. But he was very intelligent and, since he was taking biology—a subject not taught at Radley—had been granted the privilege of missing both games and classes and getting his tuition in Oxford. His private tastes lay in the direction of snails and fossils. For snails we visited Cothill Marsh, where there were some rare ones, and for fossils we ransacked all the quarries and clay-pits within cycling range. Then, as we trudged or cycled along, Thornton in his quiet voice would give explanations, and so gradually the scientists' picture of the earth—its immense age, the many stages of life that had succeeded one another upon it, its origin in the sun, the relations of this to the other stars of the galaxy—were unrolled before me. I got a special exhilaration from thinking that this vast cosmic system was indifferent to me. Its sublimity could be wholeheartedly admired because one could get nothing for oneself by admiring it. If God lay out there, it would be an impertinence to expect him to answer one.

One Christmas holidays I went to spend a few days at my friend's home. I had expected—for the postal address was Northampton—some sort of suburban villa, but to my surprise I found a Jacobean manor and several men in scarlet coats and splashed riding-breeches eating hot buttered toast before an open fire. Thornton's father was the master of a famous pack of hounds. It required a considerable adjustment of my views to see my plebeian-looking friend as the eldest son in such a family, with an attractive sister too and a taste for dances and tennis parties. Till then I had only associated him with trilobites and gastropods. He left Radley soon after this and I never saw him again, but today he is a Fellow of the Royal Society.

As I grew older I tired of fossils and became more interested in scenery. It was Mr Wilson Green who introduced me to the Berkshire Downs. On summer afternoons he would take me and another boy on bicycling expeditions which generally led in their direction. Passing through Abingdon, we would make for some point on that long string of villages that lie between Aston Tirrold and Compton Beauchamp, where the springs well out below the chalk and sudden cliffs of elms rise above harbour-like meadows. On the way we would stop at a diminutive cottage beyond Steventon which had in its window a card inscribed *Minerals*, and buy from the old woman who lived there a glass of fizzy red liquid known as Raspberry Vinegar. Then, mounting again, we would push on, either towards the Astons and Wallingford or westwards to Wantage and the Letcombes. Most of these Downs villages had a pub that served tea with new bread and home-made jam and slabs of shop cake, set out as often as not on a rough-hewn table in a patch of garden planted with tulips and forget-me-nots. On other occasions we would go to Dorchester, visit its beautiful Perpendicular church and climb to the twin beech clumps that crown the Sinodun Hills. In this way the Berkshire Downs came to be my favourite English landscape. I began to read Richard Jefferies, the first discoverer of the beauty of this country, and so stumbled on his autobiography, *The Story of my Heart*.

This book, which I cannot read today, made a deep impression on me then because it gave a name, 'Nature Mysticism', to certain experiences I had had which seemed to me very important. I have already described the first of them which took place one moonlight night at Dinard. Since then I had had another even more overpowering one. I had joined the Officers' Training Corps—this was obligatory for boys on the Modern Side—and, when the school broke up, had gone into camp with them at the foot of Silbury Hill near Tidworth. One evening after a long dusty route-march I left the other boys outside the tent that served as canteen and set off to climb the grass slope that rose behind. From the top there was a view over the whole Plain. As I reached it the sun was just about to set. Its long horizontal rays, a little blurred by the dust and heat, fell lazily and with a stroking accent upon the great expanse of turf that stretched below and seemed to turn it into a lake. Out of its surface, like tiny islands, rose a number of round barrows, each of them with its shadow beside it. In the distance, tree clumps and dust rising. I looked, and all at once a feeling of extraordinary force and violence welled up within me. I wanted to leap, to run, to fly, to join myself in some unimaginable way with this grassy plain and its ancient cup-shaped mounds. Instead I plunged down the hill and ran shouting and gesticulating over the turf.

These feelings and experiences, as well as others concerning wild flowers and birds, which made up my private life at Radley, spoke to me of the future. They were glimpses through a prison window and bore that accent of longing and deferred hope which the prisoner feels. Without them, I imagine, I should either have succumbed to the conventionality of the world I had been born into, or else, had the impulse to free myself become too strong, I should have lost in the process my faith in the essential goodness of life and become one of those people who carry about with them a grudge against the world.

CHAPTER VIII

Life in the Cotswolds

During the four years, 1908–12, that I spent at Radley my character did not merely develop—it went through a revolutionary change. I was a different sort of person, with a different approach to life, when I left that place from what I had been when I arrived. The principal reason for this was of course the misery I suffered there. The public schools choose the time when their victims are going through the critical stages of puberty to inflict their screwing and mangling process upon them. But there was another reason in my gradually worsening relations with my parents. To explain these I must go back a year or two and give an account of my life during the holidays.

Like most solitary boys of my age, I was very active and never at a loss to amuse myself. In the winter I would generally go riding in the mornings (we had now taken to horses again) and spend the afternoons and evenings in reading and arranging my collections. But on fine spring and summer days and when the snow fell I liked to set off after breakfast on some long expedition. Sometimes these were on foot— I was turning into an enthusiastic walker—but in the summer months they were more often by bicycle. On my three-speed Rudge-Whitworth I explored the country within a range of thirty or forty miles, occasionally, when the distance was not too great, taking my young brother with me on my back carrier. Abbeys and churches were the principal objects of these excursions—I had a special cult of Norman architecture—but during the time that I was under Morton's influence there were also quarries. Later, when I began to tire of churches, houses and villages took first place.

I lived on the Cotswolds and for this reason professed a certain local patriotism. But there were really two entirely different types of country that went by that name. On the west lay those deep, thickly wooded valleys that ran down to Stroud and the Severn estuary: on the east were the bare uplands that fell gradually in long flat curves to the Thames. Our house stood just within the western region and ever since I had first penetrated its recesses with my governess the romantic possibilities of this country had excited my imagination. But as I grew older I began to understand that it was really the eastern slope that was the more important. This, the books told me, was the true Cotswold country, distinguished from all others by its cold, grey-roofed villages, its sagging contours and its stone-walled fields. The cult for it, like that started by Belloc for Sussex, was just beginning, and I took it up, as I did everything that was new, with enthusiasm. From now on the principal object of my rides became the search for that village or landscape (or even farm-house or stretch of road) which would display in its purest possible state all the various features of Cotswoldism. It was only in my last year at Radley that I realized that I did not after all like this cold, inhospitable country, but preferred a thousand times the gay, windy Downs with the larks climbing airy ropes above them or the lush, willow-whiskered Thames valley. I had been led by the books I read and by the talk I heard to vamp up an enthusiasm that I did not completely feel.

Just as there was a hydrographical frontier that ran within a mile of our house, so there was a social frontier too. One crossed the wooded valley that plunged steeply below the Mills' croquet lawn and found a mode of life that differed in various ways from ours. The centre of this was the large, humped-up village of Bisley, whose spire, putting to shame the squat towers of the ordinary churches, could be seen from a great distance round. It was a place that provided accommodation for a number of retired people, most of them of a rather quiet and stay-at-home sort. It also contained a nucleus, which was later to grow considerably, of Catholics. There was no squire and the five circumjacent villages—Eastcombe, Bourne Green, the two Oakridges and Waterlane—were squireless too, having been settled for the first time by squatters in the eighteenth century.

Round Bisley and its ring of hilltop villages, as far as Sapperton three miles to the east and Painswick four miles to the west, a colony of architects and painters, poets and art-craftmen was beginning to establish itself, attracted by the low rents and by the sacred feelings that had gathered round the word Cotswolds. Three architects, Edward Gimson and the Barnsley brothers, who were disciples of William Morris, had laid the first stones and soon after them had come the flower-painter, book-illustrator and general art-craftman, Alfred Powell. He settled in Oakridge and became what one might call the high-priest of the movement.

The people who composed it were for the most part the sons of manufacturers who had made their money in the big cities of the

Midlands. They had inherited comfortable though not indecent incomes and a sense of sin which made them revolt against the ugliness of the industrial age. Ruskin and William Morris had taught them that England was to be saved by honest craftmanship and so they had settled in this remote country district, where a medieval tradition in architecture still lingered on, to devote themselves to a life of plain living and fine workmanship. But there was a flaw in their reasoning, because they expected that the furniture, the curtains, the ironwork, the flower paintings, the puppets that they made with such skill and care would be bought by the cottagers and factory workers, whereas they were so expensive that only a wealthy man could afford them.

As time went on, a second wave of poets and painters, who confessed to somewhat different artistic creeds, began to make its appearance. The Rothenstein brothers, Paul and John Nash, Bernard Adeney, John Masefield, all for short or long periods resided here, drawing their spiritual sustenance less from the Cotswold mystique than from the blue tint in the shadows. Some of them met the local gentry, whose sedentary tastes or lack of means prevented them from going in for hunting and shooting, and infected them with at least an adumbration of their feelings and ideas. Daughters of vicars began to 'spoil a little canvas', retired majors discoursed on Morris and Tolstoy, while at Painswick a musical society given to folk-singing was formed. High Church and Romans, their backs turned to one another, competed in ritual and incense. In short, country life, in this small and very special region, began to break with the philistinism of the Victorian age and to assume that varied, cottagy, mildly arty-crafty complexion which it has in many parts of England today.

My parents naturally did not mix in this artistic world. The deep valley of Holy Brook divided us from the people who wore homespun trousers instead of knickerbockers and let their hair grow a shade longer than the well-groomed man thought right. Then what sort of conversation could one have with a poet—that namby-pamby sort of a person who existed chiefly as a subject for caricatures in *Punch*? And would not a painter be a person who did not keep his fingernails clean? Besides, my father thought it undesirable to see much of Jews. If they were rich, then, as he put it, they 'stank of money', while if they were not, what reason could there be for knowing them? It was not exactly that he was an anti-Semite, but that he believed in a stratified society in which everyone knew his place, and in such a society a Jew, bound as he was through his sense of racial difference to be 'a pusher', could never achieve the natural unselfconsciousness of the English country gentleman. In any case, there was on our side of the valley a general bias against this *côté de chez Swann*. Our faces and our motor-cars were turned resolutely towards Cheltenham and Cirencester (pronounced by us Ciceter), those cities where the gentry paid their hunt subscriptions as one body and left their cards in the prescribed manner. When the postal address of our area was changed from Cirencester to Stroud, my father and all his neighbours protested, in spite of the fact that their letters now arrived earlier.

Yet for all this we did know a few of the Bisley people. On our first arrival we had had cards left on us by the Hewitts and the Drummonds. Captain Hewitt was a retired naval man, short and brisk, who lived with his eye on the clock. His wife was a bridge player who had a drawing-room full of Chippendale chairs that were too precious to sit on. A lively woman, with the air of a Colonial Governor's wife, she liked to express startling views. Thus she professed a belief in euthanasia and once disturbed my mother by maintaining that people should be given a painless end as soon as they ceased to be useful to the community. I remember reflecting that, if this were literally carried out, not many—indeed none at all—of my parents' friends and neighbours would survive. However, the Hewitts did not remain at Bisley for long, for round about 1908 they came into money and left for a 'better' neighbourhood beyond Cheltenham.

The Drummonds were very different. Major Drummond had been in the Scots Guards. After a career as one of the most dashing men about town, he made a runaway match with the daughter of a Scottish laird and settled down to live in dowdiness and obscurity. He had, I remember, an odd love for bright colours, which made him paper the walls of his drawing-room with coloured picture-postcards and assemble a glowing collection of South American butterflies. The only drama in his life—for he was a very retiring man—was his quarrel with the rector upon some fine point of theology. To show his disapproval he would go to church in state, sit in one of the front pews and, as soon as the sermon started, get up with great noise and clatter of feet and walk out. When on one occasion the rector had the door locked, he rattled on it so loudly that the sermon had to stop till it was opened. His wife, a stiff, silent woman with semi-Calvinist views, brought up their two children so strictly that I scarcely saw them till I was grown up.

But the Bisley people we got to know best were the MacMeekans, who in 1908 built themselves a Cotswold house across the valley at Waterlane. Major MacMeekan was a man in the middle forties who had been in the Artillery: alert and interested in new things, he made friends with the Rothensteins and others of the incoming arty tribe and also with my father, who found in him a good tennis player and a man of exact and positive mind. His wife, an Italian by birth but brought up in Egypt, was a pretty and vivacious woman who had a pleasantly ironical way of speaking. I had never before met anyone who used irony to give a gay flavour to conversation, and I was completely captivated. This was the only house in the neighbourhood that I always visited with pleasure. I went there alone and was treated as a person, not simply as the son of my parents. And from these visits I came to see that English country society was not invariably the elderly, wooden, philistine thing that it was on our side of the valley.

Through the MacMeekans my parents, and therefore I too, got to know Edward Gimson. He was the architect and furniture maker of whom I have already spoken who had built himself a house at Sapperton. Next to him lived his partners, Ernest and Sidney Barnsley. The three of them had come to this district some dozen years before, when they had taken between them an ancient and very isolated house called Pinbury. Gimson used to tell a story about his confrères which has always amused me. When they first settled at Pinbury they were all unmarried: then Ernest Barnsley took a wife and brought her there. As she found the housekeeping too much for her, it was decided that they should bring in a lady help, on the strict understanding, however, that she must be so plain that neither of the other two young men would take an interest in her. This was agreed to unanimously because they did not wish to break up the establishment. So in due course Miss X arrived, not only as plain as anyone could wish for but stone deaf as well. However, the god with the arrows is not so easily foiled. Before many weeks had passed Sidney Barnsley began to complain that too much work was being left to Miss X and that this was not fair, especially as she was delicate. Sidney, in fact, was in love, and when he married the lady help, the Pinbury *ménage* broke up and they moved to separate establishments in Sapperton. It was a good marriage, for she made him happy.

Gimson was a pleasant man, simple and without pretensions. I used to go and see him often. Among other things he taught me a grand revolutionary tenet—death to the drawing-room. The rock-garden not having yet come in, it was through their drawing-rooms that the women of our society competed with one another. Crowded with little silver and china knick-knacks, which it took £50 a year in housemaid's food and wages to dust, cluttered with cheap mahogany furniture, these rooms were a perfect example of Veblen's theory of Conspicuous Waste. Mrs Hewitt's chairs which were too valuable to sit on, Mrs James's bowls of potpourri and early spring bulbs, Miss Nichol's crystal chandeliers and cupboards of Dresden figures were soldiers in an army that marched to triumph over my mother's less tasteful decorations (both my parents had a natural inclination to the ugly) and her always a little faded chintzes and cretonnes. For this reason Gimson's doctrine that the functional is the basis of the beautiful came to me as a draught of fresh air in a stuffy lumber-room. Both his own house and the MacMeekans', which he had designed, offered admirable illustrations of it. Bare stone walls displaying the mason's chisel marks, or else linen-pattern panelling: heavy waxed tables, rush-bottomed chairs and iron fire-dogs: for only ornament the fine grain of an elm-wood cupboard or an old silk hanging. My mother and grandmother complained of the bareness of such rooms, which seemed to them a reversion to those coarse ages of the world before the influence of women had brought in refinement, but to me they were not only beautiful but moral. I welcomed the Ruskinian identification of the aesthetic and the ethical because like him I believed that the power to create beautiful objects sprang spontaneously out of the good life. And by the good life I meant the simple and primitive one.

Gimson and his partners the Barnsleys represented what was most valuable in the Cotswold cult in our part of the country. They preached to a world that had ceased to use its eyes the beauty of the Medieval or Early Tudor style of farm-house building and revived, as far as that was possible, the old crafts of stone-cutting and plastering that had made this what it was. By so doing they reformed the art of restoring early buildings, thus helping to put an end to the vandalism of the Victorian era. Their teaching had another result. Gimson died during the first German War, a comparatively poor man, but within a few years his influence had raised the value of house property on the Cotswolds to extraordinary heights. Farm-houses that in 1914 were worth £500 were sold in 1934 for £5,000. Even a cottage of no architectural merit sometimes realized high figures, simply because it was in Cotswold stone. It was the landlords who had laughed at his impracticable notions that profited by them.

Curiously enough there was in our neighbourhood another and quite different group that practised the simple life. This was the Whiteway Colony. A few months after our first arrival at Miserden a family of Russians bought a cottage and a few acres of rather featureless land along the Cheltenham road. Other families, also Russian, joined them, wooden huts were put up and soon a settlement of a very odd sort came into existence. They were said to be Tolstoyans, for they dressed in long white robes, had long untrimmed hair and beards, ate only vegetables and made it a principle to make or grow everything they needed. Although they could not avoid buying certain raw materials such as iron and wood, they built a forge on which they fashioned their own tools and a loom on which they wove their clothes and blankets. Some of them, however, did not need clothes because they were nudists. When one day our rector, Mr Earée, paid his professional call, the door was opened by a naked woman who invited him to step inside. 'Not till you have finished your toilet,' he replied in his self-possessed way and, getting onto his tricycle again, rode off.

As a small boy these Colonists, as they were called, had greatly intrigued me. My governess and I would follow the dull, stone-walled road, marked halfway by a single thorn-bush, till we came to a fork known as the Speaks. This was said to take its name from the fact that, in olden times, the people of Miserden and of two neighbouring hamlets would walk out here on a Sunday and 'speak'. Then we would come to a second fork, where the Stroud road branched off down a steep hill, and after another bend would arrive in sight of the Colony. This was the place where we turned (my governess always had a special place where she turned) but not, if we were lucky, before we had caught sight of some wild-eyed man, all tangled hair and beard, who called up in my mind John the Baptist. Policemen too were sometimes to be met with. The authorities had been alarmed by this foreign invasion and once, driving past in the dog-cart, we had come on half a dozen policemen hiding ponderously behind a hedge.

When, towards the age of sixteen, I began again to take an interest in the Colony, its character had changed. Although sandals lingered on, both nudism and white smocks had vanished. English families had drifted in, usually of a socialist or anarchist way of thinking, and the place was prosperous. A bearded Russian known as Peter wove linen, an unbearded Oxford M.A. called Prothero had a bakery which sent out bread all over the county, and there was a Hegelian philosopher. The Colonists, in short, made money and since money saps the foundations of the collective life, the idealist character of the settlement had declined. Only a certain freedom in sexual relations remained. I visited the place a number of times, but my father's position in the neighbourhood made familiarity difficult. Besides, their grey socialist mentality did not attract me.

It was, I think, in the spring of 1911 that we went again to Brittany. My parents took a furnished house at St Lunaire, a few miles along the coast from Dinard and close to the golf course. A small-gauge train, like that described by Proust in *A L'ombre des jeunes filles en fleur*, connected the two places, meandering across the countryside with an air of gentle indecision, as though not quite sure whether it had the dictatorial rights of a railway or the customary ones of a tram. It had been decided that I was to spend the mornings learning to play golf, but my father could not hope to succeed where the myrmidons of Radley had failed. After one wild drive into a gorse bush, I would take my copy of Shelley from my pocket and settle down to read it on the beach. Another favourite place of mine was by a stream, where the gorse, the primroses, the bluebells and the cowslips covered the banks and made the air sweet with their scent. A blackbird warbled in a bush nearby as I declaimed aloud *The Cloud* or *The Sensitive Plant*.

One conversation stands out among vague recollections of walks and bicycle rides. It took place with a very plain young woman called Miss Cooper who had been brought over as a holiday governess for my brother. I took a liking to her when I discovered that she did not care for games, but approved of poetry, and we used to go for walks together. Then one day she confided to me that there was a problem that greatly worried her. She could get no peace of mind until she had solved it because it seemed to her of the utmost importance. It was one of those questions that lie at the root of everything one thinks and believes and yet she could not come to any decision about it. It was—but no, I had probably not yet reached an age when I could understand its urgency. 'Oh, come on,' I said, 'tell me.' Well, it was the question of the Apostolic succession. To put it in a few words, if a certain Archbishop Parker, who lived in the time of Queen Elizabeth, had not been consecrated in accordance with the rules of canon law, then the inheritance of grace passed down by manual contact from the Apostle Peter had been broken and the Anglican Church was not a church at all but a collection of schismatical laymen. (She pronounced these last words with great energy.) The difficulty in coming to a right opinion was that the historians disagreed. I felt so speechless with amazement on hearing this passionate declaration by a person who was both young and well educated that I could not say anything. The magical side of religion was new to me. I gazed at Miss Cooper's slim tweed-skirted form striding beside me, saw beyond her the tiny figures of the golfers dotted over the green turf and felt that here was a mental world I should never have the key to.

Towards the end of my holidays I went off by myself on a four days' bicycle trip. The route I took lay inland through the great *landes* of the interior and then curved back again in a half-circle to the sea-coast. In those days the peasants wore their full costumes: this meant for the women the starched *coiffe* of their *pays* and for the men a short jacket or blouse topped by a broad-brimmed black hat, from which two ribbons hung down over their shoulders. When one entered the market-place of a small town one seemed to be entering the seventeenth century. All round the air smelt of gorse and hawthorn and every now and then one came on a dolmen or menhir or on a roughly carved stone calvary. Under its scalp of flowers and leaves one felt the granite hardness and uncouthness of an ancient civilization. Then wherever one went one was aware of the proximity of the sea, which with its creeks and estuaries, alternately filled with mud or water, penetrated deeply into the land. The sea, the sad northern sea with its rocks and its tides, was beginning to take hold of my imagination.

The four days of my trip went all too quickly. I passed them in an intoxication with my new-found liberty. So desirable did this state seem that I decided that all I wanted was to travel on for ever, visiting one after the other the different regions of the world and satisfying my curiosity about them. I came back with the conviction that I had discovered how I wanted to spend my life.

I have now to speak of my relations with my parents. I do not find this easy to do because from the age of sixteen on my recollections of them are vague and scattered. I had entered the cave of adolescence and was too shut up in my own ideas and projects to notice anything that did not in some way bear upon them. But certainly there was a steadily increasing friction. I was beginning to rebel against everything they stood for and this was a situation that neither of them was fitted either by temperament or by education to deal with.

Their first mistake was that they had fixed long before on the pattern I must conform to. I was to be a soldier and therefore I must be fashioned in the mould of a typical Army officer. When, as I approached seventeen, Mr Wilson Green wrote to say that he did not think I was suited for such a career, my father replied with an angry letter of complaint to the headmaster. No one was to tell *him* what his son was or was not suited for! But actually it was my mother who was the most set on my joining the Army. The military life was for her the only romantic life, and since my earliest years she had dreamed of seeing me in uniform. This had led her to shut her mind to any evidence that I might be a different sort of person from what a peace-time soldier is required to be. I was a normal boy, she declared, because everyone in her family was normal and for that reason the Army was bound to agree with me.

I was thus a victim, not so much of my father's military ideas, as of my mother's obsession with 'normality'. This had come on during her adolescence when, finding herself odd, peculiar, unlike other people, she had at first tried to develop a bookish line of her own and had then gone over with all the strength of her family loyalty to a worship of those hearty, popularity-giving qualities which everyone round her seemed to possess. For her failures as a girl must have humiliated her. She had played tennis, which was just coming in, extremely badly, and was too nervous to enjoy riding, much less hunting. She liked people, but, except with those she knew well, was ill-assured and awkward. In the world in which she had been brought up these defects were serious and so, she was determined, they must not recur in her children. When therefore she saw some of these same aberrations coming out in me, she reacted, not so much by trying to repress them—for she was too gentle to behave in that way—as by refusing for as long as possible to admit their existence.

A double barrier thus began to grow up between my mother and myself. I was in revolt against her social beliefs and conventions: she did not want to know what I really thought or felt. To make things worse, she developed a habit of teasing me. This teasing, which was always carried out by the buffoonish person who played one of the less attractive roles in her character, offended me deeply, all the more since, like most adolescents, I was oversensitive about everything that concerned my ideas. Gradually, therefore, my childish adoration of her came to be buried under a coating of resentment and irritability.

My father's place in my life was quite different. With his deafness and his abrupt, dictatorial ways he stood at a far greater distance. In his dealings with me he was never unjust or even intentionally unkind, but he could not help being often disagreeable. He believed too that in certain respects he must discipline me. He had quietly allowed me to give up shooting when the sight of rabbits gnawed by ferrets and the screaming of wounded hares had upset me, but he insisted on my learning to play golf and tennis in spite of my feeling that they were a waste of time. Perhaps the only things he really approved of in me were my love of riding and my independence. Today I can be fair to him and recognize that for a man of his irritable temperament he showed a good deal of self-restraint. I can also respect his sense of duty which made him do what, according to his lights, he judged best for me. The thing that could not be got over was that we were temperamentally at opposite poles to one another. If for that reason I found it impossible to love or admire him, he must often have regretted being saddled with a son as uncongenial as I was.

My grandmother is the person whose image rises most clearly in my mind from this time. She filled the drawing-room, the verandah, the garden—all the sunlit parts of our rambling, shadowy house—with her calm, vegetable presence. I can see her now on the chintz-covered sofa, a bowl of hyacinths by her side, working at her embroidery and whispering slowly and sibilantly to herself. 'Hugh says he can take me in to Cheltenham tomorrow.' Pause. 'He says—he can take me in to Cheltenham.' Pause. 'To Chel-ten-ham.' Whisper and pause—the tissue-paper voice went on with the monotonous intermittency of a mouse scratching in the wainscot.

The interest she took in exotic religions gave me a special link with her. We both believed that all wisdom came from the East. When I first began to take notice of these things she was going through a Buddhist phase and read or rather browsed on (for she couldn't really *read* anything) large books with long unpronounceable words in them. I remember my mother, annoyed by her having stopped going to church, taking up one of these books and declaiming aloud in her buffoonish manner a chapter heading: 'Brief Prolegomena to the fourteen different kinds of Nothing.' However, since anything my mother said in that tone always produced on me a contrary impression, that phrase did not seem funny to me at all, but exciting and subtle, although when, taking over the book, I tried to read the chapter, I could not understand a word of it. Then there came in a craze for Yogi philosophy and my mother, who liked to think that there was 'something in' all religions, bought a book which was being much talked of in certain circles—Colonel Sinnett's *Esoteric Buddhism*. I remember it lying about on our shelves for many years, a small brown volume sandwiched between *Mémoires d'un âne* and *The Romance of Electricity*. But my grandmother, who had her own sources of information, did not like small books—wisdom, she felt, lay in large, heavy tomes stuck with polysyllabic vocables—and so she passed by Colonel Sinnett and plunged for Madame Blavatsky. *The Secret Doctrine* kept her engrossed for many years.

My grandmother was one of those people whom almost everyone would think he was in a position to call stupid. She had brought her dumb, gently circulating blood into my father's restless, bitter-minded, able ancestry and had passed it on in the form of a limiting curse to him. But I have much reason, her kindness to me apart, to feel grateful to her, because she taught me that what the world calls stupidity may also be a kind of passive wisdom. Even her reading, which at first sight seemed so absurd, had a sensible object. Since her religious feelings took the form of a belief in the immanence of God, of his presence in every animal and plant and growing tree, she rightly rejected Christianity, which exalts Man at the expense of Nature, and turned to the religions of the East. Yet she had, I think, no particular wish to clarify this inarticulate feeling of hers, but merely to meditate on it and reassure herself that others before her, people cleverer than herself, had worked out its consequences. Those large tomes she turned over, without understanding more than a phrase here and there, provided an incentive to her meditation. It is in this way that many people who are by no means stupid read difficult poetry.

Sorting out my memories of her from this time, I think that what I liked her for was that she never attempted to preach at me. She was too diffuse and passive. Protected by her deafness from the noises of the world; from its monkey pattern of assertion and argument, she had allowed her mind to become dispersed among the thoughts and feelings that drifted through her and to become one of the fourteen different kinds of Nothing. In this she was the complete opposite to the other members of our household—my active, bustling, optimistic mother, my noisy, positive father, who was always either blowing his nose like a trumpet or stamping up and down the stairs like a horse. They were perpetually making their presence known, whereas my grandmother imposed by her stillness.

I now come to an event which was to have a decisive effect upon the whole of my life—my meeting with Hope, or, to give him his full name, John Hope-Johnstone. I first heard of him when I came back for the summer holidays of 1910. A young man, it seemed, of no particular profession had rented a cottage at Waterlane from the Mac-Meekans. Exceedingly clever, a great reader of books and a brilliant talker, he created an impression, as my mother put it, wherever he went. Unfortunately, she added, he imagined it made him look more original to go about dressed like an artist—that is to say, in odd and peculiar clothes. This was a pity because he was not an artist at all but a man of good family. One of his cousins was the Duchess of Buckingham, another was a well-known master of hounds, while Mrs Shaw, the wife of the rector of Edgeworth, who, being Scottish, regarded herself as related to all the 'good' Scottish families, had discovered that he was her second cousin twice removed. This had given him, in spite of his strange attire, the entry into our little society, and the Millses in particular, who would not have cared to know artists, had taken him up because they found him amusing.

To add to my curiosity, my mother told me that this Mr Hope-Johnstone had expressed a wish to meet me because he had been at my prep school, Winton House. She thought that, as he liked poetry and was so very clever, he would be an interesting person for me to know. Then a few days later a letter from him arrived, written in a thin, spidery hand, inviting me to tea. I wrote accepting and set off.

His cottage stood on the edge of a wooded ravine that ran down to the valley of Holy Brook. It was not an easy place to find when one approached it from below and I arrived hot and flustered because I was ten minutes late. Indeed, I felt such alarm at the prospect of meeting this strange man—till then I had never met anyone who read poetry —that as I walked through the woods I had twice been on the point of turning back. However, I plucked up my courage and opened the garden gate.

What followed then was something so breathtaking, opened so many doors, displayed so many new vistas that I can give no coherent account of it. I saw a slim, dark-haired man, dressed in a pale buff corduroy suit. He had sandals on his bare feet and a brightly coloured silk handkerchief round his neck and he was sitting at a kitchen table playing a tune on a penny whistle. He got up as I came in and I noticed his black horn-rimmed glasses with their thick lenses. They were a novelty at the time—all other glasses had metal rims—and I learned later that he had bought them in America. He began to speak in a rather hard and definite voice, one of those voices that one cannot imagine as ever becoming confused or hesitating, but with such naturalness that I felt at ease at once.

Of the conversation that followed I cannot remember any consecutive pattern or sequence. What I do recall is a series of things said or done by Hope, each of which produced on me a shock of surprise. Never before had I had such a battery of new ideas and impressions fired at me. The first of these came when he asked me if I had read Yeats. On my replying that I only knew one poem by him, he took up a copy of *The Wind among the Reeds* and read from it in a strange, chaunting, resonant tone which seemed greatly to enhance its beauty. Till then I had had no idea that poetry could be read in that way: I usually declaimed it. After that he began to talk about Nietzsche and, opening a copy of *Also sprach Zarathustra*, he read some pages aloud in German, using the same tone and translating as he went. Then, as I still lay under the spell of these utterances, so intoxicating by their novelty, he pulled out an illustrated copy of Blake's *Jerusalem* and, after that, some drawings by Aubrey Beardsley.

Meanwhile, in the intervals of looking at books, I was glancing round me at the cottage. It was very small, a single whitewashed room with a staircase leading up to the bedroom above, but the walls were lined with books and other books were stacked up on the window-seat and floor. There were books upstairs as well, a bed that had not been made, clothes, china and suitcases scattered about, plates and teacups unwashed—an extraordinary medley of refinement and untidiness.

At some time during these proceedings he made tea and for the first time I tasted the tarry flavour of Lapsang Souchong. As we drank it my host explained that he bought it from a special firm in the City and nowhere else could one get a Lapsang Souchong—'which after all was the only tea worth drinking'—that reached precisely that degree of sublimity.

'And try this quince jelly,' he went on. 'I flatter myself that I am one of the very few people who know how to make it. The secret lies in leaving in both the pips and the rind, which most people throw away. I learned to make it from the housekeeper of old Dr Mercier— a nice man—kept a private lunatic asylum he did—then went mad himself—whom we used to have tea with as children. I always maintain that no other jelly or jam has quite the same subtle flavour.'

As soon as we had finished tea he began with a casual air to show me some of his things. There was the polychrome Delft bowl with the blue peacock on it, the white-and-gold Worcestershire teacups, the Old Naples shaving soap with its harsh-sweet attar of roses perfume, the cottagy rag-mat, the Morris curtains. There was also a pair of shoes, whose elegant boat-shaped build he invited me to feel with my hand, which he had just had made for him by Moykoff in Burlington Arcade. All these things seemed to have some special significance for him, as though they were heirlooms he had bequeathed to himself, spontaneous emanations from his own taste and personality, but what particularly struck me was that though his income was very small— it was said that he depended on lunch or dinner invitations to get a proper meal—everything he possessed had some peculiar elegance or beauty, and when he could not get that he did without.

It is only by fits and starts that I recall his conversation that afternoon and I am conscious of confusing my immediate reactions with those that came a little later. It must, however, have been after he had shown me the blue peacock bowl that he told me that he had just taken on the job of tutor to Augustus John's children. This made, he said, a pleasant sort of break for the time being. For one thing John was the greatest living English painter—a natural genius who drew almost as well as Michelangelo. Then too he was a man built on a heroic scale, if possible even greater as a human being than as an artist. From this we got on to the subject of gipsies, to whom John had introduced him, and he took from the window-seat a Romany grammar he was studying and began to run through it line by line. The declensions of the nouns, he pointed out, were even more elaborate than in Greek, though the full system of inflections was only employed by certain of the Welsh gipsies, as for example the Wood family from Lake Bala.

'Here is a little Romany poem,' he said. 'See if you like it.'

And he recited from memory some verses about the gipsies' barn and a pretty girl who used to give them bacon.

However, Hope's linguistic interests were not, it seemed, confined to Romany and before long he was discoursing on the difficulties of Arabic. The East, I gathered, had the same fascination for him that it had for me, and we talked for some time on it. If I cannot remember anything he said about it, that is perhaps because, feeling myself at last on familiar ground, I did most of the talking.

The afternoon was now drawing to an end, but not before I had been dazzled by the display of yet another of my new friend's attainments. Pulling out some books on Symbolic Logic he started to expound in suitably elementary terms some of the paradoxes propounded by Peano. Mathematics and poetry, he said, were the subjects that interested him most, but some day, he thought, he would put everything aside to travel. He hoped before he died to see something of every part of the world except Australia. When at length I dragged myself away I felt that I had been left with a good deal to think about.

My meeting with Hope brought a great change into my life. Here was the guide and mentor I needed so badly. If I had not come across him in such a providential way, I might have imagined that I was the only person of the poetry-loving species in England. Yet during the next two years—that is, until I left Radley—I saw little of him. So far as I can remember we did not meet more than five or six times, on only two of which was I alone with him. It had to be enough for me that he existed. However, even when I was back at school I did not entirely lose touch with him. My mother, who was flattered by thinking that such a clever man could interest himself in her son, would mention him from time to time in her letters. On one occasion, she reported, he was seen on Stroud platform dressed immaculately in a morning coat and top-hat: he was catching the train to London. On another my father met him driving a light dog-cart, clad in sandals and buff-coloured corduroys, with two barefooted, ragged boys, Augustus John's children, beside him. This had made a bad impression and led my mother to express the fear that if he went on in this way he would lose the position in the neighbourhood that his cleverness had gained for him. But in her next letter he was playing in a croquet tournament at Cirencester—presumably in ordinary clothes—and doing well.

These two aspects of Hope—the bohemian and the conventional— especially intrigued me. I found it difficult to fit them together. Why, when he was the sort of person that I knew him to be, could he think it worth his while to lunch and dine out so much with the Millses? He had his own life, yet he also, without boredom or indignation, mixed in theirs. I could not understand this and for a long time it remained inexplicable.

His appearances in our society were always rather extraordinary. From his first entry into a room he displayed all the self-confidence of the Balzacian hero, fresh from Paris, disporting himself among the provincial bourgeoisie. That is to say, he set himself to amuse, to shock, to startle, and above everything to make an impression. He had certain stock subjects he drew on freely, as for example the natural antagonism between men and women, wives and husbands. He would tell stories and make jokes on this subject, starting off in a special tone, faintly indicative of contempt, with such phrases as 'Women of course always think that . . .' and leading up to some statement that they denied vigorously. This war-of-the-sexes theme was very successful with Mr Mills, who kept up with his wife a continuous, public, but at the bottom quite amiable *fronde*. But then Mr Mills was a business man who liked above all things to be made to laugh, whereas the rest of us Cotswold dwellers were staid and rather squeamish people, on whom this sort of conversation, delivered in a loud, self-assured voice by a young man recently arrived in the district, was apt to be jarring. I could see that my father did not like it though he made no comments, while one sensitive soul, a Cotswold artist who did woodcuts of farm horses standing under sycamore trees, remarked that he reminded him of the advertisement of Johnny Walker's whisky. This advert, as everyone knows, represents a sort of Gilbert the Filbert figure, mechanical and jaunty, with a top-hat and white teeth.

Since Hope had become a hero to me, I wished to see him universally acclaimed, even by those people I did not like. For this reason I was always on tenterhooks when I met him in the sort of company where tact and reserve—and, one might add, dullness—were required. I noticed that he had little power of sensing the feeling of his audience. Whenever he was excited by the presence of more than two or three people, he raised his voice and said things that, if not positively tactless, were somehow in the wrong key. Thus he was very fond of repeating the *bons mots* of Oscar Wilde, prefacing them with the words 'As Oscar once said . . .', apparently oblivious of the fact that at this time Wilde's name could not be mentioned in public. This led, quite wrongly, to his being regarded by many men as a homosexual.

His social manner was always very positive. It conveyed the idea of his being made of a harder and brighter substance than other people, less tentative and less sensitive to his surroundings. For this reason, wherever he went he aroused either sympathies or antipathies. Those who did not like him were usually men—they thought he showed off too much—whereas most women turned a kindly eye on him. And it must be said that he did a good deal to deserve their sympathy. He would go to great trouble to entertain even the least entertainable among them, fetching out his little stores of *bons mots* and erudition on the slightest sign of interest. This readiness of his to condescend to his intellectual inferiors used to puzzle me. All he appeared to ask of people was that they should like listening to him. He took everyone at their face value, judged them by their readiness to be civil—a favourite word of his—and never looked below the surface.

Since I am trying now to present Hope in his social role—and, it must be remembered, in a very limited and conventional society—I will give an example of this rather engaging affability of his which I remember because at the time it half-pleased, half-annoyed me. He had come to tea with us and stayed on to dinner (a somewhat frequent and, seeing that he disliked cooking, very natural practice of his) and my father had retired on some excuse to his study. My mother and my Aunt Nellie, a pleasant but decidedly *borné* second cousin, were the only other people present besides myself. My recollection begins with his describing how his mother had cared little for her four elder children but had adored the last two, who were now, he added, in the Indian Cavalry. On the wave of sympathy created by this—for most women feel drawn to make it up to a motherless man—he went on, by what transitions I cannot now remember, to speak of the difficulties of pronouncing Arabic, illustrating his remarks with some very guttural examples. From here he got—again I forget how—to the subject of Fourth Dimensional Geometry. On this he dilated for a little, it is true in very elementary terms and bringing out all the entertainment value the subject provided, but getting a perceptible pleasure from the dazed and respectful expressions of his listeners.

Meanwhile I had observed that although my Aunt Nellie's face had gradually taken on that look of a wooden idol, stiff and ageless, which came over it whenever anything was mentioned that lay outside the range of her immediate experience, my mother sat in furrowed concentration, pleased and flattered that such a very clever man should talk to her of these things. I however felt differently. As I walked part of the way back with Hope along the white limestone road, picking my way between the puddles on which the stars were reflected while the owls hooted in the deep woods around, I wondered how he could open his secret stores of knowledge to people who could not even begin to understand them. To people who might (though I exempted my mother from this) betray him. The dangers of the world in which I lived had made me, contrary to my real nature, cautious and secretive and, although I knew that it did not really matter to him what any of these people thought of him, his lack of awareness of these dangers, the innocence that under his hard-boiled manner stared out at one, aroused in me a feeling of wonder, almost of apprehension. For a person of sensibility or intelligence there was, I thought, only one receipt for living in middle-class society—the cult of hypocrisy. If one did not want to be hypocritical, one must escape from it.

When I try to recall what my personal feelings towards Hope were at this time I see that they varied. Immediately after my first meeting with him he became an extraordinary and dazzling figure, too strange and foreign to understand or criticize, but as I got to know him better my blind admiration changed into a more realistic appraisal. It was of course important that I found him attractive to look at. He was a slim, well-built man with finely cut features, raven-black hair and an ivory skin. His only physical blemish lay in his extremely short sight and in a slight squint in one of his eyes. When my mother first remarked on this squint I felt indignant because I did not like any criticism of him, but later I came to see a peculiar and subtle charm in it. It seemed to correspond to a certain oblique way he had of picking on a line of poetry or a feature in a landscape whose beauty was not at first sight obvious. After this it was the people that did not have squints who seemed to me defective.

His manner with me was friendly, impersonal and simple. He never focused his attention directly on me, but was as casual and offhand as though he were one of my school companions. He had besides the gift of being able to convey in clear, easy language the information and knowledge that I craved for without the least assumption of infallibility or superior wisdom. Indeed he invariably treated me as his intellectual equal—I would almost say, as a person of the same age and experience. Actually he was eleven years older than I was, but by the time that I was eighteen and had ceased to be dazzled by his superiority, I had forgotten it. It was this same simplicity and naturalness that, twenty or thirty years later, when life had disillusioned him a little, made him a sort of Pied Piper, perpetually surrounded and sought after by children.

However, in the early years of our acquaintance there was something else that appealed to me about him. This showed itself in various ways, but especially when he read aloud poetry. At such moments there was no romantic part into which I could not fit him: Bedouin by the desert thorn-scrub fire, Alastor on the lone Chorasmian shore, long-sleeved, flute-fingering magician, playing the air that brought the puppet world to life. Whenever I saw him at such times he diffused strangeness and mystery.

I remember, however, one moment of doubt and hesitation. Not long after our first meeting he invited me again to tea. I found at his cottage a tall man dressed in a heavy check overcoat of a kind I imagined to be worn at race meetings. This man had a loud, confident voice and—I noticed with repulsion—only one ear. As I listened to their conversation, another side of Hope's background—I imagined, the aristocratic side—rose before me, a sort of Regency world in which the men were tough and heartless and nothing but money and horses counted. Where then were the eagles and the trumpets? Where the vision of the East and of poetry? A feeling of his utter remoteness from my life came over me and also of his worldliness. Hitherto I had supposed that the cynical remarks he liked to throw about, his allusions to a different, racing and gambling background, were purely hypothetical: now I saw that they might refer to a side of his life and character that really existed. I was very pure and high-minded at this time, very ignorant of the world, very set against position and money, and the thought that he might possess a coarse and ugly side to his nature (by this I meant a rich and heartless side, lacking in poetry and the finer feelings) dismayed me. Then the man left and Hope became simple and serious as he always was when alone with me. Later I gathered that this visitor was a journalist whom he had only met once or twice before.

I put down these things as I remember them, conflicting and at variance with one another though they sometimes are. Now I must record a later impression that occurred when I knew him rather better: it arose out of a remark he made to me about a neighbour of ours, Mrs Chrissie James.

The lady was a widow on the right side of forty, the sister-in-law of two middle-aged bachelors who lived at Edgeworth Manor, only a mile away. In appearance she was a tall, handsome, large-boned woman with a profusion of reddish-purplish veins that spread like the map of a river system over her cheeks, and who was always dressed from head to foot in black. She had never recovered from the early death of her husband and her face in repose was severe, cold and sad. When caught off her guard, with her large, expressionless, stony eyes, she looked like Niobe, and one rightly guessed that she had little love left in her heart for anyone except her children. In company, however, she was quite different. Conscious of the need to bridge the gulf of feeling that separated her from others, she assumed an animated, gushing manner that offered the greatest possible contrast to her face in repose. She smiled, she laughed, she poured out a stream of breathless, panting conversation, couched in affectionate superlatives and making a frequent use of the word 'dear'. 'That *dear* Mr Mills . . . that *dear* Mrs Shaw . . . poor *dear* Alfred . . . *dear* you . . .' and so forth.

One day, as I was walking with Hope in Lord Bathurst's park, he began to speak of her. Her manner, he declared, had seemed to him rather extraordinary, had in fact puzzled him a good deal till, on thinking it over, he had realized that she must be a little in love with him. Otherwise there was no accounting for her being so 'all over' him. I said nothing and he went on to talk of women and of what incomprehensible creatures they were. But his remark had torn down a veil for me. Until this moment I had regarded him as omniscient, or at least as knowing immensely more than anyone else about the things that mattered. Now I realized with a shock that he had little understanding of people, but walked as a blind man among them. For ten minutes perhaps I suffered from the sense of there being a flaw in my idol, then I adjusted myself to it. In many ways it was a relief to feel that he was not always going to be right.

Since our lives were to be so entangled later it is not easy for me to mark off what I had got from Hope up to this time. Advice, direction, encouragement—all those I would have got sooner or later, though less perfectly, from others. What I would say that he especially gave me was the picture of what a superior man ought to be. For he was made of a different material from the people I had met up to this time. Glossy, preened, living like a cat for himself alone, bound to his mysterious ideal of self-perfection, with an outline that was as clear and unambiguous as the drawing on a Greek vase, he stood out in a muddy, moralizing world as a unique and altogether dazzling sort of creature.

In his dealings with me he was of course subversive. He spoke as the immoralist, the enemy of families, on the duty of living only for oneself. He professed to despise professions, marriage, politics, altruism, all forms of earning a living—everything of a social kind except good manners. The aim of a sensible man should be to get all he could out of the world and to give as little as possible back. There was a beauty in uselessness. But at the same time he took it for granted that the only things that could matter to an intelligent person were the study of the arts and sciences and the cultivation of one's own higher faculties. This in the long run was the most important thing that I learned from him.

CHAPTER IX

Rebellion and Escape

When I shut my eyes I see a white cottage room with an iron bedstead in one corner. There is a bookcase over the fireplace and on one side of it a heavy Breton chest of drawers. The only other pieces of furniture are a small writing-desk, a triangular wash-hand-stand and a couple of chairs. One of these occupies the deep embrasure that ends in the lattice window, and it is here that I sit when I wish to read.

Below the window lies the garden. In a thick matted surge the jasmine comes climbing up and the path is so close that I can jump out onto it. Immediately opposite is a sumach or smoke tree, raising its crown into the air with some of the elegance of a palm. Once when I was fifteen I had spread my bed under it (on summer nights I often slept on the lawn) because I believed it to be a relation of the upas tree and wished to test its poisonous qualities.

But the queen of our garden trees was the yew. One saw it on moonlit nights, crouching in a huge rounded mass like a limbless animal and drawing to itself all the deepest and intensest shade around. One could climb it—there was an easy way up; one could sit on the summit; one could taste the red, insipid berries that it was said to be death to eat and imagine that one was sinking into a dreamy swoon. Out of its side, like Eve emerging from the flank of Adam, grew a bamboo, and its green, rustling plumes particularly attracted me because they called up the tropics.

I loved our garden because it was at once so formal and so varied. The main part—three terraced lawns with their flower-beds—ended in a ha-ha fence, beyond which a grassy field, planted like a small park with walnut trees and sycamores, stretched away to a row of horse-chestnuts: beyond this again, though out of sight, there opened the great wood-choked chasm of Miserden Park. But this was only one compartment. On the right, following the edge of the field, a gravel path led into the 'upper garden'—a plot of thin soil, open and airy, overlooked by the grey roofs of the village, where my mother might often be found, kneeling with her trowel and basket before the long flower-bed; while on the other side, approached by a little gate, lay the 'lower garden', adjoining the cowshed and overhung by trees— a slightly lugubrious and forsaken region where our Irish gardener, Hegarty, retired to smoke his pipe and dig his potatoes. Here the syringa flowered, here the barren almond tree, the giant angelica and the enormous rhubarb, the trailing periwinkles and violets. Here the trees dripped dankly on rainy days and the Roman snails hid their white whorls under the ivy.

But I must return to my bedroom. On the further side of the fire-place there was a large cupboard let into the wall. In this I kept my collections. Until I was seventeen these had consisted of trays of worked flints and fossils, samples to show the grain of different sorts of wood, birds' eggs and butterflies and, most bulky of all, a sack containing two complete skeletons, it was thought of Danes, which I had got from a gravel pit near Abingdon. (Later my mother had these buried, after a conversation with the rector on the probability or otherwise of their having received Christian baptism, in an obscure corner of the church-yard.) Then, as I grew out of these things, they were removed to one of the empty cottage rooms, where my brother had his toy railway, and their place taken partly by books and partly by a collection of a different sort.

This new collection requires a brief explanation. My interest in wild flowers had shifted to an interest in their uses. I had begun some time before by brewing various herb wines, which everyone was expected to sample at Christmas, and then I had bought a copy of Culpeper's *Herbal* and set about experimenting with herb medicines. The more dramatic ones—belladonna and stramonium—were among those that appealed to me first and with them various edible roots and tubers such as the Spotted Orchis, out of which salep is made. Soon, however, I tired of this and began to give my attention to perfumes and essences. I bought a glass retort and with the help of books by such authorities as Piesse and Hubert, tried, though without success, to extract them. Then I got from Hope the address of a chemist called Lowe in Stafford Street, Piccadilly, who could supply samples of Oriental drugs, es-pecially of those employed in making incense, and started a collection of them.

As it happens, I still have a list of some of these drugs which I bought from Lowe and also part of the draft of a letter ordering further samples. The list includes storax, olibanum, galbanum, labdanum, frankincense, liquidambar, benzoin, acorus calamus, Balsam of Tola,

Balsam of Copaiba, Balm of Gilead, ginseng, galingale, ylang-ylang, ambergris, attar of roses, and the letter runs as follows:

'Dear Sir,

'I received with thanks the five drugs you sent me. Can you obtain samples of the flacourtia leaf, which grows on a tree known as the talisput tree? It must not be too expensive. And can you get cheaply from Java some *Antiaris toxicaria*, from a tree whose sap is poisonous? And also some gambir, the product of the *Nauclia* or *Unicaria gambir* from the East Indies: it is taken by the Malays to chew . . .'

I did not get these drugs. Sad to relate I have never to this day seen a flacourtia leaf or handled a grain of gambir or *Antiaris toxicaria*. But in their place I obtained a fine blackish-green lump of *Cannabis indica* or hashish, and a bottle of *Anhalonium lewinii*, the active principle of mescal, which Messrs Lewis of the United States had recently put on the market. In my quest for new and exotic sensations, I proceeded to take first one and then the other, though at first in such small doses that I obtained little result from them. Today it amazes me to think that my parents, to whom I had boastfully shown my purchases, raised no objection to this. My mother had so deep a horror of narcotics that she would not keep even aspirin or bromide in the house and had once allowed me to suffer agonies from a whitlow on my thumb rather than administer a sedative. I can only suppose they were so taken aback by the change that had come over their son that they no longer knew where to draw the line.

One had only to enter my room to become aware of this change. Fresh herbs were strewn on the floor in place of a carpet and bundles of roots and dried herbs hung from the walls. The letters *Om Mani Padme Hom* were written in charcoal over the bed and on the opposite wall was a piece of cardboard inscribed *Aum Shivaya Vashi*. From the ceiling hung a revolving incense burner of my own invention that sent out three different sorts of incense smoke at the same time, while the window recess contained a coloured plate of Buddha sitting under a Bo tree, which I regarded as a good subject for contemplation. Not exactly the sort of room, my parents must have felt, for a youth who would shortly be applying for a commission in His Majesty's Forces.

Meanwhile my habits began to assume more and more ascetic forms. I gave up lunch and took only a snack for breakfast—partly because I thought that digestion coarsened the mind and impeded vision and partly because I wished to harden myself. Sometimes I forced myself to rise from my bed at five o'clock in the morning and to go for a long walk in the hope that I might get a special revelation from the sunrise. I wore my hair as long as I dared—long hair was the symbol of liberty—and for the same reason took off my tie and collar when I was at a safe distance from the house. I was also much given to attacking middle-class ways of life, choosing a ground where I could do this without giving away my secret opinions. One subject that I was fond of bringing up in conversation with my mother was that of how Jesus Christ would comport himself if he returned to earth. Could one, for example, imagine him wearing a bowler hat? Or putting on evening dress? And would he, if he attended Ascot, as he might do to preach to the worldly, assume a morning coat and a grey topper? My mother said yes, he would wear whatever was appropriate, but I said no and went on to argue that one could not be a true Christian unless one gave away everything one had and lived as a poor man. And how, I added—this I regarded as my most effective shot—could a Christian possibly become a soldier?

I can still recall my mother's worried face when I attacked her in this manner. She was a deeply religious woman who sincerely tried to follow, according to her lights, the teaching of Christ in the Gospels. She suffered, no doubt, from conflicting loyalties, but she had not a trace of hypocrisy. And here was I, a horrible little prig of seventeen, selfish, self-centred and absurdly opinionated, trying to teach her her duty in a religion in which I did not believe.

My sartorial eccentricities particularly annoyed my father. Like all military people at this time, dress was a fetish to him. Correctness in these matters was such a prominent feature of the old guard—witness the stand taken by Edward VII and George V—that an unconventional attitude was forced upon the revolutionary. Yet my father's outbursts were so greatly to be feared—an open collar acted as a red rag to him —that, beyond letting my hair grow as much as possible, I did my best not to provoke him openly.

To illustrate his extraordinary and almost reflex susceptibility where dress was concerned I will relate an incident that happened much later —in 1919. I was at this time a recently demobilized officer, an infantry captain who had been through the war and survived. My military rank was the same as his. One evening—a most exceptional event—he took my mother and myself to a dance at Bisley and, as they wished to return early, it was agreed that I should spend the night at a friend's house and walk back across the valley next day. I did this, but as I opened the drive gate in my evening dress I met my father. He came up to me with his short, sharp step, his eyes hard and pebbly with

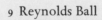

7 Gerald Brenan, November 1915

8 Ernest Taylor in 1914

9 Reynolds Ball

10 Ralph Partridge

11 Gerald Brenan in 1915

12 Anna Maria von Dummreicher, about 1919

13 Postcard of the ruined church at Hébuterne after the bombardment, sent by Gerald Brenan to his mother. The message reads 'Wed 26th July [1916]. All well.'

anger. 'What are you wearing those clothes for?' he asked. I explained what he knew already. 'Go and take them off at once,' he said. 'And in future remember that as long as you are staying in my house I expect you to be properly dressed.' For two days after this he did not speak to me.

As I have already said, I had become so engrossed in my own ideas that I had very little notion of what my parents were feeling. I merely sensed their concern at my behaviour and interpreted it as hostility. One evening, however, I got a disagreeable insight into what they thought of me. This happened in the following way. Before going to bed they used sometimes to talk together in my father's dressing-room and when they did this I found that by opening my bedroom door a little I could hear what my mother said, though not my father's answers. On the evening that I am speaking of I was the subject of their conversation. My mother began by lamenting my 'utter selfishness'. I thought only of myself, she said. I cared nothing for anybody. Then the word 'cracked' came up—then the word 'mad'. I strained my ears to listen and thought that I caught the words 'asylum' and 'reformatory'. Was it really possible, I wondered, that they were considering having me locked up? Yes, I said to myself, they were capable of anything, because they were my enemies.

On thinking this over afterwards I decided that I must have been mistaken. My mother could not really have thought, even for a moment, that I was out of my mind. Yet some years later Hope told me that she had once spoken to him—apparently in a playful way, yet, he thought, with anxiety in her voice—of my being 'quite mad'. She had, under her usual shrewdness, a violently emotional streak in her nature: when agitated she was easily carried away, and it is possible, therefore, that I heard her right.

My real feelings at this time were simple. I wanted to make my life a thing of great importance. That is to say, I wanted to live every day, every hour, every moment with the greatest possible intensity, with the most complete awareness of being alive. But how could I do that unless I escaped from the middle-class environment that I lived in and which I saw stretching forward inexorably and with stifling dullness into the future?

For these middle-class people, I said to myself, were dead. They lived by habit for petty material ends. When I looked round me and saw how they spent their lives, among what futile pleasures and occupations, without serious aims, I felt that I should never be able to be like them. I preferred poverty, misery, sickness, the risk of an early death to that sort of stupefied existence. My situation was not unlike that of a Catholic youth who feels a call to enter a religious order, but is prevented by his family. Only there was no order for me to enter because I had no faith in any established religion.

In this predicament I began to look round for some means of escape from the rut that I was caught in. I got my first ideas of how this might be done from a book that had formed part of my mother's early collection—*Walden*. Thoreau had found himself in the same sort of situation as myself and had broken away. His book was a guide, showing in detail how a person who has no private means can free himself from the fetters of society and lead his own life. It also gave me encouragement in my belief that the world in which I had grown up was radically false and bad and that I was therefore right in wishing to escape from it. The last pages of this book with their bitter invectives against society corresponded so precisely to my own feelings that I felt that I might have written them myself.

I read *Walden* when I was just seventeen and it did more to turn my life into new channels than any book that I have found since. Yet there were, I reflected, no primeval forests in England to which one could retire and make lead pencils. Nor did the idea of a sedentary life, even though it might be of the most austerely primitive kind, appeal to me. I wanted to travel. Yet how can one travel without money? Just as I was asking myself this question I came across a book, recently published, that gave me the answer. The artily dressed young lady who kept the Stroud Poetry Bookshop handed it to me with her innocent gesture, not thinking that it might be more dangerous in my hands than a phial of morphia. Its title was *The Autobiography of a Super-Tramp* and its author was the poet, W. H. Davies.

I read this book with enthralment. Not only was it delightful in itself with its flat, naïve style, but it gave me some new ideas for solving the economic problem that was exercising me. I began to interest myself in tramps and made several visits to Cheltenham to read up the subject in the municipal library. Yet neither Davies nor any of the other authors whom I consulted answered the question of how one could travel without money in the East. No European that I could hear of had done that, and I pondered the question of whether, if one became a Moslem, one could still travel like the Sufis or Ibn Batuta, begging for alms as one went.

I must now shift the scene over for a page or two to Radley and describe another step that I took on my road to liberation. There was a little round pond that I used to visit, lying in the middle of a grassy field, because it called up in my mind the lake of Walden. It had a few rushes growing by its edge and on fine days looked like an eye, staring up at the blue expanse above. Since it occupied a hollow, one could not be seen from more than a few yards away when one lay down beside it.

One afternoon (this was in the summer of 1911) I went there with a deliberate purpose. After reading a few pages of Shelley to put me in the right frame of mind, I stood up and said in a loud voice, 'I do not believe in God.' Then I waited, half-expecting (though ashamed of my expectations) the earth to open or the sky to fall. But the Universe gave no sign, the birds continued to sing as though they had not heard my important statement, so I repeated my words again and then sat down. A feeling of relief came over me. I had severed the last intellectual link that connected me with the conventional world. I had renounced not—what shall I call it?—that something indefinable and reassuring in which, whether or not I used words to describe it, I have always believed, but the God who has made so many atheists, the crude and repressive Father Deity who had cast over the world the image of his frown.

The sense of liberation I got from the success of this exploit found release in a fit of boastfulness. I wrote a long letter to Hope in which, without mentioning the scene by the pond, I remarked that 'of course I no longer believed in God or in that sort of thing'. And when I won the scripture prize at the end of term and was asked what book I should like to be presented with, I put down *Thus spake Zarathustra* by Nietzsche. On this the headmaster, Dr Field, sent for me and inquired in a friendly way how I had come to hear of this writer and, on my stammering out some vague explanation, advised me to take instead *Romola* by George Eliot.

When one is young and given to reading poetry every new poet one discovers has the effect of a new love affair or of the conversion to a new religion. For a time one's mind is filled with his cadences and images and one feels the world through his sensibility. The poet I was now reading was Yeats, which meant in those days his Celtic Twilight poems from *The Wind among the Reeds*. This intoxicating book ran through my generation like an epidemic. It offered us in the guise of poetry a collection of magical incantations and for this reason we did not read it aloud, we chanted it. But it could not take us out of ourselves into any authentic world: its effect was overwhelming precisely because it offered our stagnant and purposeless age a sort of poetical masturbation. It was able to do this because, though false in sentiment and indeed, in its languid way, very rhetorical, it had the facture of good poetry.

I was just as susceptible to these magical verses as any other young man of my time. I read them until I knew long passages by heart. They corresponded in my life to those collections of scents and drugs that I was making: to those Indian or Thibetan charms I hung on the walls of my room. The romantic costumery of the nineties was a necessary part in the make-up of any young man of poetical inclinations before the sudden breach with the past that came in with the first German War. Yet I must point out that in my case this costumery was of secondary importance. I was much too concerned about my future to think much of anything but the means to escape.

In the Easter holidays of 1912 my parents took rooms at Seaford. Getting up one morning before breakfast I walked over the hill to Cuckmere Haven and on to a hollow in the Downs above Alfriston. Here the sight of the thin turf and of the blue sky pressing above it brought on another of those ecstasies of which I have spoken. I now regarded them as promises, announcing the paradisical state that awaited me when I should be free.

It had been decided that I was to take a fortnight's cycling trip round Brittany. My father was glad to have me out of the house and my mother was eager that I should improve my French. Early one morning I started. Stopping on my way through Brighton to see the house where Richard Jefferies had spent his last years, I took a boat from Southampton to St Malo and then the train to Morlaix. From there I set out on a tour round the Breton coast.

I had been travelling for some days when, on my return from the Point du Raz, I came to a tidal river at Bénodet, close to Concarneau, which was crossed by a ferry. As I stepped off this ferry I noticed an old white-bearded man leading a very small donkey that had attached to it a vehicle of a kind which I had never seen before. Rain had begun to fall from a passing cloud and the old man drew up under a tree and threw a piece of sacking over his shoulders. I went up to him.

He told me that he was an ambulant knife-grinder who travelled round a small district between Quimper and Lorient. He had followed this trade all his life and it had taken him over most parts of Europe. Italy, Germany, Austria and Russia were all well known to him and he had visited the Balkans and Turkey as well. I even understood him to say that he had been in the Caucasus and in Anatolia. In every country in the world, he said, it was possible to earn one's living at this trade, because wherever there were men there were also knives to be sharpened. And the further east one went the more knives there were and the sharper they had to be.

The rain had stopped and I pressed a coin into the old man's hand and rode on. I saw at once that he had provided me with the clue that I was looking for. I had only to buy a knife-grinder's cart and set out, and the whole of the fertile East as far as Samarkand would be open to me. The problem I had been puzzling over for so long had been suddenly solved.

The next days passed in a state of continual excitement and exhilaration. At last my future was settled. There seemed to be no obstacles. I saw nothing to be afraid of in hardships or poverty, because I believed that I had trained myself to live without luxuries, though, to tell the truth, only two days later I was revelling in the delicious meal I had at Lorient. I drank a good deal of wine, strolled afterwards about the quay, took a few puffs at a cigarette and when at length I went up to my bedroom found a pretty, dark-haired chambermaid folding back the top of my bed. She was from Nantes, she told me, and as if to prove it pulled up her skirt almost to her hip to adjust her garter. I looked at her and longed to put my arms round her, but did not have the courage to.

A fortnight later I was back at Radley and in the infirmary with a touch of bronchitis. Here a new idea occurred to me. I wrote a long letter to Hope, whom I had not seen since the previous summer, describing my meeting with the knife-grinder and announcing my fixed resolve to set off in the following August with the aim of reaching Asia and settling down, somewhere to the east of the Pamirs, among the tents of the Khirghizi. Then I suggested that he might like to come with me. We need not travel all the way together, I said, for it was important that we should each of us retain our independence, but we might do so as far as the Balkans. Then later on, perhaps at Damascus, we would join forces again for the desert crossing.

For three weeks I waited and then the reply came. He thought my idea a good one and, as he was tired of his present life with the Johns, he was ready to come with me. We could fix up the details when we met early in August.

When I think about this today I can hardly get over my amazement at Hope's reply. Here was a man verging on thirty who was ready at a moment's notice to set off for the Far East, on one of the most difficult routes in the world, with a travel-struck boy. He had no special feeling for me—indeed he has since confessed that he had often found my youthful enthusiasms boring. And we had neither of us more than a few pounds apiece. It seems that it had been my luck to strike the one man in England who would even have considered such an adventure and then to have approached him at just the right moment.

This, however, was not the way in which I looked at it at the time. I found his acceptance of my proposal perfectly natural. Would not any man of poetic feeling jump at the chance of leaving Europe with its deadening conventionality and its hatred of the imagination and launching out into the unknown countries of the East? I was merely relieved to feel that I should not have to take the first steps of my journey alone.

I must now try to give some account of the general ideas on which my plans for the future were based. On a scrap of paper that has come down to me from this summer I find, written below some deplorable verses, the following four sentences:

'1. I have never desired and will never desire anything else but happiness.

'2. Happiness is the feeling given by the consciousness of absolute freedom.

'3. No one can be free so long as he has material possessions.

'4. Therefore nomadic life rather than settled.'

These sentences explain fairly well my philosophy at this time, but they do not say how an itinerant knife-grinder can be happy when he is starving, or even when it does not stop raining for a week. These were contingencies that needed to be fitted into my system and it was not long before I discovered how I must do this. My starting-point was, I think, an experience I had had some time before at the dentist's. There were no injections of novocaine in those days, and twice every year I would spend an hour or two in the dentist's chair with a rubber gag in my mouth while Mr Peake drilled and drilled at some nerve-riddled cavity. Then one day I made an interesting discovery. Outside the window some clouds were scudding by and as I watched them, so far away, so free, so remote from the scene of my pain, I became aware of their peculiar beauty. It was a beauty of a different sort from that which I was familiar with, for it was purer and more detached from earthly things and at the same time, like a paradise I was forbidden to enter, it had a quality of pathos. I noticed too that as soon as the drill ceased to turn and the pain ebbed away, the clouds gradually became ordinary clouds again.

I do not know that I drew any particular deduction from this at the time, but gradually it became clear to me that certain states of exaltation may have to be paid for. It is true that Shelley's *Hymn to Intellectual*

Beauty, which was one of my favourite poems, suggested that there was no law in this matter: ecstasy came and went for no reason at all. But I did not think that he was right about this. States of mind must have their causes like everything else and in fact my own experience showed that those which I sought had their rise in sudden changes of circumstance. Now surely the essence of travel lay in its being an up-and-down affair. One suffered hardships in crossing mountains and deserts and it was as a result of these hardships, at the culmination of them even, that the moment of illumination came. I should therefore be able to rely upon the natural incidents of a life of travel to raise me periodically to that exalted level of feeling which I regarded as the principal aim of existence. Such a view modified the theory of uniform happiness following automatically from liberty which the four sentences I have given above implied.

Closely connected with my belief that ecstasy was the state to be desired above everything were my theories on poetry. I had written my first verses that summer and they were pastiches of Shelley of an exceedingly juvenile kind—very different from the clever verses contributed by sixth-form boys to *The Radleian*. If they were not better, that was due, I thought, to the sort of life I was leading. For poetry, surely, was written under the influence of inspiration and what else is inspiration but an ecstasy that finds outlet in words? That is to say, when the mind is in a suitable state of purity and freedom from material preoccupations, it can receive any strong influence that comes to it from life or Nature and throw it into rhythmical language. It stood to reason therefore that if I travelled to the Pamirs and the Tian Shan, those great mountains and deserts, that simple pastoral life of the nomads who camped on them would act on me in such a way as to make me write poetry that was worthy of their sublimity. The more severe the hardships suffered in the presence of the great productions of Nature, the higher would the mercury in the barometer that measures ecstasy rise. And this ecstasy would express itself in verses.

The life I proposed to follow could also be considered under a religious aspect. In my ideas on the importance of poverty I had been influenced not only by my need for solving the economic problem of travelling without a fixed income, but also by what I had read of St Francis and the Moslem Sufis. That is to say, I thought that poverty was a good thing in itself. The life of the poor, I held, had necessarily a greater reality than that of the rich because it was more exposed to fate and chance. It had also a greater blessedness if it was accepted voluntarily. These ideas I was to develop later when I came more directly under Hope's influence because, though not in any way religious, he was better read than I was in Catholic ideology and had a certain theoretical sympathy for its views on the danger of having possessions. But in fact the whole enterprise had from its first conception a religious colouring. Anyone who sets before himself as a way of life the ideal of Everything or Nothing is following, whether he knows it or not, a path that lies parallel to that set by the saint. My plan was secular in so far as it resembled that of the polar explorer, but religious in that I regarded the life of travel, poverty and hardship as an end in itself. Greatly though I admired Doughty's *Arabia Deserta*, I would have been shocked had anyone suggested to me that I should ever write a book on my experiences.

My last term at Radley was now drawing to an end. I took my Army entrance exam, answering the papers as badly as possible in the hopes that I might fail. But no one can fail for Sandhurst, and a few weeks later I learned that I had passed. There could not therefore be any turning back. Sandhurst would be another and perhaps worse Radley: the regiment would be another Sandhurst. No, even if Hope changed his mind, I must go forward.

The moment at last came to leave the detested place. How little I guessed that again and again, on hundreds upon hundreds of nights, I should be returning there! I have never once, I believe, dreamed of the war, though I was present at some of its worst battles, but I have dreamed continually, sometimes for years on end, of this school. Do many Englishmen, I wonder, have to suffer the absurdity of returning every night, up to the age of forty or fifty, to the place where they spent their horrible school-days?

Radley did me immense and permanent harm. Just as love has to be learned in early infancy, so must mixing and getting on with one's fellows be learned at school or at the university. I never learned this. An absurd diffidence continued to come between me and the un-familiar English face and for a long time it helped to make my life much more isolated than it need have been. People speak of the world today as being riddled with guilt-feelings, but in my case it has not been the guilt of my own bad actions that I have carried about on me (them I feel too little), but a guilt induced in me by the aggressive attitudes of others. Yet let me give the school its due. It shot me out into the world in a frame of mind to discover bearable conditions anywhere. Even in the worst moments of the war I comforted myself by the thought that anyhow I was not at Radley. For those shells and bullets whose noises filled the air were inanimate objects discharged by an impartial hand: they did not come at me dressed in the malignity of the human face.

My first act on returning home was to walk over and see Hope. Several weeks of rainy weather spent in the company of the Johns in North Wales had confirmed him in his desire to escape from England and he announced that he would be ready to start by the end of the month. He expected to be able to raise £16 as a working capital for the expedition and I, as it happened, had exactly the same sum in the savings bank. But he did not think that my suggestion that we should travel with a knife-grinding machine was a practical one because we should not be able to carry our things on it. Instead he proposed a donkey and cart, into which we could pack our tents and blankets as well as a few essential books. We should need, for example, a good many grammars—one for each of the countries we were to pass through. With any luck our money would carry us as far as the Balkans and then we could look round for some means of supporting ourselves. The argument that clinched the matter for me was that with a knife-grinding cart we should be confined to the roads, and these ended in Montenegro.

As an alternative means of supporting ourselves, I at once thought of my herb medicines. I suggested that we should take with us my copy of Culpeper's *British Herbal* and a large packet of galingale, which was the drug most commonly sold by hucksters at South European fairs. We could carry it easily in root form and grind it when needed. It had a strong medicinal smell which would encourage prospective buyers and was a remedy for dysentery. Hope agreed to this, although, I thought, without much enthusiasm, and we then discussed the route. My idea had been to cross the St Bernard to Italy and Trieste, since this was the shortest road to Sarajevo, but he said it would be much better to go south to Provence and then along the coast to Florence and Ravenna, because by that route we should see more interesting places and country. Although I disapproved of the idea of going out of our way to see Italian cities and works of art—was not the whole point of our journey that it was an escape from Europe?—I had no option but to agree.

Of the many other things that we doubtless discussed, I can now only remember one. Hope remarked that ever since he was a child he had wished to visit China: indeed he had once, while still at school, bought a grammar and started to learn Chinese. Later on he had dallied with the idea of applying for a job in Peking and so getting his passage paid, but nothing had come of it. As it had now turned out, this was fortunate, since it would be much better to reach it, as Marco Polo had done, by the overland route and to see Persia, Samarkand and the Gobi Desert on the way. I replied with all the seriousness of my youthful convictions that my aim in setting out on this journey was very different. As soon as we reached Kashgar and the borders of the Takla Makan I would end my travels and settle down among some nomad tribe. The most he could count on was that I might accompany him as far as Barkul or Hami on the borders of Outer Mongolia to give him a send-off on his desert crossing. Nothing would induce me to go further for, having once escaped from civilization to the tents of the Kashgaris or Kalmucks, I saw no point in returning to it, even when it took a Chinese form.

'We shall have time to go into that later,' he replied. 'And meanwhile don't forget to get the recipe for the cake.' (He was referring to a ginger cake made with pearl ash and cassia buds of which our new cook, the successor to Mrs Frankton, was very proud.) 'It's probably the only good thing you'll ever get out of your family again.'

With this cynical remark and the promise to meet me in Paris on August 27th, we parted.

Before leaving Radley I had arranged with a school-friend called Douglas-Jones to have an alibi. I would tell my parents that I was going to stay with him at Fareham near Southampton and, after the period of my supposed visit was over, he would do his best to delay the answer to any inquiries that might be made. For the possibility of my being followed and brought back by the police had to be taken into account. I was under age and I did not know what powers the extradition laws might have if I were traced to a foreign country. That made it very important for me both to get as long a start as possible and to conceal my tracks. In other words, I must make the journey to Paris in disguise.

My first step was to write to a theatrical outfitter in London for a false moustache and a bottle of black hair dye. I also made some inquiries about a black cloak, which I specified was to have a purple lining dotted with silver stars. This was intended, not for the journey to Paris, but for particular occasions abroad. I said to myself that such a garment would produce a good effect on the crowd when I was selling medicines, but really I wanted it because I fancied myself going about like Alistair Crowley in the garb of a necromancer. The cloak turned out to be too expensive, but the hair dye and the moustache arrived—a long bushy one. With these in my possession I rode into Cheltenham to rifle the secondhand clothing stores. My idea was to disguise myself as a superior kind of workman—why not as a gas fitter? In the clothing store, therefore, I bought a little black shiny bag, suitably worn and cracked, a very high starched collar of the kind known as 'butterfly' and the most vulgar bow-tie, purple in colour, that I could find. A lucky discovery in a dark corner of the shop gave me one of those stiff black hats that seem to have been produced by breeding a top-hat out of a bowler. It cost me a shilling. All these objects I regarded as appropriate to the gas-fitting profession, though had I possessed even a particle of worldly knowledge I would have known that no one under the age of sixty ever wore such preposterous garments. A final stroke of inspiration led me to visit a newsvendor's and buy a copy of a journal entitled *The Gas World*.

I needed an overcoat—not so much for the purposes of disguise, as to wear on the journey until I reached Arab lands. Routing among the japanned steel boxes in which my father kept his old uniforms, I came on a long black overcoat that bore a Savile Row label and a date in the early nineties. It had once, I imagine, been very smart, for it was much cut in at the waist and below this flowed out into ample skirts. He had bought it to wear at Irish race meetings a short while before his marriage, but twenty years among mothballs had made it dull and shabby. I took it out and hid it in my room.

After much thought I had decided to take with me six books—a small Shelley, a copy of Blake in the Muses' Library Edition, *The Oxford Book of English Verse*, Marco Polo and Culpeper's *Herbal*. There was also a notebook into which I had copied poems by Yeats and William Morris, together with a number of cooking recipes and jottings on herb medicines. All these I posted to Hope in London with the strictest instructions not to forget any of them. On my bicycle I should have little room, for besides the overcoat, a change of clothes, the gas-fitter's bag and the stiff hat, I proposed to carry a packet of drugs. These consisted of two pounds of galingale, a lump of hashish, another lump of labdanum, a pot of storax, about a dozen samples of incense drugs and a small phial containing four drops of attar of roses. I did them up tightly in waterproof paper and I still possess some of them.

To raise more money I decided to sell a few books, my two Viking skeletons and my stamp album. I could get no offer for the skeletons, but the stamp album was valuable. I took it to a shop in Pittville Street, Cheltenham, kept by a little man with white hair, chubby cheeks and steel-rimmed spectacles, who went by the name of Mr Pink. I had often bought stamps from him in the past and, as he was such a crushed little man and had such a wheezy, asthmatic voice and such a mild, timid air, I imagined that, when I told him that I needed the money urgently and in a great hurry, he would deal with me honestly. But from the first moment difficulties arose that I had not anticipated. He was not knowledgeable on stamps, he declared: he must show my collection to a man who would value it for him. If I came back in a few days he would make me an offer. Pressed for time though I was, I felt it best to agree to this. However, when I returned three days later, he said in his wheezy voice—he seemed to be in an even worse state of health than usual—that the most he could give me was £6. As such a sum seemed far too small—I was expecting between £12 and £20—I asked for the album back, only to be told that the valuer still had it and that he had gone away for a fortnight. I was left with no option but to close and take what he offered me. But at once a new difficulty cropped up. Mr Pink could only give me £1 in cash and asked me to come back at the end of the week for the rest. Again I had to agree. I was in his power completely. However, when I returned he was still without money—the week had been a dead loss—his rent was still owing—the wheeze worse than ever—so he suggested that I might select from his secondhand books a number sufficient in value to meet the amount he owed me. Once more I had to do what he wanted. I chose Rawlinson's *History of Assyria, The Book of Mormon*, a work entitled *An Explanation of King Solomon's or the Greater Seal*, a history of Freemasonry, *A History of Gloves through all the Ages*, with illustrations, and left the outstanding amount to be collected at some future date. None of these books except the first had much interest for me, but Mr Pink's library did not offer a wide choice.

Almost at the last moment there was a hitch that nearly ruined me over the business of drawing my money out of the savings bank. The post office at Cirencester refused to give it to me and I had to make a special journey to London to get it. Then the question arose as to whether I should take any money from my mother's bureau. I had some time before got into the habit of stealing small sums, making to myself the excuse that, as my aims in life were higher than hers, the money would be more useful in my hands. In fact, it was always spent on books. I had never taken more than a few shillings at a time for fear the theft should be discovered, but even so it used to rack my conscience a little to see my mother doing her weekly accounts and getting worried because she could not think what she had done with the missing half-crown. Finally I decided to take nothing, because if the loss were discovered, as it obviously would be, my high ideals in setting off for the East might be called in question. For the same reason I did not sell any of my clothes.

I knew very well how important it was, when one wishes to elude pursuit, to lay a false trail. With this in mind I wrote to various English and French shipping companies for particulars of steerage passages to North and South America. When I got their answers I hid some of them where they would be found among my clothes and left the others, torn up, in the wastepaper-basket. I learned later that they were all discovered and had the effect that I intended.

My last night I spent in writing a long letter to my mother. In this I poured out all the ideas, feelings and irritations that had been seething in me during the past year. I quoted the New Testament and *The Little Flowers of St Francis* and declared that, though I had no pretensions to being a religious person, I was all the same renouncing the world to lead a life of poverty. There were also, I remember, some hard words about the Army, which I declared was an anti-Christian profession, some general remarks on hypocrisy and conventionality, those sins of the Pharisees, and a cruel phrase about my father, who, I declared, had forfeited my respect. 'And if you want', I added, 'to know anything more about my ideas, read the last chapter of *Walden* by Thoreau.' I left a copy on the table (I have it on my bookshelves still) suitably underlined. But nothing about my misery at Radley, which, by making me an outcast, had done more than anything else to drive me to this break. The letter was posted next day under seal to my school-friend, Douglas-Jones, with the request that he should hand it over to my mother as soon as my flight had been discovered. I added a postscript that she would hear from me again within two months.

The day of my departure, August 26th, at last came. The chauffeur drove me to Cirencester Station and left me there. Depositing my suitcase in the cloak-room, I fastened my overcoat, a suit of old clothes, the parcel of drugs and the gas-fitter's bag onto my cycle and, holding the black hat wrapped in brown paper in my hand, rode off. There was a strong south-east wind and it was raining. I had to pedal hard to make any progress. The going was indeed so bad that when I reached Swindon I decided to change my plans, and, instead of riding all the way to Southampton, where I should not arrive before the shops had closed, to sell my bicycle for what it would fetch at Marlborough and take the train from there. This meant putting on my disguise immediately. At the top of the hill, therefore, that leads up to the shallow pass in which the Og flows, I wheeled my cycle to a corn-rick that stood a little on the left of the road and changed my clothes. I poured the hair dye over my head, not realizing that it ran in trickles down my cheeks and neck, put on the strange collar and tie, put on the absurd hat and got into my heavy overcoat. The false moustache I thought it more prudent to keep in my pocket. Then I buried my waterproof cape and tweed suit with a trowel that I had brought with me for the purpose and, holding my black bag in my hand—it contained nothing but a few of my father's car spanners and a copy of *The Gas World*—set off.

The rain was driving hard when I got to Marlborough. I had a cup of tea and went to the nearest cycle shop. My machine was a very good one, almost new and beautifully kept. I therefore expected a fair price for it. But the shopman, looking at me sharply, said that it was now the end of the season and that he did not want it. However, Marlborough has many cycle shops and I went on to try them one after the other. To my amazement I was always met with the same reply. Cycles were not wanted. Even when in despair I offered to sell it for a pound, they would not take it. Deeply perplexed and disappointed I went to the railway station to catch the train.

I was waiting there when a policeman came up to me. He was one of those large bumbling types, all swollen torso and mental vacuity, whom one gets in country districts. He had been informed, he said, that I was trying to sell a cycle. I agreed. 'And to whom,' he continued, his voice swelling up from deep inside him into a menacing boom, 'to whom does that cycle in question pertain?' 'It is mine,' I answered. 'And can you, supposing that to be the case, produce proof of lawful ownership?' I saw what he was driving at and became extremely alarmed. Even if he were not able to arrest me, he could detain me on suspicion while he communicated with my parents.

I realized that my air of innocence and my public-school voice were my only assets. In those days the educated voice, especially in country districts, could do wonders. It was the weapon that, among the gentry, had supplanted the sword. Speaking therefore in my most upper-class accent, I produced a visiting-card of my father's, which I had kept in my pocket for emergencies, and explained that I was on my way to visit a school-friend and had dressed up to surprise him—as a lark. To confirm this I pulled out the false moustache I had in my pocket and showed it to him. As he still hesitated, I offered him my cycle, which I said I should not need any longer. At this moment my train came in. Leaving him still blank and ruminative on the platform, I got into it. The train pulled out. A few hours later, clutching my parcel of drugs, my black bag with its clinking spanners and the latest number of *The Gas World*, I crossed the gangway onto the boat. Next morning I was in France.

This unlooked-for event produced an unlooked-for sequel. On the evening of my passage through Marlborough the local constable of the Miserden area called at the back door of my parents' house and inquired of the cook if the young master had left that morning with his cycle. On her replying that he had, the constable went away, merely remarking that the police had the cycle in safe keeping and would return it. The cook at once reported this conversation to my father who, imagining that the cycle had been stolen, decided to drive down and make inquiries of the Cirencester police. However, the car would not start and when my father looked for his spanners to repair it, he found that those he needed were gone. By the time that he had managed to borrow other ones and to get the engine running, it was late, so he put off his visit to the town till the following day. From this moment things moved rapidly. A police call to my friend's house brought the reply that I had not been heard of, a detective was engaged and my letter to my mother handed over and read. The detective traced me to the Havre boat, but as the police informed my father that I could not be brought back forcibly from France, the chase was abandoned. I was free—as free as anyone can be who has just sixteen pounds in his pocket.

CHAPTER X

Journey through France

I arrived at Paris on the morning of Tuesday, 27 August 1912, and took a cab to the hotel whose name Hope had given me in the Rue de Seine. This hotel, I found, did not exist, so, not to keep the cab waiting, I engaged a room at a place near by that called itself the Hôtel de Tournon. In those days the Rue de Seine was a poorer and shabbier street than it is now and the hotel I had chosen was nothing more than a rather dirty eating-house that had a single bedroom to let over the dining-room. It was this room that I occupied.

After inquiring without success at other hotels in the street for news of Hope, I returned to my room in great despondency. He had said that he would arrive on the previous day and he had not done so. What if he had changed his mind at the last moment? He might, for example, have decided that I was too young and inexperienced to travel with. Or else that more money was needed. Or even, since I was a minor, that he ought to think twice before embroiling himself with my family. But whatever the reason, I said to myself, he will not come. The essential thing was to accept this calmly and refrain from blaming him. Superior people were not bound by the rules of ordinary morality but were a law unto themselves. For his own good reasons Hope had decided against coming and that was all.

But whatever I might say to console myself, my despondency remained. I lay on the dirty bed of the little ugly room, staring at the blotches on the ceiling where water had soaked through from above. There was a blotch that was like Turkey, another blotch that was like Arabia and another that might have been the Caspian Sea. From below, the barbarous, unfriendly voices of the restaurant keeper and his wife came up through the boards and filled the room with their angry vociferation. So this was travel! How many nights, how many days, how many years must be filled with moments like these!

Yet it was not so much the fear of going on alone that moved me as that of being discovered and sent back to my parents. I imagined that the French police were already searching for me. Tomorrow, perhaps, my name and photograph would be in the papers. How unfortunate then that I had got myself noticed by several people! The cabman, for example, had given me a surly look: was that because I had offered him too small a tip or because he thought that there was something suspicious in my appearance? The *patron* of the hotel where I was staying had eyed me in an unpleasant way, the porters of the other hotels where I had inquired for Hope had stared at me and answered curtly. Did they too suspect me of being a thief or was it merely my wretched dress that had drawn their attention? I realized by now that my choice of disguise had been a mistake—in Paris it seemed even more monstrous than in England—but for the moment I could do nothing about it. Even the hair dye that had run down my cheeks and neck had to remain because it would not wash off.

I got up from the bed and went down to the restaurant. I had had nothing but a cup of tea since the previous day and, though I was not hungry, I felt the need of taking something to restore my strength and spirits. I ordered therefore an onion soup, an omelet and some bread and cheese. Then as I ate, and drank glass after glass of wine from the carafe before me, I began to see the brighter side of my situation. Although some things had gone badly, I had at least escaped from the clutches of my family and had reached Paris. I would wait one day longer, buy some workman's clothes and start walking south.

All at once I remembered that Hope had given me an alternative meeting-place—in front of the Botticelli fresco in the Louvre—and set out to see if he were there. But no sooner was I in the street than a fresh wave of terror assailed me. I was wearing a black coat that was much too small for me and a pair of trousers, ragged at the bottom, that did not reach my ankles. Then there was that butterfly collar that stood up almost to my ears, that purple bow-tie, that preposterous hat. A sense of the utter absurdity of my appearance came over me and also a fear that it would attract notice and lead to my apprehension. As I walked, I kept turning round to see if people looked at me, ready to take to my heels if anyone stopped and hesitated.

Then, as I was crossing the Pont Neuf, I saw a familiar figure coming towards me. It was Hope. 'Oh, there you are,' he said in his casual way. 'I was just wondering if you had got here yet.' And in that cheerful, offhand way of his he began to tell me of the trouble he had had in getting off in time, while I wondered how I had ever imagined he could let me down.

While he had lunch at a *brasserie*, I poured out the long story of my adventures and then we set off to buy clothes. At a workmen's shop in the Rue de Seine we purchased for a few francs two blue cotton jackets, buttoning to the neck, with trousers to match, and for winter wear two pairs of heavier trousers. Hope selected blue velveteen ones, very wide at the hips and narrow at the ankles, and I straight black corduroys. To go with them we bought long flannel sashes or cummerbunds to wrap around the waist, he a black one and I a red one. Then, to replace my stiff hat, I got one of those very full Breton bérets that fall down on one side to below the ear. This gay costume was that ordinarily worn by the Parisian navvies, but it had been taken over by many of the Left Bank painters and poets.

I was still so afraid of being apprehended by the police that I wanted to leave Paris on the following morning. Hope, however, insisted on our remaining another day. 'Then, if you like,' he said, 'we will take the train south to where the olive trees begin and buy our donkey and cart there.' After looking at the map we pitched on Valence as our starting-point.

That evening after supper we went to a café in the Boulevard Saint Michel that not many years before had been frequented by Verlaine. We ordered green Chartreuse—it was the first time I had ever tasted a liqueur—and a couple of rather jaded-looking tarts came up and sat down on either side of us. They also were novelties to me and it amazed me to think that for only ten francs I could achieve that enormous, that almost inconceivable thing—going to bed with a girl. However, the warmer their attentions grew, the more acute became my embarrassment at the ridiculous garments I was wearing. I longed to get away quickly and hide myself from all women until I could sally out in my new clothes. I was also afraid that Hope would be led into extravagance by their repeated demands for drinks. When we finally escaped, I had parted with my purple bow-tie—the girl, pulling up her skirt, said it would look well on her garter—and also with a gold safety-pin which I carried under the lapel of my coat.

Next morning early I moved into Hope's hotel. We put on our new clothes and sold our old ones to a secondhand clothes merchant. To find out if we attracted attention we then walked down opposite pavements, keeping an eye on one another. No one looked at us. I was enchanted to think that I was at last dressed in a way that was both inconspicuous and beautiful.

After this experiment we crossed the river to the Louvre. I had not visited a picture gallery since I had been here many years before with my mother. Those great naked, globular-breasted women, floating on clouds, lolling on banks, sprawled out upon beds or bathing in rivers, had then filled me with astonishment. This was Art, my mother had said, these pictures were Beautiful. I had found them boring because they were unlike anything that I wanted to think about. Now Hope took me down the long corridor of Renaissance canvases, stopping every few yards and offering explanations. But the masterpieces of the Cinquecento had nothing to say to me. It was not till we entered the gallery of wood and gesso and I saw the Sienese primitives and Paolo Uccello's battlepiece that some dim idea of what painting might be came home to me. Then when, that afternoon at the Luxembourg, I saw a still-life of green apples by Cézanne, I received a different sort of impact from their mysterious immobility. Even today I prefer those pictures where everything has been made to stand still.

That evening we went back to the hotel to do our packing. When I opened the door of Hope's room and saw the amount of luggage he had brought I was appalled. The first thing my eye caught was a paint-box and a bundle of canvases: he intended, he said, to spend part of every afternoon painting landscapes. This seemed to me very wrong because it was at variance with the serious aims of our journey and gave it an arty, amateurish flavour, but since he had made up his mind I could do nothing about it.

Next I looked at the pile of books stacked on the floor. There were some twenty volumes of reading matter and a rather larger number of grammars and language books.

'This is terrible,' I said. 'We can't possibly take all these. On mountain roads no donkey will be able to pull them.'

Hope rather reluctantly agreed, so we sat down, like the barber and the parish priest in *Don Quixote*, to go through the books and decide which must be taken and which left behind.

'I think,' said Hope, 'that we ought to proceed in this matter by some general principle. I propose therefore that we take with us one grammar for every country that we expect to pass through until we reach the borders of China. After all we shall need to make ourselves civil to the people we meet. And when no grammar of the language exists, then we must take the Gospel of St Mark, or, as the case may be, of St Matthew, in the British and Foreign Bible Society edition. These last hardly weigh anything.'

'That seems to me reasonable,' I answered. 'So let's go through them.'

Sitting on the edge of the bed, I took the books up one by one. There were Otto's *Arabic Grammar* and Otto's *Persian Grammar*—both rather substantial volumes. Then there were the thinner grammars in

the German Hartleben series—Italian, Serbian, Greek, Osmanli Turki.
All of these I passed.

'But what,' I demanded, 'do we want with the Bulgarian, Rou-
manian, Russian, Kurdish and Armenian grammars if we are not going
through those countries?'

After some argument, in the course of which Hope said that we
ought to allow for being sometimes carried off our course, he agreed
to jettison them, though, as I later discovered, he slipped the Armenian
back into the pile when I left the room. This language interested him
because it was that in which George Borrow had made love to Belle
in the dingle.

'And is this book on one of the dialects of Balkan Romany really
necessary?' I inquired, holding up a tattered volume in French.

'We can't possibly leave *that* behind,' he answered. 'Why, who knows,
we might want to settle down for a bit with one of the gipsy tribes.'

We next came to the Bible Society booklets. There were gospels of
St Mark in Tosk, Gheg, Jagatai Turki, Khirghizi, Kalmuck, Southern
Mongolian, Easy Wen-li and Mandarin Chinese. All these would
clearly be needed, but why Kurdish, Uzbeck Turki, Buriat, Georgian,
Samoyede and Vogul?

'Only three hundred families speak Vogul,' I said, 'and they live in
northern Siberia.'

'I know,' he answered. 'They sound an uncommonly interesting
people and I should very much like to meet them and learn their ways.
But I agree with you that we can leave these books behind. After all,
we have to be practical.'

The books of general reading followed. We rejected half a dozen
whose titles I now forget and decided to keep the following: the
Bible, the *Little Flowers of St Francis*, Angela de Foligno's *Visions*, the
Bhagavadgita, Book 777 (this was one of Alistair Crowley's productions),
Shakespeare's tragedies, Gibbon's *Decline and Fall*, Sweet's *Handbook of
Phonetics*. I strongly protested at the inclusion of the six volumes of
Gibbon, both because they weighed so much and because they seemed
to me out of keeping with the aims of our journey, but in fact they
were the only books we took with us that I read from beginning to
end.

'But where is my Culpepper's *Herbal*?' I burst out as we picked up the
last volume. Alas, though Hope had brought the other five books I
had posted to him, he had forgotten this, the most important of all.

The question now arose of how we were to pack these books, because the suitcase in which they had come had fallen to pieces. We

tried doing them up in Hope's camel-hair sleeping-bag, but, since it buttoned down the side, they fell out as soon as we lifted it. As we were struggling with straps and bits of string the Paris clocks struck two.

'All this is pure waste of time,' exclaimed Hope. 'We must put off our start tomorrow and buy a sack and some cord.'

Very unwillingly I agreed.

Forty hours later we got out of the train at Valence. The sun had set as we passed Vienne and it was now dark, but we could see the lights of a fair and hear the music of the roundabouts from the open ground beside the river. We took rooms at the Café-Restaurant Joubert, close to the square, had supper and went to bed.

Next morning we disclosed our plans to M. Joubert, and asked him to help us. He was a short, dark, exuberantly cheerful man with a Southern wine-drinker's paunch and large bushy moustaches. He immediately became enthusiastic over our project and told us that we should easily buy a donkey in the town that would carry us to China—'and, if necessary, beyond'. Thus encouraged we went out to search and at the end of an hour had secured an admirable cart for, I think, forty francs. But though we spent the morning chasing from house to house, we could discover no donkey.

'Let's buy the blankets and cooking things,' I said, 'and maybe a donkey will turn up tomorrow.' And with this I began to enumerate the articles I thought we should need: a large knife, a grill for grilling meat, a kettle, tea, a packet of cornflour and a cookery book. Hope scornfully swept all these things away. In the first place, he declared, we would be vegetarians and live on fruit, cheese and vegetables. Then cornflour was a disgusting preparation and a cookery book would be quite useless. As for tea, he proposed that we give it up altogether. Tea, coffee and tobacco, he asserted were insidious and deleterious drugs that sapped the moral system and from that day on we ought to make it an absolute law, never to be infringed under any circumstances, to do without them. The only drug permitted to us should be hashish, which by its power of giving visions promoted virtue. I agreed to these pronouncements with enthusiasm: in our new way of life strict rules of conduct were a necessity.

We bought therefore, besides the blankets we needed, a large iron cooking-pot, a rod to suspend it from, earthenware bowls and cutlery, two baskets to hang from the cart and a green *bâche* or tarpaulin to cover it. I also bought a woollen shirt, chocolate in colour, that came down to my knees: actually I think it was a woman's nightgown. Since my only other shirt was one I had worn at Radley, I left it behind and wore this chocolate garment every day and night—washing it occasionally in a stream—till I returned to England. The rules of our régime required us to do without luxuries.

Seeing that no donkey could be bought at Valence, we set off on a two days' walk into the Ardèche to try if we could find one there. But no trace of such an animal could be discovered. Reluctantly we realized that we should have to pull the cart ourselves down the Rhône valley till we came to the region of Montelimart where, M. Joubert assured us, donkeys were as common as hens. Bidding goodbye therefore to our hosts and to the wonderful dishes of stuffed *courges* and *aubergines* which Madame Joubert prepared, we set off.

I pulled the cart, Hope pushed behind. As the days passed I was sometimes to feel, as those who know him will readily believe, that he did not push very hard. But on that first afternoon we had not many miles to go. Halting by a willow plantation on the edge of the river, we cut the poles we needed for our tent and camped a short way further on. Our method of putting up the tent was as follows: first we sank the thick ends of our six poles at proper distances from one another in the ground, then we bent their tops over and passed them through the holes cut in the ridge-pole which a carpenter at Valence had made for us. Over this framework we threw the blankets, pinning them to the tent poles by skewers, which road people call 'spiggers'. In this way we obtained an excellent tent, warm and rainproof, which never let us down.

Then, as night fell, we made supper. Into our iron pot we put water, potatoes, carrots, green vegetables and one Maggi soup tablet, together with a sprinkling of thyme and other wild herbs. For second course we had dry bread with grapes, and thought we had never tasted a better meal. So satisfied were we that during all the time we travelled with the cart we did not vary it. There was another merit too in this repast—it cost little. Our rules, which became fixed and set within the first few days, required that whenever possible we should steal the fruit and vegetables we needed, choosing for that purpose the plot of a rich man rather than of a poor one. Under our conditions of life small pilferings of this sort became highly meritorious actions, as they are in certain primitive tribes. Besides we felt that, in view of the high nature of our enterprise, the land owed us this contribution.

For some days we pushed the cart down the Rhône valley. The country was ugly and the white dust of several large cement works covered the grass and the vine leaves like flour. In the evenings we camped outside the villages where we usually found other families of travellers squatting beside their patchwork tents and tending their fires. Road people are not persecuted in France as they are in England: in the *droit de vingt-quatre heures,* as it is called, they have a charter that gives them protection from the police and for that reason the South of France has a larger population of pedlars, circus folk and strolling musicians than any other country that I know. We found them reserved, suspicious, unamiable people, going their own ways and keeping closely to themselves. When we met someone we could talk to it was generally a man who was only temporarily in the travelling line.

I think it was outside Viviers that such a person came up to us. A cheerful-looking type with long black moustaches, he stopped as he passed us and said, 'Well, you've got a nice cart there. What d'you sell?'

'Oh, we sell everything,' said Hope.

'That's good. But you'll find business bad in these parts.'

'We don't care. The customers we want can only be found in Nice.'

'Isn't that extraordinary?' the man said, throwing out his hands. 'Everyone in this country wants to go to Nice. Someone ought to explain to them that there are too many travellers that way already and that all the women have been spoiled. I'll tell you what to do—go to Béziers. There's a town for you! Large, rich, crackling with life, a tavern every five yards. And the women—whew'—here he kissed his fingertips and opened them like a fan in the air—'why, they're the most tremendous in France. Breasts like this—*nom de Dieu!* Thighs like that—*tonnerre!* And you don't even have the trouble of asking them. They ask *you.* Yes, *mon vieux,* hurry on quick to Béziers. Once you're there you'll find there's no need to hang about, *tu peux demander a toutes les portes.*'

Next day, overcome by the heat and cement dust, we stopped at a tavern to have a glass of wine. The girl who served the drink, a blowsy, pock-marked creature dressed in nothing but a cotton frock, planted herself on Hope's knee and began to stroke his face.

'Come into the back room, *chéri,*' she said. 'It'll only cost you five francs. I'll make it worth your while.'

And with that she pushed her hand down inside his trousers.

Hope disengaged himself with an embarrassed laugh and we went out.

'I like this frank method of approach,' he said in his most man-of-the-world tone as we pulled the cart on down the road. 'No nonsense about sentiment. Just a proposal and a price. That's as it ought to be.'

But I felt my whole body on fire. I would have given anything to have run back with the money in my hand and taken my chance of a dose of venereal disease. The fact was that, though she was still quite young, her bloated, overripe look gave her a special attraction for me. Lust apart, I hankered for sordidness—sordidness of situation, sordidness of act—because I thought that that would help to wash away my sheltered upbringing and to plant me more firmly in reality.

We crossed the river at Bourg St Andéol and heard that a donkey was for sale close by at Pierrelatte. It was a very small donkey, by name Guébir, delicately made, with a sensitive face and an excellent character. We bought him for a hundred francs and rechristened him Mr Bird. The drudgery of pushing the cart was over. Our road now lay through some of the most beautiful country in Europe—Orange, Avignon, Arles, Aix, Draguignan, Grasse. A country of olive trees and cypresses, of rock-crowned mountains and of splendid cities. I remember the weeks we spent travelling through it as some of the most idyllic in my life. Our rule was to rise with the first glint of daylight and to be on the road before the last stars had disappeared. Breakfast of bread, milk, butter and honey followed a couple of hours later and we camped as the sun was reaching its greatest heat. Since the donkey's pace was very slow, we had by that time made scarcely more than twelve miles. Then, after pitching our tent, we ate a piece of bread with grapes and cream cheese and spent the rest of the day, till it was time to think of supper, as we pleased.

As we walked, we read. I ploughed my way laboriously through the Italian and Serbian grammars, while Hope, with many uncouth sounds and facial contortions, grappled with Sweet's *Phonetics*, which his theoretical approach to every subject made him regard as the best preparation for speaking Persian and Arabic. I see him now, a slim figure, sky blue in his velveteen trousers and cotton coat, a broad-brimmed black velvet hat jammed on his head, pacing slowly along in front of the cart. Sometimes he took out his pipe and played, either the Old Jamaica air or else that other even more lovely one to which Mistral's song, *O Magali*, had been set. At such times the whole landscape with its bushes and its olive trees would seem to bend and dance to the tune. Or else, putting his pipe away, he would chant the words of the Provençal song in that strange manner of his that gave me such delight, so that to this day Mistral's love lyric, with its contest in Protean transformations, seems to me one of the most beautiful in the world.

The early hours of the morning were the most memorable. The

cone of the Mont Ventoux rose, a pale lavender blue, into the sky:
the mountains above Draguignan stood one behind the other like the
pink and lilac waves of a coralline sea. Each little pebble, each little
stalk of grass cast its shadow. Then, as the sun mounted higher, the
mistral got up and the olive trees showed their silvery under-sides.
Quickly the heat increased, the dry shrubs of the heath popped and
crackled. But the afternoons were tedious. Sometimes I went for a
walk and came on a village fair or some boys bathing, but usually I
yawned over a book and waited for the evening. At length it came. We
ate our supper by a fire of twigs under the olive trees while the crickets
came out and made the air reverberate with their trills. If the moon
were up, Mr Bird would become restive, curling back his upper lip,
dancing about and braying, but when it was dark, a fit of loneliness
would come over him and I would wake to find his head bent over
me and his nose a few inches from my cheek. We tethered him at
night because experience taught us that he would go a long way to
find a plot of vegetables or a vineyard of juicy grapes.

During this time I was getting to know something about Hope's
family and early life. It was so different from mine and so mixed up
with money and racing and the smartest possible clothes, which had
always to be bought at some particular shop, that I found a fascination
in hearing about it. Both his parents had been great spendthrifts. His
father had in a quiet way run through a considerable fortune and had
then settled down in the seclusion of an apartment at Brighton to
taking morphia. His mother, on inheriting a second fortune, had spent
it in a few years, almost without knowing how, on horses and cards.
The crash came when he was at Cambridge and nothing was left.

This was, I realized, the decisive event in my companion's life. He
had been brought up to expect an independent income and had been
suddenly deprived of all hope of ever having one. The knowledge that
from now on he must live by his wits, for apparently the idea of adopt-
ing a profession never occurred to him, led him to turn a cynical eye
on the world. Cynicism was in any case a normal attitude in his family:
all the Hope-Johnstones were temperamentally cold and obsessed by
the importance of getting hold of money. The sisters, who were very
good-looking, married well: the younger brothers went into the Indian
Cavalry where they made up for their lack of private means by their
skill at cards. Only the eldest brother, G., took an independent line by
setting up in a shady way as a racing man and for a time doing well out
of it. He had been both the bully and the hero of Hope's childhood and
now his sudden success combined with his brilliant and rather flashy

qualities made him a figure of the greatest prestige in his brother's eyes. Most of Hope's anecdotes about his family turned on him.

The legend was all that the story of a gentleman crook of the type of Raffles ought to be. G. had made his first impression on the world by going up to Cambridge with ten polo ponies. Then the family crash had come and he had sailed for South Africa with a hundred pounds. Here he hired a hansom cab and drove about Johannesburg taking fares. The principle he adopted was never to accept any coin lower than a sovereign: if people did not wish to pay this, he took them for nothing. Most paid and he returned to England with a substantial sum in his pocket. This he laid out on the turf and did so well that at the end of a year or two he was the owner of a racing stable in Wiltshire.

The position that G. held at this time in his brother's estimation might be compared to that which Caesar Borgia held in Machiavelli's. He was the successful man of action whom the intellectual, who is deeply aware of his own helplessness, romanticizes. His unscrupulousness seemed justified because it was exercised against an absurd society. The man who, making use of his superior intelligence and daring, preys on the moneyed classes, who are themselves in their more cautious way equally unscrupulous, has some of the qualities of a hero. But what especially charmed Hope about his elder brother was his cynicism. He was the person who had seen through the pretences with which people veil their greed and their go-getting and had no illusions left about them. 'Men are divided into mugs and crooks,' he used to say, 'and since there is a mug born every minute the odds are all in favour of the crook.' This was not only his theoretical judgement on the world, it was the system on which he acted. Exquisite in manner, witty in a tired enervated style, extremely good-looking, dressed in the most perfect taste, he suggested a Don Juan whose field of action lies not in seducing women but in fleecing men.

This attitude of G.'s towards society had an added attraction for Hope because it provided an explanation of the ways of the world that was flattering to his vanity. When anything in his affairs went wrong it was not, he would say to himself, because his intuitions had been at fault, but because he had been too unsuspecting and innocent. From now on he must cease to be one of the army of mugs and learn like his brother to keep his eye on the ball. But these resolutions always remained rather theoretical. He was much too sociable, much too easy-going, much too little bitten by the craving for success, much too respectful of established usages really to adopt the lone-wolf stance. Yet his brother's views did in some indefinable way influence him. In the first place they made him feel that money was something to be picked up rather than earned. Although he was not in the least lazy, there was always something slightly immoral for him about working for a living. Then, by flattering his *amour-propre*, they helped to keep him discrete and unattached, ready to mix with people of all kinds but never to throw down roots among any of them. Although he completely lacked the predatory instincts, he was, like G., a rolling stone who would never find a fixed place.

It thus came about that, of the various persons who occupied a place in Hope's private mythology, the first niche was occupied by his elder brother. And since all his gods were necessarily at this time my gods, G. passed on in some sense to mine. He was real to me because my companion, with his exact verbal memory, was able to repeat to me so many of his sayings. I accepted him as a wit and arbiter of fashion and as a man who played a sort of Nietzschean role in society. And when, a year or two later, I met him, I found him to be exactly as his brother had portrayed him to me.

I will describe this meeting now because it belongs here. Some time during the war I had called at G.'s flat in Bruton Street to ask his advice on the possibility of borrowing money on my parents' marriage settlement. I found a slim, dark-haired young man with a small mouth and finely cut features smoking a Turkish cigarette in an armchair by the fire. His handshake was limp and his voice high and rather trailing, as though he found it exhausting to talk at all. I noticed too that his complexion was of a marble paleness—the result of taking morphia. But there was nothing weak about his conversation, for it ran entirely on fraudulent means of making money. He was so frank and explicit over this that I realized that being a crook was the thing on which he most prided himself. It was more than his means of livelihood—it was his role in life. And how well he acted it! There was such a perfection in his whole appearance and manner, such a sense of his having grown into his part, that for the first half-hour I felt that I was talking to a character in some new play by Oscar Wilde. Even his wit had a ninetyish flavour: 'As I sometimes try to tell people,' he remarked to me in his languid way, 'the passing of the Married Women's Property Act has been the downfall of the English gentleman.'

At eight o'clock his valet brought in a light supper of claret and caviar sandwiches. As we ate it, he commented on the fact that caviar was not what it used to be. 'The worst of war is,' he said, 'that in it all the higher things decline.'

After a little the telephone began to ring and, feeling that I was in the way, I asked him if he could recommend me a cheap hotel.

'Yes,' he replied meditatively. 'I know a little place that might do you just round the corner. It's called Claridge's. I don't think you'll find it too uncomfortable.'

I went—I had never heard of Claridge's before—and was astonished at the bill I had to pay next morning.

G.'s taking to morphia proved both his salvation and his downfall. A dozen years later he was the leading figure in the Mr A. case, when an Indian maharajah was successfully blackmailed for an enormous sum. But when the case came into court he could not be prosecuted because, owing to his drug-taking habits which kept him in bed till six o'clock every evening, his more active accomplices had stolen a march on him and secured the swag. The publicity given them at the trial upset his vanity. Approaching the press, he told them his tale and they printed his photograph in a morning coat and top-hat with the caption, which must have pleased him greatly, of 'The Wickedest Man in London'. After this he sank into obscurity and died by his own hand some time in the thirties, when keeping a herbalist's shop in Nottingham.

I have written at some length upon this strange person, because he played such a part in my companion's conversation. But there were other people of whom Hope talked to me during this journey. Literary and journalistic figures in New York, gipsies in Surrey, women (he pronounced it 'wimmin') who had been a little in love with him, a young cottage girl at Chedworth for whom he had had a sentimental attachment. As will be seen later, almost the only girls about whom he could feel in this way were either under sixteen or else poor and in some way pathetic and unfortunate. But the people of whom he had most to say were the Johns. He had the deepest admiration for Augustus John and a devotion not far short of idolatry for his beautiful wife Dorelia. In his eyes she was the perfect woman and when later on I got to know her, I agreed with him.

As I sat listening over the evening fire to his stories, the John family, their caravans, their ponies, their naked children, the gipsies who visited them, their absurd battlemented house, the strange and romantic life that went on there, became deeply impressed on my imagination. Who could have supposed that there were people in England who lived like that? But in this oasis in the desert of mediocrity there was, it seemed, a serpent known as Edie who was Dorelia John's sister. Hope never tired of describing her vulgarity, her stupidity, her typically

suburban attitudes, so that she came to symbolize for me all that
is most obnoxious in the lower middle-class mentality. Judge then
my surprise when, on visiting Alderney a couple of years later, I found
a rather downright but decidedly likeable woman who by her energy
kept the place together and was adored by the children. Although not,
like her sister, of the race of the Homeric Gods, I could see nothing
vulgar about her—only a great deal that was human. But she was the
watchdog in that house where no one else could say Go to a guest who
had overstayed his welcome and she had fallen foul of Hope in his
more or less nominal role of tutor to the boys. Besides she was one of
those people who cannot endure a breakfast-table argument and for
Hope the argument—long, persistent, remorseless, carried back to
first logical principles—was an almost indispensable element in the
day's hygiene. Slow to realize how he was affecting others, he was apt,
when someone boiled over, to feel a deep and surprised indignation
and, for lack of any other explanation, to attribute to them the
character of demons.

CHAPTER XI

Italy and Dalmatia

We had fine weather until we reached the Italian frontier, but then the rain began. Since it was impossible to pitch our blanket tent during a downpour, we had each evening to discover some sheltered place where we could sleep. On this villa-studded coast that was particularly difficult and so, as the evening wore on and our slow procession of donkey and cart and two blue umbrella-bearing figures crept along the road, a great anxiety would come over us. Would we succeed in getting in that night or not? On one occasion we were obliged to camp in a road tunnel near San Remo. On another a peasant allowed us to sleep in his hay-loft. I remember this last particularly well because it was attended by an alarming experience. We were munching our supper of bread and cheese in the dark when a light appeared below. A noise of humming and mumbling followed and then steps on the ladder. A moment later and a dishevelled, maniacal head appeared above the floor, carrying an enormous double-edged knife in his teeth. A slouching, ape-like body followed, bearing a lantern. The creature passed within a couple of yards of us without noticing us and vanished into the back of the loft. Then the light was extinguished. We realized that this must be one of those idiots whom Italian farmers keep to do odd jobs, and made a point of getting off in the morning before he stirred.

The weather cleared as we entered the Apennines. The woods near Bagni di Lucca were beginning to turn brown and crowds of women and children, dressed in brightly coloured clothes, were busy collecting chestnuts. The sky overhead was the most transparent of blues and a damp smell of leaves was in the air. Autumn had come and down by the river the grass was scattered with mauve colchicums.

We reached Florence and put up at a *stallaggio* or mews, close to the market. Mr Bird after his exhausting all-day journeys had a rest and, since both our rules and our purse forbade beds, we slept at night in his manger. But now a new and to me disagreeable element entered our life. In France our gaudy clothes had passed unnoticed, but here everyone stared at us, the children called after us and hooted, and the concierge at the Uffizi Gallery refused to admit us until we defeated him by appealing to a higher authority. I found this publicity so painful that in the end I gave up going out by daylight and remained in the manger reading Gibbon beside Mr Bird. Yet my costume had become necessary to me, marking me off as it did from the rest of mankind as a person engaged on a sacred mission, and I would not for anything have changed it for the dress of an Italian workman.

The peculiar nature of our life, its difference from that of other people, its semi-religious rules, the immense pride we felt on account of it had become more strongly marked as we travelled eastwards. To express it we invented a special language, special terms, special values. The supreme value we called 'virtue' and it comprised all that aided us to conduct our life upon the highest possible plane, as well as those acts on the part of other people that favoured us. Below this there were subsidiary values, such as the one to which we gave the name 'mumply', which defined the precise degree of squalor that seemed appropriate to our mode of living. The special language, on the other hand, grew out of our habit of interlarding our conversation with quotations from English poetry and the Bible, to which we gave of course an ironical sense. In time these came to form a network of allusions which to a third person would have been completely unintelligible. Most of these quotations originated in Hope, who carried in his head a dictionary of usable phrases, but I made such additions as I was able. Thus my frequent adjurations to Mr Bird—for I had the task of getting him along—were thickly studded with lines from Shelley's *Epipsychidion*. We had invented a mode of life which no one had ever thought of before and which I at least seriously regarded as one that could be offered to other people for their worldly salvation. We needed therefore a language to express it in.

I had written to my mother some time before and now I got an answer. My letter had been couched in a high-flown argumentative style that aimed at convincing her that I was leading a life of voluntary poverty analogous to that prescribed by Jesus in the New Testament. I felt the falsity of this line of approach, yet could think of no other way of impressing on her the seriousness and indeed the semi-religious nature of my undertaking. We lacked a common ground of understanding, yet I had to justify my conduct and to prove to her that I was not engaged on a mere escapade. Now the answer, or rather answers, came. Half the members of my family, including my positive and worldly Aunt Maude, had been roped in to reply in the same vein.

What the post office handed me was a bundle of moral and theological dissertations.

Hope expressed the greatest disgust for this correspondence. His nature reacted tepidly to the word 'ought' and any sort of moral uplift gave him a cold feeling down the spine. He blamed me strongly for having written as I had done, declaring that all that needed to be said was that I was having a pleasant journey and that the weather had been fine. At bottom I half-agreed with him—it would have been gratifying to have been able to take such a superior tone—yet the temptation to gain moral points was too strong for me. It was not for nothing that I had had a religious upbringing.

My parents had sent me a couple of pounds with the request that I should sew them into my clothes in case of emergencies. We both agreed that it would be out of the question to act in such a craven way and then in a fit of euphoria decided to blow the money at once on one or two good meals, a lot of Chianti and a certain wonderful nougat of which Hope had preserved delectable memories since his childhood and which turned out to be almost, though not quite, up to his expectations. We did so—our rules made provision for occasional orgies—and regretted it later.

Our next stage took us across the Apennines to Ravenna. The weather was getting cold with frosts at night. Finding that one could get a large bowl of coffee and milk for fifteen centesimi—that is, a penny halfpenny—Hope declared that he must have one every morning. This started off an argument that had been going on at intervals since we left Nice. I had been alarmed by the diminishing state of our purse and wished to economize by halving the butter ration. Hope, who had calory tables at his finger ends, had replied that this would lead to our gradually losing strength and arriving in Asia Minor in a weakened condition. Now with the onset of the cold his plea for a better diet began to take a more poignant form. He declared that he simply *could* not walk for two hours in that weather on an empty stomach. There was nothing to be done but fall in with his wishes.

Our relations during this journey were not in the least like those of two friends travelling together. To judge by our surface manner they were much more offhand and distant. We had, for example, no names by which to call one another. To have used surnames would have seemed too formal, whereas Christian names were taboo because they were too intimate. We therefore addressed one another as 'Hullo' or 'I say', pronounced in a particular tone, and for more than thirty years stuck to that. This no doubt came chiefly from the fact that Hope shrank instinctively from any personal note in his dealings with people. Without being particularly reserved, he liked to keep others at a distance. But I was touchy too about my independence and therefore grateful to him for the tact with which he respected it. Although we often argued—a daily argument was a necessity for Hope—we had the real intimacy of people who are partners in a difficult enterprise. We were, turn in turn, Sancho and Don Quixote.

Autumn was passing into winter when we reached Ravenna. A cold sun shone through a whitish haze, giving a pale and wintry unreality to the grass-grown squares, the empty streets and leprous houses. I had reached the chapters on the Ostrogoths in Gibbon's *Decline and Fall* and the abandoned aspect of the city with its pitted walls and marble-columned churches glowing with gold mosaics recalled vividly the invasions of the barbarians and the ruin of Italy. We lodged at an inn close to the gate of Forli. Its stable, where as usual we slept next to our donkey in the hay of the manger, gave onto a yard which was used as a dump for broken carts and gigs and rotting harness. Against its back wall men and women could be seen squatting at all hours of the day to relieve themselves. No place could have been more 'mumply', yet in that cold misty air transfused by a wan sunlight, which distended streets and houses and elongated figures to Greco-like proportions, even the most grotesque postures seemed unearthly and spiritual.

It was in this town that we met a person who till his death in Poland in 1919 was to be one of my best friends. As we were looking at San Apollinare in Classe we saw a tall rather shabbily dressed man, unmistakably an Englishman, who appeared to take a great interest in us. For a time I kept him away by making a remark in Serbian whenever he came near us, since I had no wish to break the charm we lived under by meeting a compatriot. But Hope was more sociable and, after tantalizing his curiosity a little longer, went up and spoke to him. We then learned that he was an artist, by name Reynolds Ball, the son of a canon of Peterborough, and at present staying at Venice. After a meal together at a tavern, we agreed to take him with us as far as Cavarzere, where he could get a boat back.

Our road onward lay by a sandy track that skirted the pine forest. Flocks of rooks and starlings flew up from the fields and a ghostly sun shone through the haze. Ball interested me by telling me that he was a Christian anarchist, had studied under Patrick Geddes at Edinburgh and had met Reclus. He was a vague, woolly-minded man, sexless, confused in all his ideas, but with a benevolence that shone out in everything that he did. He took a great liking to me and a correspond-ing dislike to Hope, whom he made it clear that he regarded as my bad angel. But I was not to be influenced by any of his opinions be-cause I saw that he was completely unable to understand the spirit of our undertaking. When I told him, with the single-mindedness of the young, that anyone who wished to live a real life must give up everything and do as we were doing, he merely smiled philanthropi-cally. I put him down, therefore, as a person without true understand-ing—as what would today be called 'a square'.

We spent a cold night in a shed, though outside it we had built a fire to warm us, and got off before daylight the next morning. The sun rose slowly through the thick mist and then suddenly we saw brown and yellow sails in front of us moving above the dry grasses, and after that the blue water of the lagoon, smooth and shallow, with the yellow earth not far beneath. Beyond this was Commachio, its towers and walls drinking a pale gold from the sun and every window flashing out its light. A causeway led across the water to it and we cheered Mr Bird into a gallop and ran alongside the cart with its dangling buckets and cooking-pots, shouting.

At Commachio we came up against an unexpected difficulty. The road which our map showed as leading northwards over the Po marshes did not exist and the detour by Ferrara would add another day to our journey. There was nothing to be done but hire a boat across the lagoon and a man to tow us from a footpath which had been built up above the water. The passage turned out to be tricky. The cart was too broad to settle properly and at the least movement the boat rocked violently from side to side. Then Mr Bird, who had had to be lifted in bodily, proved unable to accustom himself to the situation. As soon as the cauliflower we had bought for him had been eaten, he began to be restive and to think that with all that water around him he might be allowed a drink. With great difficulty I kept him quiet by feeding him brown paper smeared with honey, which was a special delicacy of his, till, as the last scrap gave out, we reached land.

Next evening we were in Cavarzere. Our serious journey was de-generating into a sightseeing expedition, for Hope, under the influence of Ball, was now determined that we should turn off our course to spend a few days in Venice. A boat was leaving at four o'clock next morning, so we decided to take it and leave the donkey and cart behind.

So many things happened during this long journey which, though not of any special interest in themselves, were to stand out afterwards in my memory as extraordinary experiences. Thus at Cavarzere Hope and I overslept and missed the boat and, to catch a second boat at Chioggia, had a fourteen-mile walk or rather race down the towpath of the river, with nothing to eat or drink, in thick darkness, reeds and marshes all around. The exhilaration that this forced march produced justified all I had previously thought about the value of hardships. But Hope had not the same greed for the ascetic life that I had, so when we reached Venice in the evening, not having eaten all day, he led the way firmly to a small German *gasthaus* that stood at the end of the Riva degli Schiavoni and which Ball had told him of, instead of looking about, as we should have done, for a doss-house. Here we had a good meal and slept in clean sheets—the greatest breach of our rules we had so far committed.

In Venice we visited Ball's room and saw his pictures, which were very bad, as well as the scrolled ironwork he had turned to making. We also met the Wilsons, vegetarians, theosophists and makers of art jewellery in the Byzantine style, together with their beautiful golden-haired son, Guthlac, whom Ball had been tutoring. Then, on November 21st, we left to return to Cavarzere. Here a shock awaited us. As we landed we were arrested by the police on a charge of murder and clapped into gaol. But the mistake was soon discovered. On the following morning we were released and, after harnessing Mr Bird, set off on our last lap to the Balkans.

The weather was now colder than ever. The ponds and canals we passed were frozen hard and the chink of fast trotting hooves from the farmers' gigs could be heard from a great distance. We slept out as usual. Under our blankets we kept reasonably warm, but getting off by starlight was a different affair and with our frozen fingers we were often hard put to it to do up the harness. Then Mr Bird, seized with a sudden gaiety, would break into a gallop and we would run alongside shouting and cheering. But the cold continued to increase. On our last two nights therefore on Italian soil we took refuge from it in peasant farms, dossing down on a bed of hay in the cow byres, where, warmed by the breath of the animals, we slept as though wrapped in opium.

We crossed the Austrian frontier and put up in Aquileia. On the following morning we set off without the cart for Grado, a fishing port that lay a few miles out of our road, where Hope wished to see a Byzantine fresco. Our arrival in this small place created a sensation. The entire population turned out to follow us and, as this demonstration was displeasing to the police sergeant because it upset his sense of decorum, he arrested us. Taken to the police station, we were charged, in default of any other reason for detaining us, with being spies, searched minutely from head to foot and sent under armed escort to the gaol at Monfalcone. My situation was rather awkward. To enter Austria I had had to provide myself with a birth certificate. Uncertain of what the effect would be of approaching my parents for mine, I had got Hope to ask his elder brother for a false one and he had sent me that of his office boy, Charles James Claridge. I had used this to pass the frontier while at the same time I had in my pocket a number of letters addressed to me under my own name at a post office. Anyone who looked at these would be able to see at a glance that I was travelling with false papers. But, fortunately for the delinquent, the stupidity of the police is a thing that can usually be relied on. Herr Fuchs, the *polizist* at Grado, after confiscating my notebooks which contained nothing but a few bad verses, returned me my letters and on the train journey to Monfalcone I had the happy idea of taking these out, drawing portraits on the envelopes of the two soldiers who guarded us with fixed bayonets and then throwing them out of the window. In this way I managed to dispose of all compromising documents.

At Monfalcone we were put into a cell with four or five men most of whom were awaiting trial. One was a small shopkeeper accused of bigamy, another was a Slav who had been caught riding his cycle on the footpath, a third, an excessively meek and mild little fellow called Beppo, was charged with rape, while the most talkative was a professional burglar by name Giuseppe Paretti, who had served his sentence for stealing a woman's chemise and petticoat and was now awaiting release. The cell was very clean and smelt of disinfectant.

The discomforts were boredom and hunger. Boredom was relieved chiefly by singing. Through a small hole in the wooden shutter we could see into the bedroom of the gaoler's daughter across the court and whenever she appeared, which she did frequently, a burst of song would greet her. She would then kiss her hand, pretend that she was going to undress and—close the window. Other more crudely worded serenades were directed to two prostitutes who occupied the cell next door. They had been arrested for pulling up their skirts when, at some early hour in the morning, they had met the Mayor returning home from a carouse and, as we passed their cell on the way to our daily exercise in the courtyard with the other prisoners, we would look in by the peep-hole and they would repeat their performance.

Hunger was the other thing we suffered from. The daily ration consisted of two small rolls of coarse bread, a canister of thin gruel and another of beans. Boredom leads the mind to concentrate on food and we found that, whatever we might do to distract them, our thoughts ran continually on eating. However, since we had not been convicted of anything, we had the right to order at our own expense an evening meal. The gaoler's wife provided this for one lira fifty and we had not the strength of mind to resist the temptation. Every evening, therefore, two small dishes of spaghetti would be brought in with two quarter litres of red wine and two white rolls. This was the moment we had been waiting for all day and we sat down like wolves to devour our portions. Behind us stood or sat the other inmates of our cell, sniffing the delicious fragrance of the sauce and watching with beady eyes every movement of our forks to our mouths, but, though we felt the selfishness of our conduct, it would have required a superhuman generosity on our part to have invited them to share it.

Our burglar fellow-prisoner, Giuseppe, was a cheerful, talkative man and we made friends with him. He could speak when required a sort of pidgin-French, which, since we found the Venetian dialect hard to understand, facilitated conversation. He professed to take a poor view of our chances. The Austrian Government, he said, was in a particularly nervous state on account of the Balkan War and gave suspected spies long sentences in a fortress on very little evidence. And once in a fortress, how should we escape? He had escaped from fortresses and some day perhaps would do so again, but then he was a professional in his line with a long experience of getting into and out of locked buildings. Without boasting, he could say that there were few people in Italy with his skill in these matters.

'Then what shall we do?' I asked.

'Well, if I were you,' he replied, 'I would not wait to be condemned and sent away somewhere else, but would leave now. Nothing easier. A babe in arms could get out of this place. My sentence was for a mere couple of months, but even so I would have left by the back door if I hadn't got interested in the gaoler's daughter. A good girl, très bon cœur, aime tous les prisonniers. Moi surtout, parce que moi très connu.'

'But to get through the bars,' I said, 'we should need a file.'

'That's all right,' he said. 'I'll get you one. Nous trois camerades, alors moi vous aiderai. Comprends, moi italien pas autrichien. Alors moi aide toujours li camerades étrangers.'

The plan was worked out. He would send us the file by the underground tobacco road as soon as he was released. We would cut the bars, climb up the shutter, get onto the roof and descend by a gutter into the kitchen garden outside. There he would be waiting for us with false papers which would enable us to walk out of Austria by another route. He would charge us nothing for the file as he had several of them—anything for a foreign comrade—but the papers would cost us fifteen lire since he would have to buy them.

The idea of escaping from a prison naturally delighted me. I was prepared to sacrifice Mr Bird, the cart and all our immediate plans to be allowed to carry out such a glorious feat. Hope was less enthusiastic, for he was old enough to have lost the love of adventure for its own sake, but the prospect of spending two years in a fortress decided him. He merely insisted that we should not make our attempt until we knew the result of the magistrate's sentence. We therefore gave Giuseppe a chit on the gaoler, who held our money, for fifteen lire and sat down to wait.

The file arrived. I felt almost free already. Since I had not much confidence in Giuseppe's meeting us with the papers, I had privately decided that we should swim the Isonzo, which to my inexperienced eye had not looked very difficult to negotiate, and then cross into Italy between the frontier posts. But this plan was fortunately never tested. On the following day the magistrate sent for us to his office and told us that we could leave. As we did so, the gaoler handed us an invitation to dine at the principal hotel with the Scottish engineers who were employed at the naval arsenal. It seems that the *Daily Telegraph* had printed a paragraph on the arrest on a charge of espionage of 'two Cambridge undergraduates' and the dinner was to celebrate our release.

I still remember vividly that awful occasion. Along a table decorated with chrysanthemums and silver sports cups were ranged a dozen or more men with sandy hair and prognathous jaws, dressed in suits of heavy tweed. Their features were not capable of forming any expression, but a complete silence came over them when they saw us. What they had been expecting I do not know, but what they saw were two tramp-like figures dressed in brightly coloured but very dirty clothes, one with a black beard, the other beardless, but with hair that hung in long lank strands almost to his shoulders. Not a flicker of surprise crossed their faces, but the meal passed in silence and we left immediately afterwards.

We had now to find Giuseppe and recover our fifteen lire, but neither at the address he had given us nor at any of the taverns was word of him to be found. He had left the town, they told us. We there-fore gave him up and set off to fetch our donkey and cart from the inn at Aquileia. Having paid the bill, which was exorbitant, and complained without avail of the things that the innkeeper had stolen, we took the road back to Monfalcone. We had not gone far when we caught sight of a short, jaunty figure who somehow seemed familiar coming to-wards us. It was Giuseppe. A look of deep surprise and embarrassment came over his face when he recognized us, then he hurried forward and greeted us enthusiastically.

'Sacré nom!' he exclaimed. 'Quelle chance! Enfin li camerades inglesi!'

He had heard, he went on, that we had been released and, after failing to find us the night before, had hurried after us that morning in the hopes of catching us before we re-entered Italy. Now, since we were going that way, he could accompany us back to Monfalcone and put himself at our service.

We walked for some time along the road talking of various things, but not mentioning the subject that lay on our minds. Since he did not bring it up either, we realized that he had no intention of giving us back our fifteen lire and wondered how he would explain this to us. Hope therefore broke the ice by saying that, in return for all the good-will he had shown us, we should be obliged if he would keep the money.

'Merci, camerades,' he replied, 'beaucoup merci, but what you say is impossible. You entrusted me with the money and you shall have it back—every penny of it. Am I a German? But first I must give you a little explanation. As soon as I came out of prison, I began to think about your case. These poor camerades inglesi, I said to myself, are inexperienced in the ways of life and it would be a splendid thing if I could hand them some piccolo regaletto, just a trifle, you understand, to help them back to Venice. Then I heard that you had been released. At once I thought that I would offer you a little dinner to celebrate the occasion and present you to one or two jolies filles pour vous rigoler. I know a place where are some très gentilles petites filles who will do everything I tell them. C'est bon, eh? Ah, c'est très bon. Then I remembered—I have amused myself a little and so I am short of money. I will go to a tavern, I said, and play. As a rule when I play cards I win because I was born on a Good Friday, which is a very lucky day, and this time I felt sure of winning because I had just come out of prison. But, sacré nom, though I played all evening, I lost. Perdu tout.

'But no, I said to myself, but no. Those poor forestieri are not going to be losers on that account. I am a man of my word. I shall find some other way of benefiting them and making them glad that they ever met Giuseppe Paretti. So I thought to myself of a certain shop where every night the proprietor leaves in the safe a considerable sum of money. I entered by the window, I cracked the safe—such things are part of the day's business to me—and took out the money-box. C'est bon. C'est très bon. But then, nom de sacré Dieu, what did I find? The box was empty. That cursed shopkeeper had cleared it out that afternoon.

'But understand, a little thing like that was not going to upset me. I am a man of many ideas. I am that 'Giuseppe whom everyone has heard of. So, crack, crack, I broke open the store-room at the back of the house and what did I find in there but a large cheese—one of those cheeses, you know, that are as big as a cart-wheel—and a string of sausages. I wound the sausages round my waist like that. Bon. Then I got the cheese out of the window and trundled it down the street in the moonlight. Ah, c'est ça. Très bon. My luck was in for no one saw me. I took them to a place that I knew of outside the town and there I hid them under some straw. Now, I said, those poor inglesi shall have that cheese and those sausages, and they will be able to live on them for many weeks. Every time they eat they will remember that their camerade Giuseppe Paretti was a man of his word.

'But it would seem that a spell has been laid on everything I do, for when I went early this morning with a handcart to fetch that cheese it had gone. Some evilly disposed person had found it and carried it off. Ah, sacré nom! So what was to be done? Since time was short, there was nothing for it but to hurry after you and tell you what had happened. And here I am! C'est moi. Here you see me!'

We nodded our heads sympathetically.

'But, mi camerades,' he went on, 'don't imagine that because of this I shall not pay my debt to you. Would it be right that one or two little accidents of this sort should prevent Giuseppe Paretti from keeping his word? So I will tell you what I will do. At this moment I have in my house a unique collection of umbrellas. Some are rather old, but others are quite new, made of silk, and one even has a gold band with a bird stamped on it below the handle. I give them to you. I give them all to you—every one of them. You shall carry them away in your cart and whenever you need money you can sell one. You'll find they are a mine of gold. For you are inglesi, the police won't meddle with you any more and you can hide them safely away under your tarpaulin.

Then whenever you take one out you will think of what your camerade italien has done for you. C'est bon, eh? Tu crois, c'est bon?'

We refused. It took us the rest of our journey back to Monfalcone to convince Giuseppe that nothing would induce us to touch his stolen property, because the more vigorously we refused it the harder he tried to persuade us. Thus we never discovered whether these umbrellas had a stronger claim to existence than had the cheese and the sausages. So, after standing him a drink and offering him many assurances of our gratitude, we separated.

Our aim was to reach Trieste that night, even if we arrived late. Darkness fell and still we pushed on hour after hour, neglecting the signs of fatigue that our donkey gave. At length, turning a corner, we saw the lights of its waterfront spread out in a long line before us. Like living creatures they blinked and palpitated, sending out signals that seemed to denote the godlike delight and assurance in which they dwelt. But another two hours had to pass before we reached them.

We spent the morning in Trieste to rest Mr Bird and see the Consul and then continued on our journey to Fiume. This was to be our last postal address for some time and it was an important one because we were expecting to receive money. Hope had been promised some by his elder brother, while my parents had offered to send their usual birthday present. With this and the sale of the donkey and cart we thought that by taking a boat round Albania to avoid the Balkan War (the Turkish front then ran along the southern edge of Montenegro) we might reach Athens and thence Constantinople by the end of the winter. My original idea that we should take out a pedlar's licence in Italy had had to be given up because it would have delayed our progress. Now I wished to get as quickly as possible to the Near East and to put off till I arrived there the thorny question of maintaining myself. Possibly, I thought, if I asked to be instructed in the Moslem religion I should find that some post was offered me while I learned Arabic.

Since no mail had arrived for us when we reached Fiume, there was nothing to be done but find quarters there and wait. Then a day or two later a bundle of letters for me arrived. But how different they were from what I had expected! From Monfalcone I had written my parents an excited account of my imprisonment and of the near chance I had had of making a dramatic escape. I had also done what I could to explain Hope's presence. Hitherto I had let them suppose that I had been travelling alone, but the paragraph in the *Telegraph* had given this away, so now I told them that I had run into him in Venice and that he had agreed to come with me as far as Fiume. The answer I got to this letter was what anyone less simple than myself might have expected. My father was furiously angry, declared that I had been 'having a walking tour at his expense' and *commanded* me to return home immediately. My mother spoke of his being unable to sleep at night, dwelt on her own increasing grey hairs and said that even my young brother had cried all night on hearing of my imprisonment. (Later I heard that they had never told him of it.) Only my grandmother wrote in a gentle tone, excusing herself from sending her usual Christmas present, two pounds, because my father did not approve of her doing so. Naturally the two pounds I had expected from him and my mother were not sent.

Our situation was now very serious. We had only thirty lire left between us and, as we were continually being stopped and questioned by the police, we dared not separate for a moment, because for one of us to have been caught with less than twenty lire in his possession would have meant his being taken off to gaol as a vagabond. We were sleeping in a particularly sordid doss-house and living on bread, cream cheese and dates. Besides, our travelling papers were out of order. The British Consul at Trieste, who had received us in a very friendly way and shown us the portrait of his predecessor Richard Burton, had given us a letter to the Consul at Fiume, who, he told us, would provide us with the necessary *reisekarten*. But this man, a sort of dwarf dressed in black knickerbockers and buttoned boots, so mean and porkish-looking that at first we took him to be the German secretary, drove us out of his office in the most violent and abusive way, refusing us the documents with which it was his duty to provide us. I afterwards learned that he had been put up to this by one of my uncles.

There remained the proceeds of the sale of the donkey and cart and blankets, and the money which Hope's brother was sending. While waiting for this to arrive and because Hope wished to see yet one more Byzantine fresco, we set off without Mr Bird on a rapid three days' walk through Istria. It was exhilarating to tread Balkan soil for the first time and to feel the East, by small, almost imperceptible signs, drawing nearer. The fiord of Albona too, the coast and the view of the islands were beautiful. But our last day's march—we had started at dawn from Parenzo—was extremely long and we did not get back to Fiume till after midnight, hungry and in a state of exhaustion. Before going to bed we went to the Trattoria Napoleone to have a glass of wine and a roll. There we were told of an Englishman who had heard about us and wished to make our acquaintance. He turned out to be a certain Richard Brinsley of Liverpool, a steward on one of the emigrant ships plying to New York. He was deeply impressed by our journey—he had once run away from home himself—and on my telling him of the disappointment I had just suffered he pulled out two five-pound notes and offered them to me. But I had scruples about taking his money for fear that he might regret it next day, and refused. He then said that he was sailing in a few hours' time for New York and pressed me to come with him. My berth would cost me nothing and he would find me a good job on the other side. But I was still obsessed by my desire to get quickly to the East, and so I refused this offer too. Had it come a day later I would probably have accepted and then the whole course of my life would have been different. The same might be said had we got back a few hours earlier from Parenzo.

For the following morning brought our financial crisis to a head. To begin with, Hope found the money that had been sent him by his elder brother waiting for him at the post office. He did not tell me how much it was, for he was beginning to separate his interests from mine, but it was less than he expected. This led to an immediate revision of our plans. Hope, who was tired of austerities and wanted to spend the winter in comfort, declared that he would return by boat to Venice and find a job there till the spring. I said I would go on alone. Since the last shilling of the money I had brought with me from England had just run out, I would have to depend for my support on the share that accrued to me from the sale of the cart and donkey. With this I hoped that I might get as far as Greece, failing which I would take a job for the winter on a farm in Bosnia or Montenegro. But the next thing that happened was that the donkey and cart proved impossible to sell. Small donkeys, it seemed, were not used round Fiume and fodder was dear. We had no option therefore but to exchange them for what we owed the *padrone* of the *stallaggio* and to accept the thirty shillings he offered us for the cooking-pots and blankets. Bitterly I reflected on the succession of small incidents that had led me to this pass: the swindle over the stamp album, the orgy at Florence, the unnecessary trip to Venice, the sightseeing expedition to Grado which had led to our imprisonment, the similar walk to Parenzo which had caused me to arrive back too late to accept with a good conscience the steward's offer. Certainly I would be better travelling alone from now on because, unlike Hope, I had it in me to resist the fleshpots. But meanwhile I was in his hands. Generously he offered me the whole of the sum the *padrone* had paid us and added enough from his own pocket to bring it up to two pounds.

It was on a dark afternoon a few days before Christmas that I set out. I had tied my long overcoat up into a roll with two blankets and had made loops of string, padded with brown paper, to pass over my shoulders. Through the bundle I stuck the large blue umbrella that I had bought in Italy, and the only other things I carried were a pocket Bible, a Blake in the Muses' Library Edition, some grammars and a cake of soap. Hope and I ate a last meal of dates and bread together and then he walked with me as far as the main road.[1]

That night I slept supperless in an empty shed and the next day a calamity occurred. My boots had been in poor condition for some time and now the sole of one of them dropped off. I wore no socks, so there was nothing for it but to go on barefoot. In Zenj I found a cobbler. He convinced me that my boots were unmendable and offered me a new pair. The only ones he had that fitted me were city boots with high heels and elastic sides and for them he asked the equivalent of twenty-five shillings. I could certainly have found something cheaper and more suitable had I looked around, but a great timidity had come over me because people stared at me so much and could not understand what I said when I spoke to them in my halting Serbian. The cobbler cut down the heels and I went on.

Soon after this the road left the sea and it began to snow. It snowed steadily as I climbed up through rocky country and I wondered what I should do if night fell before I could find a lodging. But just at dusk I came to a farm that stood a little way above the road and from it came the sound of someone playing the fiddle. I went up to the door and was invited inside. There I found a number of people seated on chairs and boxes along the sides of a small kitchen. A tankard of home-made beer was passed round and soon a meal was served of curdled milk followed by cabbage soup that had a little meat in it. A few couples got up and began to turn in the confined space.

One of the men of the house had been in America and spoke English. He interpreted for me and everyone expressed surprise that I had come from Paris, which seemed to them to belong to another world. They were accustomed to Germans, who they declared were paid by their government to travel on foot. Soon, under the influence of the beer, the language and gestures became very free and a girl, coming up to me and raising her skirt well above her knee, asked me

---

[1] At this point ends the document I have been following—a detailed account of our journey from Paris to Fiume which I wrote down in 1916 from a memory that was still reliable. I also checked this story while I was writing it by conversations with Hope. But my journey on into Bosnia was never recorded because I felt too ashamed of my failure.

to hold it while she adjusted her garter. Then, egged on by the others, she sat on my lap and, among much laughter, promised that night to sleep with me. But, when bedtime came, I was led up to a hay-loft which I shared with a very old, white-bearded man, and no girl followed to keep me company.

I passed the next week or two in a sort of dream. I have no consecutive memories of how I went or of what places I stopped at. Even with a map of Yugoslavia on the table before me, I cannot always be certain of which road I took. The blank, denuded look of the country is what I best remember—bare stony plains scattered with thin clumps of oaks or fir trees, bare stony valleys without streams or rivers, hills that when not snow-covered were ribs of whitish limestone rock. High above, a ceiling of greyish clouds passed slowly with a purposeful movement, like that of birds migrating, and the air had the unbreathed purity of the air on mountain tops. Then as I travelled south and east the character of the landscape began to alter. I came on mountain ranges that were dark with forest, valleys with clear rivers flowing in them, small towns and villages that in place of churches had minarets and mosques. Yet wherever I went there was the same emptiness—the land too poor or too rocky to cultivate, the settlements rare, the farms few, and the ground either greyish white or ribbed and streaked with snow. Often, to compensate for the silence, there was a delicious smell in the air like incense which came from a grey-leaved plant whose name I later discovered to be helichrysum.

I imagine that the chief reason for this vagueness and lack of order in my memories is that I suffered from an acute anxiety which began every morning at about noon and mounted steadily as the day wore on. Should I or should I not get in that night? My only map, a sheet torn from a cheap atlas, was almost useless since it showed neither roads nor villages. Much less did it give information about the lie of the country, which was what I chiefly needed, since from that I could have judged the likelihood of my coming on peasant farms where I could get shelter. Whenever possible I stopped at these because they offered free hospitality, whereas in the villages there would be an inn where I would have to pay. I thus found myself every afternoon facing a grave predicament: should I waste an hour or two of precious daylight by stopping early—and the farm wives were less willing to admit me then—or risk getting caught on a lonely piece of road by the dark? For that was to be feared. No one could approach a Balkan farm after nightfall without being torn limb from limb by the dogs.

Once in a stretch of wild country this happened to me and it was an experience that I did not forget. Darkness fell before I could get in and although soon after I passed the lights of several farms and heard their dogs barking, I dared not approach them. Then the road, which had been climbing steadily, entered a forest. The snow, which had drifted a good deal, became deeper, and the going was bad. In the distance I could hear a wild, eerie sound which I took to be the howling of wolves. Fear gave me an addition of strength. Soon my clothes were drenched with sweat from the struggle and whenever I stopped to listen I could hear my heart beating like an underground ram and the sudden rustle as a load of snow fell from a branch. Then the unearthly howling would begin again, this time a little closer.

After perhaps a couple of hours of this, the road began to descend. The trees thinned out, the snow no longer rose above my calves. I caught a glimpse of a valley and of distant, ghostly mountains. But at this moment I happened to look around. Among the rocks and trees that bordered the road, I saw an animal about the size of a dog following me. Was it a fox or a wolf? Running a few steps towards it, I shouted and opened my umbrella and it immediately vanished. Although for some time I had the impression that it was still following me, I never saw it clearly again.

Before long the road was winding down into a valley and I was half-running. Surely now, I thought, I will come to a village. But, though I heard the barking of dogs in farms, no village appeared. Instead it began to snow, a thick, gentle snow that fell on my face and hands and cooled them. I kept on and soon I began to enter a trance-like state. All thoughts of finding shelter that night left me. A white curtain cut me off from the world, making beds and houses and human faces seem unreal and unconvincing. I was alone and in that aloneness I found a sort of melancholy exhilaration. Even my tiredness seemed to have fallen away, for while my legs moved mechanically, my thoughts floated above them in a thin, ethereal stratum that had little contact with reality. The only thing that I clung to was the valley. So long, I felt, as I did not have to leave it for the forests where I should hear the wolves howling, I should be able to keep on till morning.

It must have been some time after midnight when I turned a corner and saw houses. A furious barking of dogs broke out as I entered the village street, but only one or two came towards me and I was able to keep them at bay with my umbrella. I saw a door that, from the bush hanging over it, I took to be an inn and knocked loudly. A man opened it. Soon I was sleeping uneasily on a straw mattress and when I woke in the morning I found both my feet blistered.

This was my worst experience on this journey and it frightened me badly, but I ought to record that there were also pleasant ones. I especially remember the evenings I spent in certain mountain farms. Round the open fireplace, which sometimes was built on a raised dais in the centre of the room and protected on three sides by curtains, would be seated the old bearded grandfather, the women preparing the meal, the young men and the girls. After my long walk in the snow, the food and the beer would go to my head and I would sit in a dazed state, feeling that to live in a peasant family like this, to marry one of these free-spoken girls and join in the farm work would be the height of human happiness. They sat on my knee, laughed as I tried to repeat the obscene words that the young men spoke out for me with explanatory gestures and pretended to quarrel as to which would spend the night with me. But when I asked the men if they would take me on as a farm-hand for the winter, they always shook their heads. There was no work in winter on the land and very little in the summer because the farms were small and the families large.

Discouraged by this, I determined to strike inland to Sarajevo and see whether there was any better chance of finding work in that neighbourhood. I gathered that the farms there were larger and that there were saw-mills and other industries. I therefore turned east by a branch road across the Dinaric Alps and then, after walking for a whole day across a plain, crossed another and then, if I remember right, yet another range. But scarcely had I gone far along this road when all my fears and anxieties began to increase. Although the weather had changed to fine, the snow on the passes was deep and the thought that I was moving away from the sea, placing mountain ranges between myself and it, gave me a feeling like terror. In the coastal steamers lay my line of retreat and when I turned my back to them and began to move inland, I seemed to feel something dragging my feet backwards. At the same time one of my teeth began to ache and in the cold air this turned to neuralgia. I tried to tell myself that this was the supreme test and that if I failed to pass it I should be disgraced in my own eyes for ever. But no arguments were strong enough. One morning, just as it was beginning to snow, I turned and began to race by an easier road for the coast below Spalatro.

It was dark when I arrived at a fishing port whose name I think I never knew and there I found that a coastal steamer was leaving at daybreak on the following morning. I had the money to pay the fare (at two or three places round Christmas-time collections had been made for me) and by the second day I would be in Fiume. I embarked.

The coast with its black rocky islands was beautiful had I been in the mood for admiring it, but I sat dejectedly on a coil of rope thinking of everything that I had lost by my cowardice. When the sun came out and the fishing ports gleamed like white shells across the blue water, I felt that I was not fit to look at them.

We reached Fiume after dark and I at once made inquiries as to when Richard Brinsley's ship would be returning. Not for a week or two, I gathered, but a boat was leaving for Venice on the following evening. I visited Mr Bird, whom I found exactly as when I last left him, and sold the blankets I had been carrying for a few shillings. This allowed me to have a good meal, which I needed badly, but did not provide enough to pay for my passage. However, this did not matter, since I had already been promised one at quarter price if I helped in the loading. One more night and I was in Venice. A feeling of immense relief came over me, drowning my former sense of guilt, to think that I was among friends again and in a civilized country. It did not matter that I had only twopence left or that I could not remember the Wilsons' address. Quietly I sat down on the steps of St Mark's to wait for them and after an hour or two they came. Someone had told Mrs Wilson that the second of the two foreign brigands had returned.

I found Hope installed in Ball's place as tutor to the Wilsons' son. He had solved his problem of finding winter quarters that were congenial to himself and for that reason was not too pleased to see me. Wilson, however, in spite of his reputation for parsimony, was extremely kind, for not only did he put me up at his own expense at Neumann's, but he tried to get me a job. After a few inquiries he found a restaurant keeper who offered to take me on as a waiter on condition that I could provide myself with an evening suit. Wilson promised to lend me an old one of his own, but when the man saw me with my long hair and my sulky adolescent's expression, he changed his mind. Another possibility of employment then arose. One day, in the public gardens that lie close to the Arsenal, I was sitting on a bench in the wintry sunlight eating my lunch, which consisted of two buns, when a working-class girl sat down beside me. She looked at me, I offered her one of my buns and we began talking.

She was a girl from the mainland, an orphan, who had come to Venice to earn her living. She worked in a small factory close by and shared a room in an attic with another girl. One evening she took me there: we sat demurely on the single truckle bed while her friend lay down on the further side with her back turned. I then kissed her. She was, I imagine, one of the mothering type of women, for when I told her that I was looking for work she became very concerned and proposed that I should get a job at the factory where she was employed and share her attic. There was room in the bed, she declared, for three and the other girl would soon be moving out to live with her boyfriend. I agreed at once, for the idea pleased me in every way, went to the factory with her and, as I understood it, signed on. But when I turned up next morning, I was stopped at the gate and, since I knew very little Italian and could scarcely follow the Venetian dialect at all, I failed to make out what had happened. I only knew that when I saw Giulia that evening, she told me that I must wait a week and then all would be settled.

Meanwhile I had been corresponding with my parents. Both Hope and Wilson urged me to accept their offer and return home, and I could scarcely refuse to listen to Wilson's advice because he was supporting me. Then, though my determination to reach the East and Central Asia had not in the slightest degree abated, I realized that, if I were to succeed, I must set about it better. Deeply though I blamed myself for having turned back, I saw that to be able to live on the roads in Oriental countries I must have a trade that I could practise. If I could not be a knife-grinder, at least I could be a travelling smith. Why should I not ask my father to apprentice me to a good blacksmith for a year? It would cost him very little money and after that he would be free of me for ever.

Among the various relations and friends of my parents who were trying to entice me home was Mr Mills. He wrote me such a calm, sensible letter that I thought that I could not do better than put my proposal to him. As a practical man, he would surely appreciate my reasonableness and moderation. I therefore did this, adding at the last moment, because I thought it sounded better, that I wanted to be an 'art blacksmith'. That, after all, was the career that Ball had chosen and he was a Cambridge B.A. and the son of a canon.

Mr Mills' reply came by return of post. He did not think it would be proper, he said, for him to make any comment himself on my suggestion, but he felt sure that my father would give it his closest attention. However, these things needed to be discussed round a table rather than by letter. He therefore advised me to return home at once and put my wishes personally to my parents. I wrote agreeing to do this and the money for my journey was telegraphed to me.

I spent my last days at Venice in an orgy celebrating the end of my liberty. I took hashish and on coming round from my trance wrote a number of poems. It was snowing and sleeting outside, but the only poem which I now remember was a description in rhymed sextets of a tropical forest. Then the money arrived. There was enough to pay for a second-class ticket so, as I intended to travel third, I bought a number of peasant pots in the market, some photographs of Byzantine mosaics at Alinari's and a kilo of *marrons glacés*. Going to the post office, I wrote out a telegram 'Prodigal son arriving lunch Thursday. Prepare fatted calf.' But I had the sense not to send it off, though I later boasted that I had done so.

A suitcase of clothes had been dispatched by my parents to a hotel at Southampton and a Cook's agent met me on the boat and led me to it. I had my first hot bath in six months and (alas, for long hair was sacred) my first haircut. Then I took the train to Cirencester and found my parents awaiting me on the railway platform. My father had evidently laid down in a family conclave precisely what degree of affection tempered by silent reprobation should be shown me, but my mother found it difficult to repress her delight on having me back. She was astonished to find how I had grown. At school I had been small for my age—now I was tall. It was as though I had discovered for the first time that there was air above me.

My own impressions were different. I was amazed to see that, while I had lived and travelled and become a new and changed person, my parents and my home had stood still. There were the same habits, the same tones of voice, the same family conversations that I remembered, only they seemed to have become even more unimportant and trivial. I who had breathed the free air of the world must now learn to live in this cramped little burrow.

On the following morning, as soon as breakfast was over, the moment that I had not been looking forward to came. My father ordered me in a curt tone (on occasions of this sort he always settled his tone beforehand, as a woman makes up her face, and could be heard rehearsing it while he was dressing) to come into his study. There, lighting a cigarette, he began by saying that he was not going to speak of the past. No one, neither he nor anyone else, would refer to that again. It was a subject which—and at once he launched into a long retrospective sermon upon it, in which all his grievances against me— waste of an expensive education and so forth—were brought out. For it was part of his character that he could never leave the past alone, even when he was, with one part of his mind, anxious to do so.

Then he came to the question of my future. 'I've taken a good deal of trouble,' he said, 'to look into this because I want to give you the widest possible choice, but I find, after exploring every opening, that there are today only two careers open to you. You have yourself ruled out the Army. You are too old for the Navy. I think you will agree that you are not suited to the Church, and I cannot afford the Diplomatic Service. This year there are no vacancies in the Consular Service. There remain the Indian Police and the Egyptian Police. Here are the syllabuses for their entrance exams. Have a look at them and tell me tomorrow which you prefer.'

The words 'Father, I want to be an art blacksmith' died on my lips. Not only was the courage to pronounce them lacking, but I felt the uselessness. I therefore took the papers he held out and, on finding that for the Indian Police it was necessary to know French and German whereas for the Egyptian Police foreign languages were of little importance, I announced that I was ready to work for the former.

'That's a very sensible choice,' said my father. 'The pay will give you enough to live on without requiring an allowance from me and after thirty-five years' service you will be able to retire on a good pension. Then you will find that your hobbies come in useful.'

My mother too wanted to encourage me. 'India's a wonderful country,' she said when my father announced my decision. 'I know you'll simply love it. Really, I'd give anything to be in your shoes.'

And so it was settled that I should go off at once to Clifton, where I would stay with my great-uncle Vincent, and be coached at a crammer's. My father, who, having nothing else to do, loved making arrangements, had fixed up everything while I was still in Venice.

'Only,' he said, 'there is one thing that I must insist on. The cause of all this extravagance in your conduct has been poetry. I must ask you to give me your word that you will read no more of it until you have passed your exam. After that, of course, you may do as you please.'

I gave my word without having the least intention of keeping it. Was it not generally agreed that oaths made under compulsion were not binding? Give up reading poetry indeed! Why, it was no more in my power to do that than it was in my mother's to give up going to communion. And in dealing with my father one had either to agree with him or to face an explosion.

CHAPTER XII

Bristol and Germany

I now set off for my Uncle Vincent's house near Clifton. The occasion —meeting a great-uncle—seems to call for some account of my ancestry on my father's side. If this requires a brief interruption of the narrative, the time will not be wasted, since no family can be seen in its proper perspective unless those ghosts who bequeathed it their habits, their money and their innate characteristics are shown pulling the strings from behind the scenes.

Of my eight paternal great-great-grandparents all except two were Lancashire and Westmorland people who drew their income from the shipbuilding and cotton-spinning industries which had been built up by their ancestors during the preceding century. Simpsons of Harthill near Eccles, Hobsons of Hope Hall, Hawksbys, Borodailes, Greens, Wrights and beyond them Arkwrights and Swabeys—all of these were at one time very wealthy people who began to shed their money and their estates when, a little before the Victorian epoch, they moved south and severed their connection with business. Their descendants remained county families of a sort, living till the end of the century in manor houses which as a rule they rented together with the circumjacent shooting, but rarely striking roots anywhere or acquiring local responsibilities. After deserting the cold and overpopulated north, they lived for their comfort and their pleasure as *rentiers*.

It is good to have rich ancestors, but it is not so good to have dull or idle ones. Few writers, I fancy, have had poured into their blood so much of what Gertrude Stein calls 'stupid being' as I have had into mine. Since 1820 none of these persons from whom I trace my descent has had any profession (unless one can count as that a few years in the Army) and so far as I know none of them ever said or did anything in the least remarkable. They ate their dinners, entertained their friends, who were other people like themselves, and corresponded with their stockbrokers. As an illustration of their general attitude to life let me cite the diary which my great-uncle Simpson kept through the Crimean War. He recorded every day with varying comments the menus of his luncheons and dinners and the number of times he had to take a blue pill. Of the battles he fought in, of his brother officers, of the climate and country, nothing. Yet he was a good soldier as soldiers were then, was recommended for a V.C., and rose by sheer staying power to be a general.

Into this indolent, somnolent, stagnant, good-natured stream, smelling of pheasant shoots and of beds of tulips and of four-course dinners, there ran however a thin, rapid and decidedly bitter rivulet. This is the line of my patronymic ancestors. They begin with an Irishman from County Kilkenny who in 1814 was paymaster in the 54th Regiment in Nova Scotia. His eldest son, born in that year, quarrelled violently with his parents while he was still in his teens, renounced his Catholic faith and became a radical. This had consequences that to us today are familiar. A civil war having at this moment broken out in Spain in which his political opinions were at stake, he anticipated the young men of 1936 by throwing himself into it. Granted a commission in the British Legion under General de Lacy Evans, he rose to be major, was wounded and awarded two decorations. Soon after this the victory of the Liberals brought his military career to an end. It was not until the Crimean War that he got employment again as major in the Bashi Bazouks and finally as colonel of a regiment of Osmanli cavalry.

Colonel Edward FitzGerald Brenan brought his Irish blood into my all too English stock through meeting in 1840 the Simpson family, who were touring Spain in their carriage, and running off with their daughter Emily. The irate father chased them as far as Irun in a post-chaise ('Papa left in pursuit of naughty Emily' is the entry in her sister's diary), but the young man and his bride-to-be got away. They settled at Dinan in Brittany, where there was a large English colony attracted by the cheap living, and had five children. Old Mr Simpson never forgave his daughter for marrying a penniless soldier and refused to give her more than a meagre allowance.

My great-grandfather seems to have been a lonely, sarcastic, embittered man maintaining his family on an insufficient income in Brittany and Jersey. He spent his days reading the papers at the English club and at home talked little. He took all his meals alone, his wife and children eating at the same table when he had finished. Since he brought up his children to have no religion, his sons became atheists, while his daughters ended as Plymouth Sisters.

It was through this man that the black blood of the Brenans entered my otherwise placid family. He hated his own parents to such a point that he would not speak of them. He destroyed all his family papers and when his eldest son became engaged to my grandmother and begged him for some information about them, he refused to tell him even their names. For this reason I know almost nothing about them.

Of his three sons the eldest, Gerald, had a sad history. Put by his Simpson grandfather into a crack regiment, he was not given a sufficient allowance to maintain his position. Running into debt, he deserted, enlisted with Gordon in China, became correspondent to the *New York Times* during the American Civil War and was later sent by that paper to the Balkans. His marriage to my grandmother, whom he met in Vienna in 1869 (her father, Mr Green, was touring Europe in his carriage), was unhappy, for he had a difficult temper and was unreliable in money matters. He died of a fever in, I think, 1878, thus saving my father, who would not have appreciated parental discipline, the trouble of rebelling against him.

I now reach, with his two brothers, the end of this family tree. The elder, Vincent, started in the Merchant Service and ended as a senior official in the Chinese Customs. The younger, Byron, entered the Consular Service and rose to be Consul General at Shanghai. But for his sarcastic tongue, which made him enemies, he would, it was said, have succeeded Sir Robert Hart as Ambassador at Peking. Apart from my maternal grandfather, who made money, they have been the only two successful members of my family. But then they started from nothing and worked, while the others merely lived to enjoy what they had inherited or obtained by marriage.

My Uncle Vincent's family occupied a suburban house on the further side of Durdham Downs. It was one of those drab, roomy villas with thick privet hedges and a rough tennis lawn that get taken by people who have more children than money, and its cupboards told their tale in the jumble of tennis rackets, golf clubs, old shoes of a dozen different sizes, cycle lamps, spanners and school books that they contained. Here lived my uncle, his second wife who was much younger than himself, and a boy and two girls who still went to school. Three other sons in the Consular and Diplomatic Services were out in the world.

My uncle was a lean, rather dried-up man with vague, watery eyes and a prominent Adam's apple. His speech was slow and of a nautical simplicity and he talked little. One came across him reading the newspaper (a Liberal one) by the gas fire or wandering uncertainly about the garden in his baggy trousers with a bicycle pump in his hand. Every morning he would go off with a string bag to do the household shopping and now and then, when the weather seemed to promise well, he would cut some sandwiches, get on his bicycle and disappear for the day.

A stranger might have supposed that this vacant-looking man of sixty-five, who rolled a little as he walked, counted for little in his home. In fact my uncle never had to raise his voice or speak emphatically to find his word law. The reason for this was the quality that had made him famous in every treaty-port in China—his kindness. He had spent his life doing things for other people. He mended their punctures, he did their commissions, he took their sickly children back from Hong Kong to London without a nurse to look after them, he even, though he had little of it, lent them money. And he was no fool. He had made his way in the world by his shrewdness and eye for character almost as much as by his patience and reliability.

This unobtrusive selflessness of my Uncle Vincent made him the saint of our far from saintly clan. His brother Byron was a totally selfish man with a rasping tongue, my grandfather had been a weak and furious egoist, my father—I have already given some account of him. Yet in other ways my uncle bore an unmistakable likeness to his kin. He had the Brenan leanness of mind, their flat two-dimensional outlook, their caustic matter-of-factness. This came out clearly when he spoke of what he called 'humbug'. Under this heading he included everything that did not fit in with his utilitarian conceptions, such as, for example, titles, fashionable life, inherited wealth, art (whenever his daily paper gave him a momentary awareness of its existence) and above all religion. His dislike of everything connected with this was so great that a clergyman had only to be mentioned for him to come out with some heavily ironic remark. Although he said nothing when, for the sake of respectability, his wife took his daughters to church, he regarded every kind of religious ceremony as an imposture.

I spent the spring and summer of this year in my Uncle Vincent's house. Bicycle rides, tennis, exchanges of repartee with my schoolgirl cousins—the atmosphere was friendly and pleasant. However, I cannot say that this quiet family existence made any real impression on me. I was far too absorbed in my memories of the recent past to take much interest in other people. I had entered a stretch of my life when I was to live with my head turned backwards.

Yet I could not escape altogether the claims of the present. I had never lived in a suburb before and as the mild spring drew on I felt the charm of those straight, quiet roads bordered by gardens and shrubbery-encircled houses that seemed to be wrapped up in their own privacy. Fish-shaped leaves of laurel, dusty smell of red hawthorn or privet, delicate freshness of lilac called up for me visions of girls in flowered cotton frocks, girls in airy muslin dresses who lived their sequestered lives behind these hedges. In the evenings, at the hour of lighting lamps, I would walk slowly up and down, hoping against hope that suddenly one would come out and speak to me. At the same time I began to read Ernest Dowson and to find in his weak languishing verses an expression of the passion I longed to feel. By placing 'not' in front of a word, by writing 'lost' instead of 'found', the evocative power of the image is increased. I was far from being a decadent, I wanted to find, yet the whole of my present life lay under the sign of deprivation.

Another and more serious subject of interest lay in the city of Bristol. I explored its streets, its docks, its slums from one end to the other. I got a particular pleasure from walking through its lowest and poorest quarters because my nostalgia for the past made me feel that I belonged to them. Had I not once slept in doss-houses myself, side by side with out-of-work sailors and tramps? Had I not found satisfaction of mind in the company of thieves and poor factory workers? How happy I should be, I thought, if only I could return and live among them!

It was, I believed, my craving for reality that made the poverty of the down-and-outs and road people so attractive to me. They alone lived a 'real' life because they alone were fully exposed in their daily affairs to the hazards of the world. Everyone who was in receipt of a regular income was protected and therefore in some degree deadened and tame. Here I was more logical than those young communists of the twenties who were romantically drawn to the proletariat yet wished to destroy in them those qualities that they admired by raising their level of life to that of the bourgeoisie. For it was precisely in the low standard of living of those people that I thought I saw the possibility of a new and higher sort of liberty. I explained this by my recollection of something that had happened to me when I had first set out on my travels: everything that I could afford to buy had then had a small price label attached to it—½d., 1d., 2d., 4d. My income being so very low, I was obliged to keep within these figures. And this, contrary to my expectation, had given me a feeling of relief and liberation. I felt free because the dissipation of the will caused by giving way to casual desires had been suddenly suspended. 'In necessity,' I said to myself, 'lies the idea of liberty.'

Of course this life of poor streets, these vistas of red-brick houses and smoking chimneys were sordid. But beyond them in expanding circles lay the cinder heaps and the black canals, the open spaces and the football fields, the elder bushes and the flower-filled meadows. It was the contrast that seemed to me appropriate. Each made the other. The boy of the poor streets had a world of purity and innocence to escape into: the country boy had a picture of human vice and pullulation to quicken his inertia. Bristol offered the double view of the poems of Blake.

I went up for my exam in July 1913 and failed. As I had had only a short time to prepare for it, my father was not too disappointed. However, since German was my weakest subject, he decided to send me to a crammer's in Baden. The place chosen was Mr Adams's establishment at Freiburg-im-Breisgau.

Meanwhile Ball came to stay with us and made a conquest of my mother and grandmother. I was allowed to pay him a return visit in London. Here I met Francis Birrell, who later became a great friend of mine, and Hubert Waley. Hubert introduced me to his brother, Arthur, a haughty young man with a thin, high, cutting voice and the profile of an Arab sheik, who was then reading the *Arabian Nights* and wondering whether he would take up Arabic. We went (without Arthur) to the Café Royal, drank a good deal of green Chartreuse and walked through Leicester Square arm-in-arm in the early hours of the morning. Ball rented two rooms in a house in Cumberland Market: as he had no furniture except for a large Staffordshire dinner service and a couple of mattresses, we sat and slept on the floor.

These meetings suggested to me for the first time the possibility of my leading a literary life in London and having friends. Up to now I had ruled friendship out. This was partly due to my not having met anyone I liked, but still more to Hope's influence. Incapable himself of intimacy with another human being, he had passed on to me his belief that there was something weak and demoralizing in such relationships. One must never lower the drawbridge to another person, never leave the battlements unguarded. Now I saw with shame that I was only too prone to these weaknesses. I enjoyed their warmth and expansiveness, their easy, unthinking give and take. I came out of my reserve and self-conceit—those strong defensive positions of adolescents—only too readily. However, as soon as I was alone again, I pulled myself together. Was I not a dedicated person, whose eyes were fixed on remote and solitary horizons? The plan of a literary life, which Ball with his flattery of my poetic scribblings had put into my head, faded rapidly.

Before changing the scene to Germany I must describe a small adventure I had had the previous spring. My parents had a housemaid called Minnie, a fair-haired, buxom girl who was engaged to the first footman at the Park. A day or two after my return from Venice I made advances to her which rather to my surprise were accepted. This was my first sexual experience and, since she was as ignorant as I was, which is saying a great deal, it was conducted on both sides with the maximum of clumsiness. Besides the opportunities were limited: we could only meet in my room where at any moment someone might come in. The affair, therefore, which continued at intervals for several years, came to inspire in me a self-disgust from which a night or two in bed with her would have saved me. Yet Minnie was a decent girl, intelligent and warm-hearted, and deserved something better than the guilty lust which was all I had to offer her.

The Adams' house at Freiburg stood on the edge of the town, immediately below the Black Forest. The establishment consisted of Mr and Mrs Adams, two masters and four or five pupils. Oddly enough one of these last had been with me at Winton House. This was Troubridge, a bilious-looking youth a little younger than myself, whose dry croaking voice and long sleek black hair suggested a raven. His mother, Lady Troubridge, was a well-known novelist and he had a passion for the drama which led him to spend as much of his time as possible with his feet raised high above him on the stove, reading one English and German play after another. He talked a great deal in a loud, self-assured voice, smoked a pipe continually and never, if possible, went out of doors. Besides him there were two Jewish youths —Henry Mond, a clever, lively, very precocious boy who later became Lord Melchett, and a son of Sir Godfrey Isaacs who left soon. I did not make real friends with any of them.

The change of scene from England put me at first into a high state of exhilaration. I had long associated happiness with being abroad. I was particularly delighted by the old quarter of the town with its mysteriously closed and shuttered inns, its quiet canals and its paved squares. Still more I loved the Cathedral. Although I found Gothic architecture rhetorical and over-emphatic in comparison to Romanesque, I paid it frequent visits to stand and gaze in a sort of trance at its medieval stained glass. Then one evening I went to a performance of *Romeo and Juliet* at the State Theatre. I had never seen good acting before and was completely carried away by it. A few days later I experienced the first of those fits of possession—for I do not know how else to describe them—which have recurred at irregular intervals throughout my life. I was walking by the canal in the evening when suddenly the desire to write came over me. I pulled out the notebook I always carried and words began to flow more rapidly than I could put them down. They were, so far as I can remember, pure gibberish, a meaningless jumble of what I had been reading lately—Shakespeare, Blake, Nietzsche and the Book of Job—mixed with something that was more personal. The words came as if dictated, one phrase suggesting another, and I had not the slightest idea of what I was going to put down next. Moving from lamp-post to lamp-post I wrote till both the notebook and the loose sheets of paper I carried were filled. Then I returned to the Adams' house and the fit ended.

Every few years since this time and generally in the autumn these bouts of writing have returned. Once, as I shall describe later, I wrote in a night and a morning a poetical-satirical book which was published and got some favourable reviews. On another occasion, quite recently, I wrote a play of a poetical-symbolical sort which took me five days, writing continuously from breakfast to midnight, with no interruption for meals. What is most curious about these occasions is that they have always been unpremeditated. I have started, generally towards six o'clock and in low spirits, by putting down in a casual way a line that came into my head and then the words and ideas have suddenly flowed. Although in time I learned to exercise some control over the general import and shape of what I was writing, I have never been able to prepare the ground beforehand because I have never known when the moment would come or what the immediate stimulus—usually some book I had been reading, which acted on me rather as what in spiritualistic séances is called a 'control'—would be. This has meant that my arrow, though shot with a strong arm, has always been shot at random. Had I had the patience and intelligence to arrange my life and my work to lead up to these eruptions, when all the sleeping powers of the mind are brought into play, it is possible (or so, at least, in moments of self-conceit I tell myself) that I might have written something of value. For a poet the proper management of his talent is everything. But when at length I decided that I wished to become a writer I felt that to submit myself to the mercies of such irregular and uncontrollable impulses would be unendurable. I wanted to cure myself of the poetry disease—waiting upon the moment—by disciplined prose writing just as I have heard some people say that they wished to cure themselves of the vagaries of violent infatuations by marrying. I like the monotony of regular life and hate the spasmodic.

Our two tutors were Mr Halsey and Herr Sartig. Halsey was a short, silent, humourless Yorkshireman who looked like a dull twin-brother of Napoleon. He had only one interest in life—his collie dog, whom he called Old Girl. Every day he went for walks in the pine forest to exercise her and when I went with him I found that she was his only subject of conversation. Many years later, after we had completely lost touch with one another, I got a postcard from him. It showed a photograph of himself standing on a Yorkshire moor with Old Girl and on the other side was written: 'You'll be glad to hear she is still going strong. All the best. H.H.'

More interesting was Herr Sartig. To look at he was a caricature of a Prussian officer. Very tall, immensely thin, with arms that hung down like wires, cropped hair, high starched collar and duelling scars, he appeared at first sight severe and formidable. Actually he was a child, naïve and sentimental, very good-natured and with a clownish sense of fun.

Like myself he was interested in painting, but whereas I was all for Cézanne, Seurat, Picasso and the Italian futurists, he refused to see anything in them and stood out for the old German masters and after them for Rodin and Hödler. This led to a lot of good-natured argument in which we usually ended by admitting that there was something to be said for each other's view. But Herr Sartig was also a great walker. Since walking was a passion with me, we used to set off on week-ends with rucksacks on our backs to explore the villages of the Rhine valley. Here in some sanded inn-parlour we would both get drunk on the heady wine and he would caper about and pretend he was going to kiss the serving-girl.

I also went on long walks alone, a book of verse in my pocket. The primeval forest of the Mooswald, the vineyard-terraced hill of the Tuniberg were both places that stirred me. At Breisach there was an inn where one could sit on the terrace and eat freshly caught perch and drink white wine while the great river rolled by below. But most attractive of all to my mind were the large peasant villages of the plain. Set in orchards of cherry trees, their sprawling half-timbered houses ringed round with wooden balconies, their broad streets encumbered by huge wagons, they called up both the etchings of Dürer and the *Märchen* of Jacob Grimm which I was reading. They were medieval, they were peasant, they were Germany. When one had seen them the nature of the Romantic Movement in this country became clearer. It was a delving into the past history of the race and culture to find there materials for a new literature that should be purely German. In other countries romanticism stood for a revolutionary breaking out of the ego, an assertion of the value of the individual over society and finally a colonization of the unexplored regions of the mind. In Germany it was a half-mystical movement designed to evolve a new national self-consciousness and I could understand the resentment they felt over Shakespeare's having written in English, for he was the great poet they needed, the perfect exponent, without Latin admixture, of the genius of their race. Even his feeling for language was Germanic rather than English.

It had been agreed that instead of coming home for Christmas I should go to a phonetic institute at Berlin to improve my German. This institute was in the suburb of Lichterfelde West and was run by a Germanized Australian called Tilly. It proved to be a strange and rather disagreeable sort of place. People of all ages and countries went to it and were taught by the various members of the Tilly family, from the youngest aged nine, who gave the first lessons, to Herr Tilly himself who was fifty and discoursed on art. The pupils and the staff were subjected to a special diet, mostly vegetarian, with a taboo on drinking at meals, which I must say that I found a good deal more appetizing than the oppressive German cooking. The most remarkable thing, however, about the institute was the Tilly family itself. This consisted of five or six girls and two young men, all very good-looking, all very musical and all very neurotic. Their mother was said to be in an asylum and they most of them had an inclination to suicide. Indeed, three of the sons had killed themselves already, the last to do so having jumped off the roof the week before I arrived. Was this the result of parental tyranny? Herr Tilly certainly looked like the worst type of German professor, pompous, heartless and self-satisfied. He had forgotten his foreign origin and become one of those coldly passionate nationalists who believed that the Germans were culturally the descendants of the Ancient Greeks.

A few days after I arrived, the institute closed for the holidays. Although it was arranged that I should continue to have my meals there and even to take a few lessons from one of the daughters, my time was almost entirely my own. I had a bed-sitting-room in a house near by, warmed by a huge porcelain stove. Outside in the broad, empty streets an east wind howled and chivvied the snow, so I stayed indoors drinking cups of black coffee and giving myself up to an orgy of reading. I had started that autumn on German literature with Grimm's *Märchen*, *Also sprach Zarathustra* and *Faust*. Then, finding the new language heavy going, I had sent for three or four volumes of Verlaine. One of these was *Les Poètes Maudits*, a collection of essays introducing Rimbaud, Corbière, Laforgue and Villiers de l'Isle Adam. Greatly excited by what I read, I had spent my Christmas money on buying the works of these poets, as well as the two biographies of Rimbaud by Paterne Berrichon and his letters. The parcel arrived a few days after I reached Berlin and I shut myself up to read them.

The effect on me of Rimbaud was prodigious. Here was the gospel of adolescence I had been looking for. Although I did not at first find him easy to understand, I had only to glance through *Les Illuminations* or *Une Saison en Enfer* to come across a dozen passages which exactly and in the most moving language conveyed my own experience and which no one else, I felt sure, had ever put into words. After this all other poetry, except a few lyrics by Blake, seemed to me mere rhetoric. For of course this youth was, in a very special sense, the poet for me. All the features of his life—the search for vision, the dabbling in magic, the drugs, the cult of poverty, the determination to harden himself, the pull of the East—had been mine too. I began to identify myself with him, seeing in his meteoric passage through the world the flash of a messianic figure who showed the way—but what way? a blocked and impossible way?—to his followers. For eight or nine years, till I ended my prolonged adolescence by falling in love, he became a half-divine figure to me and I still like to think today that I understand his writings better than anyone else. For only those who have travelled along the same road can feel their full force.

The sombre Christmas weeks that I passed at Berlin come back to me like the memory of an illness. I had spent all my pocket-money on books and had only fourpence left. This meant that when I wanted to see the Kaiser Friedrich Museum I had to walk eight miles and back with nothing to keep up my spirits but a roll of bread. Every day the wind howled through the Grünewald like a wolf and around it the plain, the enormous plain, was white with snow. Excited by the *Illuminations* and by the solitude, I thought that this would be the occasion to write some poems. To reach the proper state of vision I fasted for two days, walked for hours under the blue arclights and finally took a little hashish. The poems came, but even to my uncritical eye they were bad. I reflected that I was now nearly twenty, whereas Rimbaud had written all that he was ever to write by the time that he was nineteen. I had better give up the idea of being a poet.

I must now return to Hope whom I had last seen lying in a hashish trance at Venice nearly a year before. He had a fixed income of his own of forty pounds a year and what presents his brother cared to

send him. This was enough in those days to take a man who was prepared to travel rough from one end of the world to the other. Setting
out in April, he had walked down the Adriatic coast to Montenegro,
taken a boat round Albania and got on to Athens and Constantinople.
From there, partly on foot and partly by train, he had arrived at
Damascus. His last letter showed him living in native dress in a fondak
and preparing for the next stage to Baghdad.

His journey naturally filled me with both envy and enthusiasm. I
passed over the fact that he had taken the train across Anatolia and
imagined him living in a state of austerity and 'virtue' which in reality
were foreign to his nature. He could put up with hardships for brief
periods for he had a stoical vein, but comfort and good food—especially good food—were always at the back of his mind. He was not of the
breed of Doughty. But the fact remained that he was moving steadily
eastwards. This was not only in itself immensely encouraging, but it
set up in my mind an impatience with my present life and a longing
at any cost to escape and set out on my travels again.

I have in my correspondence with Hope, which begins at this time,
a record of this restlessness which otherwise I should probably have
forgotten. My letters to him, written in an unformed, scratchy hand,
are filled either with passages copied out from poems or else with
plans for escape. Till 1918 the plan of escape, or of what I should do
when I had escaped, occupied a large part of my thinking. I had become a confirmed nostalgic, longing for a return to a life which I had
once experienced, but in a setting of new places and countries.

The only thing, it would seem, that prevented me from setting out
immediately was that my parents kept me very short of pocket-money.
My ordinary allowance was five shillings a week, to which Mr Adams
added a little for week-end expeditions. However, it occurred to me
that if I used the journey money given me for my return to England
in April and added to it my birthday money I would have enough to
take me as far as Spain. From there I could get on to Africa. This idea
provides the argument for a long letter dated February 1914, in which
I discussed the possibilities of African travel—from Tunisia to Abys-
sinia, from Fezzan to Timbuctu and the Congo. But this of course was
a daydream. The plan I finally decided on was first, so as not to enrage
my parents too much, to fail at my exam, and then to sign on as a
seaman on a long-distance voyage. As soon as I had acquired sufficient
experience of this life, I would desert in an Arab-speaking port and
there find some means of supporting myself while I picked up the
language. Or else, scrapping the East, I might go to the South Sea

Islands or Mexico. The point of being a seaman was that it would make me mobile.

Meanwhile I began to do everything I could think of to harden myself. First I made the discovery that one could walk barefoot in the snow in spite of the severe frost. I put this to the test by setting off on a week-end tramp across the Black Forest without boots. Then I went for some extremely long walks, carrying my blankets with me in a monster rucksack, eating nothing but bread and chocolate and sleeping out under the pine trees. Today the world is full of people who know the exhilaration to be got from pushing one's body to the limits of its endurance, but in those days, in a tame, devitalized country such as England was then, these sorts of ventures were rare. The revolution that was to give the young a life of their own had not yet started.

At the end of June I returned home to take my exam. On my way I stopped for a couple of nights at Rotterdam. Here I met a retired ship's purser who told me that for a couple of pounds he could at any time get me taken on as a seaman on a ship going to the East Indies and at the same time provide me with the necessary kit. I remembered Rimbaud's voyage to Java and decided that, unless something better turned up, I would accept his offer as soon as my failure to pass into the Indian Police was announced.

Hope had a friend called Ernest Taylor who had once rented a cottage at Cranham on the Cotswolds, not far from my home, and after that another cottage at Shepscombe, and who now lived at St Ives in Cornwall. Like myself he was in rebellion against his parents. But he had had—or so I thought—better luck than myself, for on his refusal to remain in his father's brewing business at Cardiff he had been given an allowance of fifty pounds a year and told never to write or speak to him again. On this sum and a few hives of bees he supported himself. Since he was reputed to know something about tramp ships, I had written to him from Germany to ask him if he could arrange a cheap passage for me to Jiddah or Hodeida on the Red Sea. My idea was, if I could raise £70 from the moneylenders on my mother's marriage settlement, to go there and learn Arabic as a preparation for travelling in the interior. Only if I failed to raise this would I sign on as a seaman.

In a second letter dated July I gave reasons for going to the Red Sea even if I proved unable to raise any money. I wanted to burn my boats. Distrusting my courage after what I regarded as my shameful turning back in Bosnia, I felt I ought to put myself in a position from which retreat would be impossible. It was at such moments, I thought, when face to face with starvation, that the important things happened, that the miracle that changed the course of one's life occurred. At any cost I must lever myself out of the rut of bourgeois comfort and safety in which I had been brought up.

These letters led to a meeting. I took a steamer from Bristol to Hayle and was met by Taylor. I found him a good-looking, rather self-possessed man of about twenty-five who had spent the winter reading Dostoevsky and Nietzsche and was longing for some more active occupation. He lived, because he could afford nothing better, on a diet of milk, butter, honey and broken ship's biscuit. This broken biscuit, which arrived in barrels from London, cost less than bread, and, since his bees made more honey than he could sell, we ate a comb of it at every meal. How quickly one makes friends when one is young! The week I spent at Penbeagle, Taylor's cottage on the Zennor road, was one of the high points of my youth. It passed in an orgy of talking, reading poetry, discussing Blake and Nietzsche and drinking the green tea I had brought with me till the dawn began to show in the sky. Fogs came and lifted, suns rose and set, the fuchsias and the hydrangeas flowered, while time stood still for two young men who felt they could never say all they had to say to one another.

At the end of my visit we walked to Falmouth to make some inquiries about boats. Outside the news-vendors there were posters announcing the Austrian declaration of war on Serbia. This meant little to either of us and we slept that night on the beach at Gunwalloe without any idea of what was in store for the world.

A few days later the Russian and German mobilizations began. At once it became clear that a general explosion was about to take place. I wanted to be in that explosion, which I saw would be one of the great events of my time, but I also wanted to be in it in a way that would interest me. I therefore wrote to the Montenegran Consul, offering my services in their army. He replied a little stiffly—he was an Englishman who lived at Harrogate—advising me to enlist in the ranks of my own countrymen. For by this time England was at war and there seemed nothing left that I could do but write to the French Consulate in London to inquire how I could enrol in the Foreign Legion, as that seemed the quickest way of getting out to the front. But before the answer could arrive my father drove down to Gloucester to apply for a commission for himself in the Territorials.

I remember that August afternoon of 1914 very well. I had been to tea with my mother at the Mills's and we were walking back along the raised footwalk that skirts the road to Miserden. On either side of us the fields of corn were ripe for the harvest and a warm misty sun shone down upon them. We began to talk about the news from the front. At that very moment Englishmen, Frenchmen and Germans were shooting at one another across cornfields like these: men in the flower of their age were dying and their corpses were lying among the uncut stalks. The world, which till a week or two before had been so smiling and so peaceful, had broken out into a rage of destruction. It seemed impossible to believe, since there was no reason whatever that we could see why this should have happened.

On reaching home we found my father waiting for us. The adjutant had told him that his deafness would prevent their accepting him, but had inquired if he had not got a son. 'We still have a vacancy or two,' he had said, 'for young fellows who have been at good public schools.' Half an hour later my father was driving back with a commission for me in his pocket.

Next day I took the train to London to be measured for a uniform by a Savile Row tailor. In the fitting-room of Messrs Hawkes' establishment I ran into my Uncle Charlie. He was in the highest spirits and invited me to have dinner with him that evening at the Cavalry Club. I refused as I was going straight back.

'Some other time, then,' he said. 'Now I must be off to the Admiralty. Got to see the First Lord at once. He was in the regiment, you know. Fine chap, Churchill, great pal of mine, nothing he wouldn't do for me. Before he took up with this political stuff, I taught him to sit a horse properly and he swore to me he'd never forget it. I shall ask straight away for a division. One of these new divisions, civilians in khaki, you know. Could hardly give me less, could he? Then you can be one of my A.D.C.s. Mind you get your sword at Wilkinsons' and tell them to sharpen it well. Nothing like a good blade when it comes to a scrap. Hi, here's the taxi. Give my love to your mother and tell her I'll look after you. Ta-ta, you'll hear from me later. To the Admiralty, main door.'

But I never heard. At the end of the war my uncle was still a major —in fact he was Town Major of Jerusalem. A week later I joined my regiment at Chelmsford.

CHAPTER XIII

The War: Armentières and the Somme

I found my battalion, the 5th Gloucesters, installed in billets on the outer fringe of the town. Its officers were business and professional men who had joined the Territorials in much the same spirit in which one joins a cricket club. They thoroughly enjoyed the uniforms and the parades and the jolly fortnight they spent every year under canvas. Mess each evening was the high point of the day and drinks cost nothing because they were put down on the general bill. The whisky and port therefore made their rounds and by eleven o'clock most of the senior officers were sozzled.

On the day after my arrival I had the alarming experience of having to take my company of two hundred men onto battalion parade because all the other officers were away on courses. The sergeant-major whispered the words of command and I had to shout them. Then followed an hour of those parade-ground manœuvres that had come down unchanged from the eighteenth century. The machine-gun had been in use for thirty years, but we were still practising for the battle of Minden. These occasions caused me more terror than anything I was to experience later at the front.

I found the long evenings in the mess so tedious and destructive of my inner life that I determined to skip them. I rented therefore a sitting-room and spent the hours after the last parade was over in reading. Instead of dinner I had bread and butter, cake and green tea. One Saturday evening I took hashish and after coming round from it wrote a prose poem in my favourite 'illuminated' style. It was as bad as anything could be. On my free Sundays I would hire a horse and ride out into the country, chanting Rimbaud's lyrics in my tuneless voice whenever it broke into a canter. Then one week-end in October Ball came down to see me and we went for a long walk on the Essex coast, getting back in the small hours of the morning: he and Franky Birrell were just off to join a Quaker ambulance in France. Ernest Taylor, now in uniform, also paid me a visit.

But the great event of the autumn for me was Hope's return from the East. He had walked down the Euphrates with some Arabs as far as Baghdad and had then set off in native dress to cross Persia on foot, his destination Samarkand. But in one of the passes in Luristan he had been robbed of all his money and had reached Teheran destitute and in the first stages of typhoid. The British community there had put him in a hospital and, after his recovery, had paid his passage home through Russia and Sweden.

I found him in a very patriotic mood and longing to enlist as a private in the infantry, but his short sight and the still wretched state of his health made this impossible. However, he had bought a number of technical books on musketry, and although he had never fired a rifle in his life he already knew more about its principles than our Regular instructor. We argued a good deal about the war, for although I supported it on the grounds that I did not wish to see the Germans masters of Europe, I did not believe any of the atrocity stories that were filling the papers, whereas he believed every one of them. But we were both in a great hurry to get to the front and afraid that the war would be over before we did so. For how, we asked, could Germany and Austria stand up for long against the armed might of Russia, France, Italy and Britain? Everyone in England thought like this at the time.

I was not, as may be imagined, popular in my battalion and now a succession of things happened to make me seem positively undesirable. First there was a scandal over a girl, the governess to the master tailor's family on whom I had at first been billeted. Her father complained that I had seduced her. In fact, nothing had passed between us but a little surreptitious petting. My brief interest in her had only been discovered because I had written her a letter saying that I could not see her again. Then from my second billet, owned by a prissy family of Methodists, there came a complaint that I had introduced a tramp into the house late at night and allowed him to sleep on the drawing-room sofa. I was not believed when I explained that he was the son of Canon Ball of Peterborough. But my crowning offence came during the three days' field operations that took place in November. They were supposed to go on day and night, but there was a gentleman's agreement that when we dossed down in a comfortable barn we should remain there till next morning. My enthusiasm did not allow me to accept this, so I roused my company, which I was then commanding, at midnight, made a forced march and surprised the White forces sleeping in a barn. I could not be reprimanded for this, but the commander whose surrender I had taken, a gentle, kindly major verging on forty, was justifiably annoyed.

The sequel came soon. Round Christmas I was seconded to a new unit that was being formed, the 48th Divisional Cyclist Company. It was intended to act as a support for the Cavalry in the great advance that everyone expected would take place in the spring. Early in January I joined this company in a village called Great Totham.

I found a collection of six young subalterns of the same age as myself. The adjutant was just one year older and the Company Commander, though he seemed to us almost elderly, was only twenty-six. Looking round the mess room I tried to guess why each of them had been rejected by his regiment. As they were well-built men who had volunteered not to play at being soldiers but to serve in the war, this was not immediately obvious, but I quickly saw that I was going to get on with them. So, feeling myself free and un-hampered at last, I threw myself with enthusiasm into the task of training my platoon. I became a stickler for drill, which I had up to now disliked, and I also took my men on long endurance tests. Twice, for example, we rode up to London through the heavy traffic and stacked cycles in Hyde Park.

It was at Totham that I met the man who was to become and remain for forty-five years my closest friend. He was an Oxford undergraduate called Ralph Partridge. On my first evening in the mess I was surprised to see someone reading *The Times* with an air of great concentration, for none of the rest of us did more than glance at the headlines of the popular press. Suddenly he dropped the sheet that concealed him with a deep, hearty laugh and I saw a good-looking man of powerful build with the brightest, bluest eyes I had ever beheld in my life. He seemed so born to lead anything from a Polar expedition to an infantry assault that I was puzzled to understand why his regiment had got rid of him till, as I got to know him better, I realized that it had been precisely for that reason. He was very sure of himself and did not easily submit to authority that he regarded as stupid or incompetent.

The day we were all looking forward to came at the end of March 1915. We crossed the Channel and moved into billets close to the Belgian frontier just behind Armentières. The sun was shining, the fruit trees were coming into bloom, the woods and fields were in their freshest and most transparent green. From a few miles away came the steady roll of guns and when one went out after supper one saw the sky lit up by their flashes and the long wavering line of flares floating above the horizon like yellow water-lilies. I remembered the accounts

I had read in General Marbot's memoirs of the stirring and exciting effect of distant gunfire. The trench line was a natural frontier like the August sea and everything close to it, including ourselves, felt its pull and attraction.

A day or two later I was able to visit it. My friend Ernest Taylor was a lieutenant in the 1st King's Own Regiment which was holding the line exactly in front of us. I set off to look for him and found him at his headquarters—he was now Brigade Machine-gun Officer—in the *curé's* house at Le Bizet. He gave me lunch and then took me down to the front line to show me his forward gun emplacements. In this sector the ground was marshy and no digging was possible. The·approach to the front trenches lay through a row of red-brick workmen's houses in which a hole had been knocked in every partition wall. The windows had been hung with sacking and we stumbled along, bending our heads at every aperture in a sort of twilight, till at the end we emerged into a narrow parapeted lane, built of sandbags, which was the front trench. It had a few strands of barbed wire in front of it and ended suddenly a little further on in a field. Since the German trenches were only seventy yards away (in one place only thirty) one had to speak in whispers, for, if a sound was heard, a rifle grenade or a catapulted jam-jar full of shrapnel or even a great lumbering trench mortar would come over. In fact, as we stood in the yard of a ruined house, looking at the entrance to one of our mines, a mortar did burst above us and a small piece of metal tore my breeches and drew a few drops of blood. It was my twenty-first birthday—a good day, I felt, for an initiation.

A young soldier's first experience of war is almost bound to be exhilarating. There is, to start off with, the thrill of danger, just enough to stimulate but not enough to frighten. Then there is the sense of new powers awakening in him, new fields of action calling for a response. All around him is the surrealist landscape of war, brought about by the reversal of the ordinary uses of things. That long line of workmen's dwellings, for example, now no more than a covered passage through which one walks; those fields scattered with dead not living cows and that prominent house that stands up only a few hundred yards away more difficult to visit than the Potala Palace at Lhasa. Or take that cottage just behind our front trenches which seems to have come down unchanged from the time of Breughel. In it there lives an old woman who cannot go out by day without being shot at by a German sniper. According to Belgian law, which we have to respect, she may not be forced to leave. And where is the enemy whom we are supposed to be fighting? He is permanently invisible, buried in the earth just like ourselves. So everything is topsy-turvy and till one has grown accustomed to it this provides a special sort of pleasure, not unlike that given by nonsense poetry. That is, it offers a relief from the expected and conventional.

A few days after my visit to Ernest Taylor our company was given a formal introduction to the front line. As we entered it another company of Territorials was coming out and I recognized its commander, who had been in the first football eleven at Radley. As he passed me his face was green with fear and he said, 'This is hell.' That at least is what my memory tells me, though today I find it hard to believe. All I can be certain of is that I got the impression that he was frightened and that this gave me a delicious feeling of triumph because I knew that I was not. As I came to discover later, the sight of fear on another man's face would produce elation if I felt sure of myself, but anger and disgust if I was trying to control my own uneasiness.

In this sector we were visiting, the German trenches were several hundred yards distant from ours. The regular troops our division was relieving were tired and dejected, for they had been holding the line all winter, but I was too young and impatient to understand this and blamed their lack of initiative and adventurousness. If machine-gun fire was the only obstacle to our taking Messines, why, I thought, could not some device of bullet-proof shields be wheeled or carried? Then stupidly I wandered out beyond the trench line, got sniped at and, as I came back, saw one of our sentries shot dead in the head as he stood beside me. But even this did not affect me. I was too green to take in the danger and privately believed that, young and full of life as I was, no bullet could harm me.

During the next few weeks I saw a good deal of Taylor. I was billeted not far away at Pont de Nieppe and would often ride over to lunch or supper with him. After the meal he would take me round his machine-gun posts, explaining things as he went, and fire off a few belts of ammunition. Both sides were very active and waspish in this sector and we were losing men every day. Thus one afternoon we went down the line together to find that half a dozen of his battalion had been killed a few hours before by a mortar bombardment put over in revenge for a mine that we had just exploded. There was no live and let live in those trenches.

But we also had time for other things. Sitting at the window of his house we would watch the shells bursting on the monastery a few hundred yards away and admire the beauty of the explosions. The aeroplanes (I had hardly ever seen one before) looked like large, slow birds, and by night there were yellow flares, green or red rockets and gun flashes. This war, we agreed, was very theatrical. Then we talked of the spring. He showed me some lilac that had pushed through the window of his latrine, saying as he did so, 'The military meaning of spring is that it gives cover from view.' I said, 'Yes, but it has other meanings.' To which he answered, 'I find it better not to think of them. This life is only endurable if one keeps one's mind on the war.'

From the middle to the end of April I had my billet in a farm-house in a small hamlet known as La Crèche. One day Taylor came to see me and I took him for a walk under the dome-shaped elms, over the grass that was sprinkled with cuckoo-pint and cowslips. After that we sat by the big open fire and had coffee with cream in it and bread with honey and farm butter. As we talked the war seemed far away, but then the sun set and he rode off on his horse. I had had my sleeping-bag put out in the orchard under a tall pear tree. As I lay there snug and warm I could feel in my nostrils the moisture of the grass and flowers and when I looked up could see the pale starry sky and the white blossom outlined against it. The flashes and lights on the horizon and the sound of distant gunfire seemed to make the spring more desirable.

A few nights after my friend's visit I was awakened by a steady tramping and rumbling of vehicles along the great cobbled road, built long before by the Spaniards, that ran close by. I got up and, dressing hurriedly, sat for a long time watching the dark column passing in the moonlight between the tree trunks. It was, I guessed, the 4th Division marching north to fill the gap in the line left by the German gas attack at Ypres and somewhere in it Taylor must be riding on his horse. Till dawn I could hear the sound of marching and the men singing *One móre river—óne more river to cross.*

Early in May we moved to a moated farm closer to the line known as the Château d'Oosthove. Here Ralph Partridge, whose mind ran much on women, courted a fair-haired, blue-eyed farm girl and I held the ladder for him to ascend to her room. My own half-hearted advances to her hard-boiled friend had led to nothing. Then on other evenings we would ride in after the last parade to Armentières. In this place there was a hotel restaurant in the station square where we could eat omelets and *pâté* and drink champagne while we flirted with the waitresses, who had not yet been browned off by the sight of troops. I remember a jolly major who pretended to be a dog and crawled round the table on all fours biting their ankles. Then once, going out into the courtyard where an acetylene lamp was burning, I saw one of these waitresses lying on a heap of straw with her skirts pulled up to her waist and a knot of soldiers queueing in a line to take their turn. So much, I thought, for the stories of public rapings that a few months before had been filling the English papers! Some of them were said to have occurred in Armentières. Really, in this country of the bacchanalian kermess, force wasn't necessary.

A strange atmosphere pervaded this rather sordid manufacturing town. The nearer half of it was still animated, in spite of the shells that frequently fell on it, but when one entered the further part one at once became aware of that something hushed and sinister that always hung about the region of the front line. The poor working-class streets, which can never have been gay, were littered with glass and rubble, but, though faces were to be seen at some of the windows, the pavements were deserted. For the German trenches were only a few hundred yards away and, rounding this corner or that, one came under machine-gun fire. One evening I saw a small shell burst in front of me and kill a child.

But in war one can see and forget things that in peace-time would leave a scar on the mind. There was the gay exuberant spring to tell us that all was well and the pervasive feeling of sex to give an air of don't care and abandon. We used, for example, to bathe—naked, of course —in the Lys and a group of wide-eyed girls would assemble to watch us and make their comments. Then the brewery at Pont de Nieppe was converted into soldiers' baths and while we plunged about in the steaming vats we would see the eyes of the laundry girls who worked in the compartment next door peering at us through the gaps in the wooden partition and hear their excited giggles.

But this pleasant, lazy life did not last for long. Soon we were riding off every evening at six o'clock to spend the night digging a redoubt for the second line opposite Messines. The place chosen was a hilltop crowned by an estaminet known as *In den Kranienberg*. The building had been a good deal knocked about by shell-fire and the fresh smells of spring were mingled with the stench of decaying corpses, whether of people or of animals we did not know. Each time that a flare rose and lit up the poles of the hopyard we had to freeze in our places, though really, I think, we were too far from the German lines to be visible. Now and then a burst of machine-gun bullets would whish by and the corncrakes and nightingales, excited by their sound, would sing all the louder. On every second night one of our men was wounded and before we had finished digging two had been killed.

Sometimes, instead of returning home at dawn, we bivouacked in the grounds of a château close by and returned to our work in the evening. This château, which was modern, stood on the slope of a small wooded hill among clumps of peonies, lilacs and rhododendrons. The grass on the lawns had grown up thick and tall and round its edges there were pools of red poppies, columbines and irises, flowering with the same abandon as the wild campion and stitchwort. One wall of the château had been ripped off by a shell and looking up one could see a brass bedstead still heaped with sheets and a mirrored wardrobe staring out over the drop, untouched by looters because the stairs had fallen in. I was reading Jules Laforgue at the time and so saw everything through his eyes. I imagined the pale anaemic daughter of the house killed by a shell on the eve of her marriage, her chaste bed preserved as an ironic memento and the flowers she used to love coming out again.

These enchanted months released in me a burst of prose and verse. Sitting in the garden of this château with a pencil and notebook on my knee while the men picked bunches of flowers like schoolchildren and green gooseberries to cook, I felt that this life was almost too idyllic. The thrushes and blackbirds sang round me: doves cooed in the woods: at night there were corncrakes and nightingales. Through the haze I could see tracts of green country—tall hedges and farms and trees. Yet I hated the war.

'You cannot imagine,' I wrote to Hope, 'the longing of every man in this army for the end of the war. My hopes cannot go beyond that. I have come out here to see corpses and shells and a rain of bullets, and I wish to see them as at Neuve Chapelle. But always, above all things, I long for peace.'

For some time I had had no word from Ernest Taylor. Then, just as I was beginning to get anxious, I heard from Hope that he had been killed near Ypres on May 1st. My cousin, Byo Brenan, who had been my companion two years before at Bristol, had also fallen there a week before as well as Hope's younger brother. In England my single childhood companion, Bob James, was dying of consumption. It was a holocaust of my friends and I decided to ride off and look for Taylor's grave.

A month before this I had visited Ypres on a sightseeing trip with Ralph Partridge. The city had then been crowded with people and little damaged. We had admired the cathedral and the Cloth Hall and looked curiously at the principal hotel which had been cut in two by a shell, revealing, like the photograph of an abdominal operation, its pathetic bedroom furniture, its flapping wallpaper and curtains and even a piano. In those days such sights were new to the world. Then we had ridden back in the heat of the afternoon and I had had an angry argument with Ralph—he always got irritable when he was hot—because he had said that pacifists were skulkers and ought to be shot whereas I had defended their right to think as they did. Twenty years later he was a pacifist himself: we quarrelled over Munich and did not meet after that for some years. He was a very emotional man and whenever he held an opinion he held it passionately and liked to have it out with those who disagreed with him.

I now set off again for Ypres with my batman, Dartnell. Although the city was out of bounds for troops, we got through it without difficulty and found the part of the line that Taylor's battalion was holding. I spoke to a man who had seen him fall. He had been wounded in the thigh while firing his machine-gun over the parapet at the retreating Germans: then, after sitting down for a moment to bandage himself, he had got up and begun firing it again. A moment later a bullet from a sniper struck him in the head, entering by the ear-hole. He was buried just behind the trench where he had fallen, but the grave could not be visited because the Germans had advanced again and occupied it.

On our way back we stopped to explore the town. It was completely deserted—not a soldier except for three military policemen, not a civilian. Whole streets were burning and packs of dogs roamed about, feeding on the corpses which one could smell everywhere. In the great market square the shattered walls of the cathedral and of the Cloth Hall stood up, surrounded by ruins. Out of curiosity we entered some of the undamaged houses. In the cafés and estaminets half-filled glasses still stood on the tables, for with the first rumour of gas the whole population had fled in panic. In one of the main streets we found a house that had belonged to an artist. Its upstairs rooms were filled with large and vulgar nudes of a woman whom I conjectured to be his mistress. In their bedroom all the drawers were open and underclothes, false hair, rubber tubes and syringes lay scattered over the floor and bed. Under some handkerchiefs I found a collection of pornographic photographs which, shocked and disgusted, I at once covered up again. The only thing that I brought away from Ypres as a souvenir was a stiff, red, clerical hat.

So Taylor (or, as I called him, Penbeagle, after his cottage in Cornwall) was gone. In this war the heroic gesture had to be paid for. I sat down to write a short biography of him in the tone of a poem by Laforgue—

Encore un de mes pierrots morts,
Mort d'un chronique orphelinisme.
C'était un cœur plein de dandyisme
Lunaire, en un drôle de corps.

In our provisional world, when we were all going to die so soon ourselves, that seemed to be the only tone to take about the dead. But
in fact I was too young to understand my friend properly. He was not
like Hope a man with sharp edges. It is only today, with the help of a
packet of his letters to me and a still larger packet of the vivid and
self-revealing ones he wrote to Hope, that I can form a picture of what
he was like. What I see then is a sad and rather fastidious man, unusu-
ally mature in character, who had a philosophy of *noblesse oblige* which
he had learned from Nietzsche. He felt deeply the tragedy of the war
and had volunteered for the most dangerous post he could find because he wished to spare himself nothing. He had suffered a good deal
from loneliness because, though getting on for thirty and decidedly
good-looking, he had never found a woman he wished to marry or
indeed any real friend except Hope. Much though I liked him I could
not claim that position, for the letters he wrote show that he regarded
me as a child: most of them began, with affectionate irony, 'Dear
Arabia', because I talked so much of that country, and he told Hope
that he did not give me many months to live because I had so little
sense of danger. He himself was full of premonitions that he would
soon be killed. 'I try to think', he had written a month or so before,
while the snow lay on the ground, 'how beautiful the spring will be
when everything, I mean the war, is intensified. I can imagine nothing
more real than the conjunction of death and, say, the first primroses
and lady-smocks.' Perhaps he did not mind dying too much because
he saw himself as a man without a future.

*

My cousin Byo had been killed at Hill 60 a few days after he had
come out in April. To please his mother I decided to set off once more
for Ypres and search for his grave. This time the city looked fresh and
glittering as I approached it, its broken, jagged towers rising white
and sharp, as though put up only yesterday, out of a ring of dark trees.
But the centre was now a complete ruin, all the roofs fallen in and the
debris piled twenty feet high inside. The plastered walls that were still
standing gleamed in the damp air like marble. Hill 60, a few miles to
the south-east, was an inconspicuous lump rising some thirty feet

above the treeless, pock-marked plain and containing an immense mine-crater on its summit. It had been continuously fought over, both above and below ground, and its surface had taken on that pitted, tormented aspect which so many sectors of the front were to show in the later stages of the war. Shell-craters, mounds, rotting sandbags, coils of wire, latrines, graves in jumbled proximity, with rats and flies and the faint, unescapable smell of putrefaction mingling with that of chloride of lime. I found the tiny cemetery where my cousin had been buried and came back.

Towards the end of June we moved south to Picardy, where a new British army was taking over the sector that stretched from below Arras to the Somme. After a week or two in reserve, among those unspoiled woods and châteaux where the brass-hats led their delectable lives, we took up our quarters at Hébuterne, a village that stood about a mile behind the front line. My honeymoon with the war was now over: I settled down in that bare, rolling country, where the front was quiet and static, to a monotonous marriage. Gone were the days of euphoria when I had written to Hope that I liked being under shellfire: that it made me want to run about and dance. I was now learning to take good care of myself in the hopes of living on into better times.

The first task that we were put to was that of repairing communication trenches. The deepest was a brick-lined one called Vercingétorix and at its lower end the dried-up hand of a dead German or Frenchman jutted out from the wall and some of the men when they passed by shook it to bring good luck. Then we were given a sector of the line to hold and I got a certain pleasure from going out on night patrols in the broad belt of country that divided our trenches from the German ones. Here, crouching in shell-holes, we would lie listening to the hammering on wooden pickets and the clanging of corrugated iron and see dim figures moving about as they worked on the wire. There was always a mystery and strangeness about this neutral zone which could not be visited by daylight, and it was safe enough, for we never met any German patrols.

The summer that year was a fine one and the trenches that the French had dug in the chalk seemed almost cosy after the miserable, waterlogged ones of Ypres or Armentières. Larks rose and sang in the sky and a carpet of aromatic plants—feverfew, camomile and wormwood—grew thick and luxuriant wherever the soil had been disturbed. These, with the famous poppies, were the plants of the front region. Yet in spite of the general lull there were still to be seen signs of past fighting. Once, exploring an old trench, I came on a strongpoint that the French had taken from the Germans: in it lay some twenty or thirty bodies, blackened by the sun and rain, and scattered round them a drift of letters, thrown out when their pockets had been rifled. I took some of them back and read them—no, the German people were not our enemies because they had the same feelings as ourselves. Whatever the papers might say, this was none of their doing.

I had a pretty little house all to myself on the edge of the village. The owners had only recently evacuated it and no one else had been anxious to take it over because a large unexploded shell was lodged in the sitting-room fireplace. There were geraniums and cactuses in the windows, a set of flower-patterned cups and plates in the cupboard, and in the garden twelve hives of bees against an old pisé wall and some gnarled pear trees. I was delighted to have managed to annexe such a peaceful-seeming place when every house round was more or less battered, though when I woke in the night and heard shells bursting close by I thought of that black iron cylinder lying only a yard away.

In the autumn we moved back to billets at a village called Bus-les-Artois some five miles behind Hébuterne. Here we were in a country of corn-ricks: on every hilltop there were clusters of them that looked in the evening light like African hut villages. The real villages were hidden among gardens and orchards and separated from one another by miles of empty, rolling stubble. In this place we settled down to spend the long, dull winter. As the staff could find no other work for us to do, we were put—what ignominy!—to mending the roads with occasional short spells in the front trenches. However, this allowed me to have the evenings to myself and I read, among other books, *War and Peace, Le Rouge et le Noir* and several volumes of Mardrus' translation of the *Arabian Nights*.

My letters to Hope and my literary effusions now begin to show a nostalgic obsession for those too-happy days I had spent in Provence and Italy, and at the same time an intense longing for the end of the war. I had also become taken up with the concept of original sin, by which I meant that lack or defect in human nature which shuts us out of the Eden we imagine we were born for. I liked to think that there must be some method for reaching that state—after Rimbaud I called it 'purity'—in which the mind and the feelings are completely awake and alive. I had begun reading Pascal to see if he had any remedy to offer me, only to find that he postponed the solution to a future existence in which I did not believe. For all round me, now, now, there existed a world of beauty and delight from which I was cut off, except for brief glimpses, by the shallowness and inadequacy of my nature.

That was why Blake's Emanation wept incessantly: here lay the tragic theme of life. Yet, though my thoughts on this subject have not changed, I cannot read these letters or literary compositions today without disgust because of the note of maudlin lamentation that fills them. When I was young I reacted to boredom and inactivity as some people do to toothache—that is, with cries of rage and self-pity—whereas hardship brought out the best in me.

My growing friendship with Ralph Partridge gave me on another level some relief from these morbid cogitations. I could not share with him my feelings about poetry or the inner life, for he was not, like Hope or Taylor, one of the elect, but on a more mundane footing we were good companions. I found his rollicking high spirits and zest for life irresistible. From the moment that he tumbled out of bed in the morning he was singing Dixieland songs (jazz had just begun to reach England) and his bright blue eyes were rolling like a negro's and his powerful body stamping and swaying as he put on his shirt or buttoned his jacket.

> *Way down in Tennessee,*
> *That's where I'm going to be,*
> *Back at my mother's knee,*
> *She thinks the world of me.*
> *All I can think of tonight*
> *Is a field of snowy white,*
> *Banjoes ringing, darkies singing,*
> *All the world is bright.*

I could not let myself go like that, but I envied his power of doing so.

Although Partridge, as I called him in those days, rarely opened a book, he had a good mind. At Westminster he had been head of the school and had shown his independence of character by refusing to play games. He who could have played them better than anyone else! Now, released from Oxford, he lived for enjoyment and girls. Yet he had another side, as when he sat in a heavy meditative silence absorbed in *The Times* or shut up like an oyster in himself. I could see him practising successfully at the bar, for there was an aggressive streak in his character which showed itself in his love of argument and in the exasperating manner in which he conducted it. 'You say . . .' he would begin, bringing out some opinion that one didn't in the least hold and then falling on it with the whole of his weight. However, these contentious moods of his were well spaced out: what I got most of the time was his exuberance and gaiety.

Although it was not till much later that Ralph became one of my closest friends, there was always an element of hero-worship in my liking for him. I admired his sexual prowess and I admired still more his obvious superiority as a soldier. One part of me was committed to the war and it was not difficult to see that under his indolent, pleasure-loving disposition there lay a magnificent infantry officer with a judgement that could always be relied on in practical matters and a complete confidence in himself. A Roman rather than a Greek by temperament, he called up—or so I then thought—Plutarch's portrait of Mark Antony. There was the same reserve of mental and physical energy, the same formidable presence when aroused and also the same tendency to indolence and sensuality. What was lacking was ambition, of which he had not a scrap. But just at present, on this quiet front, in our absurd unit, the only contribution we were asked to make towards winning the war was to fill up the puddles in the roads.

Since everything had become so dull it was only natural that we should seek some alleviation for our boredom in the hunt for girls, although in this I played a subordinate part because I was not attracted to prostitutes, who as a rule were the only ones available. The best place for them and for pleasures of every sort was Amiens, so we took to riding in there—of course without permission—whenever we were free from other duties. The distance might have been twenty miles. We would arrive in time to eat a splendid lunch at the big hotel in the square, after which Ralph would go off to meet the little tart with whom he corresponded while I, to his jeers and disgust, would visit the cathedral. Although its architecture and sculpture, so admired by Ruskin, left me cold, I would spend an hour or two staring in a trance at its stained glass. Later, while on training at the base, we made several expeditions to Le Tréport. Riding to the nearest level-crossing we would stop a goods train and make the driver give us a lift. The attraction here was the daughter of the chief of police and her cousin. They were both very plain, with pale goggle-eyes and snub noses, but as the champagne flowed their faces opened out and flowered till suddenly they were as lovely as houris. There we would lie reclining beside them on the sofa, while the *chef de police* sat replenishing his glass in the next room, with the door just sufficiently open for him to see that things were not going too far. Then at three in the morning, drunk with love, we would take a goods train back to repeat the process a few days later.

Madeleine, it suddenly comes back to me, was my girl's name. Every time I arrived and saw her I would shrink back in dismay, but then the champagne corks would pop and set her features right.

Ralph had a good voice and on fine afternoons we would sometimes walk out to a grassy bank and he would sing Border ballads. Although his ear was not perfect, he sang with great feeling, bringing the tears to my eyes. Sometimes a couple of little shepherdesses would join us, but the girls of the forward zones had been far too spoiled by the troops to allow any liberties. Their price for a chaste peck on the cheek was a gold wrist-watch. However, I did have one small and rather touching adventure all to myself. Between Bus and Hébuterne there is a village called Sailly-au-Bois where my platoon was mending the road. Just outside it there stood an isolated cottage and one day, as I was riding past it, the door opened and a girl threw a pail of dirty water over me. I got off and went inside to borrow a cloth. The cottage belonged to the village carrier and baker and he and his wife had a single daughter, aged perhaps fifteen. There she stood, barefooted and dressed in nothing but a short cotton smock that was thickly powdered with flour because it was she who kneaded the bread. Her long yellow hair fell loose onto her shoulders and her face and bare arms were dabbled with flour too. With every movement she made her smock showed her small breasts and slim figure.

I felt immediately attracted to this lovely girl, but though I went often to her house and brought her small presents I could not get a word out of her. She was petrified by shyness. Her mother, who had worked in a factory in Amiens, encouraged me wickedly, pulled up her smock to show me her thighs, pinched her breasts and once even pushed me playfully into the bedroom with her. But it was all of no use. She would not even smile at me. In the end, feeling that my presence upset her, I stopped going round.

In October 1915 I had my first leave and, concealing this from my parents, which gave me an uncomfortable feeling of guilt, went to stay with Hope in a cottage he had taken near Cranborne in Dorset. The sitting-room was very small and whitewashed inside so that with its thick walls of stamped chalk and its deep window embrasure, it looked like a white cave. All round it were beech woods, their leaves a fierce yellow against the blue sky: never had England seemed to me more beautiful. I found Hope in a depressed mood which had led him, for the first time in his life, to write some poems. They were very short—the longest had only seven lines—and in unrhymed *vers libre*. Two of them consisted chiefly of the names of towns and mountains in Central Asia. This seemed to make the writing of poetry very easy, but, as they were well phrased and conveyed a congenial mood of *sehnsucht*, I liked them. On the last day of my leave we went over for a night to Augustus John's house near Parkstone, but I will speak of that strange and romantic establishment later.

In February 1916—we were now back at Hébuterne—I went on leave again, but this time I stayed with my parents who were living in London because my father had a job guarding the Dock railways. I found my mother, like all her friends and acquaintances, full of the wickedness of the Germans. She had taken on, as she always did, the prevailing colour because she could not resist other people's opinions and also because her religion inclined her to believe that where there was a crime there must be a criminal. My father however—and I respected him for this—kept a soldierly reserve. He hated all exaggeration and later, disgusted by the carnage, came out for a negotiated peace. But in general one could not cross the Channel without being shocked by the atmosphere of unreality and hatred. The base camps were nasty too for they were full of shirkers and brass-hats who were making a good thing out of the war. The only decent and healthy place was the front line and, except during my idyllic interlude in the country with Hope, I was always glad to get back to it.

On my last night but one I went to a party at the Johns' house in Chelsea. It was the first party I had ever been to. I was feeling lost because I knew no one and was the only man to be in uniform when a woman with a rich guttural voice and a Russian accent came up to me. This was Alick Schepeler who had been a model of John's and after that Wyndham Lewis's mistress. She knew Yeats well and there was a story that he had once made a pass at her—or, as some said, proposed to her—in Coole Wood. She talked to me in her rich beautiful voice, the gins had their effect and we embraced passionately. But on seeing her next day my infatuation vanished as suddenly as it had come, for the morning light showed that she was a good deal older than I was. However, when I got back to France I had a fit of verse writing and threw off in great excitement half a dozen poems in *vers libre* upon her. They were in the ironic manner of Jules Laforgue and, thanks to his prompting, the most mature verses I had written up to now.

I think, though I cannot be quite sure—for it may have been eighteen months later—that it was on this visit to London that I met Ezra Pound. I was walking in Charlotte Street with Hope when we ran into him and on his hearing that I wrote poetry he invited us to the Eiffel Tower Restaurant for a drink. I was very glad to meet him because I had liked what I had read of his poems and particularly his translations from the Chinese. Indeed, I had written a parody of the last which Wyndham Lewis had promised, probably without meaning it, to publish in *Blast*.

We sat down and Pound started at once to hold forth on English poetry. There was a certain late medieval translation of the Aeneid (I imagine he meant Gavin Douglas's) which was fine, but after that there was practically nothing worth reading in English poetry down to mid-Victorian times. The Renaissance was rotten all through, though one might perhaps allow oneself a glance at some of the Elizabethan songs, and the Romantics were of course pure drivel. No, there was really nothing in English verse till one got to Swinburne and Browning. But French poetry—that was the stuff. First there was Villon—he was really great—and then after a long gap there were Corbière, Laforgue, Rimbaud and Paul Fort. They were the people to go to. Now it happened that I knew all these poets well except Paul Fort, whom I had not liked, so I began to talk about them. But soon it turned out that Pound had only a passing acquaintance with Rimbaud and appeared to know Laforgue merely through van Bever and Léautaud's anthology: Corbière and Villon were the ones he knew really well.

I felt deeply disillusioned. Pound's allusions to Chinese and German poets did not impress me, for what judgement could a man have on poetry if he ran down almost everything that had been written in his own language? And when later some of his crude and angry essays came my way I realized that he could only admire those poets whom he, Pound, had discovered. His vanity dictated his choice of what to praise, and he hated all the rest. I therefore put him down as a pretentious charlatan and did not for a long time read his later verse. This of course was a pity, but the young do not easily understand that a man can have enormous faults of literary judgement and even certain unpleasant paranoiac tendencies and yet in his best moments be a fine poet. And to be a fine poet is such a rare and difficult thing that it is worth the sacrifice of every other quality.

Spring came and our Divisional Cyclist Company was broken up and merged with other Cyclist Companies into the VIIIth Corps Cyclist Battalion. Ralph returned to his infantry regiment, but my application to do the same was turned down because for some time I had been running an observation post just outside Hébuterne and Corps H.Q. wished me to continue on that. My application to join the Flying Corps was also refused as had been my rather eccentric suggestion that I might attempt a one-man reconnaissance patrol behind the German front line. I was restless because, as the Somme offensive drew near, I was becoming increasingly concerned at not being more deeply engaged in the war.

Meanwhile Hope's situation was altering too. In spite of his weak eyesight he was called up and given the chance as a private in the infantry of discussing his theories of musketry with a real sergeant-major. But he was never to fire his rifle at the enemy, for, a few months later, he was transferred to the Intelligence Service and sent out to work on a Greek island under Compton Mackenzie. I was therefore left with no available friends.

Our Corps Cyclists now went back to train with the Cavalry—those fair-weather soldiers on whom it had not yet dawned that we were at war. After that two of our platoons were allotted as guards to the Corps Commander's château where they were kept busy sweeping the drive free of waste-paper and cigarette-ends. Not quite the duties for which they had enlisted, but under many British colonels and generals there lay a fussy old maid and General Hunter-Weston was one of the worst for spit and polish. Other platoons were given other peaceful tasks while I, after being attached for a week or two to the Kite Balloon Section—a post I did not enjoy because our balloons were continually being shot down in flames—was put in charge of the O.P. that I had had before. Here I was in luck, for the great attack that would drive the Germans back to the Rhine was imminent. Every day new batteries would arrive and begin registering, new light railways spring up, new shell-dumps be laid along the roads, new notice-boards make their appearance, while the woods and villages a little way behind were filling up with khaki figures till the whole countryside began to teem like an overstocked rabbit warren. The left hinge of our advance was to be an assault on the hamlet of Serre, which stood on a low rise immediately opposite my O.P., about three-quarters of a mile distant from our front trenches, and my task would be to send back reports of how the fighting went to the beautiful, well-kept château that lay so far behind the line.

The battle opened a little after sunrise on 1 July 1916, with a bombardment that shook the air with its roar and sent up the earth on the German trenches in gigantic fountains. It seemed as if no human being could live through that. Then our men climbed by short ladders onto the parapet and began to move forward shoulder to shoulder, one line behind the other, across the rough ground. They moved slowly because each of them carried a weight of 66 pounds. Then the German barrage fell on our trenches and their machine-guns began to rattle furiously. Clouds of blue and grey smoke from the bursting shells, mixing with a light ground mist, hid the general view, but in the gaps I could see the little ant-like figures, some of them keeping on in a broken line, others falling, crawling, lying still. Each of them carried on his back a tin triangle to assist in their identification by our artillery, and the early morning sun shone on these triangles and made them glitter. But as the hours passed I could not see that any of them had reached the German front line and later I knew why: our bombardment had not penetrated the deep dugouts the Germans had excavated in the chalk and their machine-gunners had come out and were mowing our men down.

I sent off a report and then set out across country to see if I could get a closer view. Just behind our front trenches, by the broken tree-stumps known as Matthew and Mark copses, shallow assault trenches had been dug to hold the second, third and fourth waves. I later learned that they had been manned in the wrong order and that this had led to confusion when the moment for advancing came. Indeed, two of the waves had never started at all. And now a terrible artillery barrage had fallen on them and was churning up the earth all round. Suddenly out of the smoke and flying dirt a man whose face and uniform were smeared with blood came staggering back, his features distorted with terror and crying out something I could not in that infernal din understand. I could see nothing ahead of me through the barrage so, as there was no communication trench and the pieces of metal were whizzing round me and the fountains of earth spurting up in front, I turned back to my O.P. which was now being sprinkled with gas shells.

The sun rose higher and higher in the sky, the heat of that scorching summer day grew and grew, but though I was never able to get any coherent picture, the failure of our assault on Serre gradually became obvious. Those three or four hundred yards of rough ground that lay in front of our lines were thickly sprinkled with silver triangles, only a few of which still moved, while the German parapet was bare. And still the pounding of our front trenches went on. Then darkness fell and the stories began to come in. They told of appalling casualties, of whole battalions reduced to thirty or forty men, and I have since read that no British army corps had ever before suffered such losses in a single day. The pick of our young men, the first to volunteer for the war, were dead and on our corps front not a yard of ground had been gained.

And this was not all. During the next few days terrible stories began to come in from the survivors of parties that had got through to the outskirts of Serre. After fifty-six hours spent in shell-holes, sleeping among and even pillowed on their dead comrades, without water, without food, having to defend themselves all the time, a few of the more determined had managed to creep or fight their way back through the German lines to tell their tale. I saw two of them and they looked like men who had been pulled out of a mine after being entombed for a week by an explosion.

It was not long before I was brought face to face and in the most repellent way with the final consequences of this battle. Perhaps ten days had passed since our attack or perhaps it was longer, when I got orders to take my platoon to Colincamps, a mile or two along the ridge from Hébuterne, for a burial party. The bodies—hundreds of them—were being brought up every night on a trench railway from the front line and bundled out onto the ground. Legs had broken off from trunks, heads came off at a touch and rolled away, and horrible liquids oozed out of the cavities. A sickening stench filled the air and obscene flies crept and buzzed about, not to speak of the worms that wriggled in the putrefaction. Our job was to cut the identity numbers from these corpses and then to shovel them into shallow trenches which we had dug near by. At the end of three days of this—and I took a shovel and worked myself—I found that my morale had completely vanished: I knew that if I were asked to go over the top next morning I should not be able to. The stench had brought the fear of death to my very bones.

Meanwhile, I had left my O.P., where my work was over, and been given the armband of an A.P.M. or Provost Marshal. I slept in a cellar at Sailly, which was being slowly bombed to bits (all the civilians had long been evacuated), and had the job of patrolling the roads under the orders of a pleasant, amusing man called Captain Coatesworth. It was the softest job I had ever had, for I was off duty every other day.

One morning as I was out on my patrol I ran into Ralph's battalion marching up to the line. There he was himself on his old grey mare, Bucephala, together with several familiar Divisional Cyclist faces. The column drew up for a five-minute halt, the men fell out by the roadside and I was able to talk to him. He told me that his battalion had gone over the top on July 1st and had suffered heavy casualties, but that he himself had been kept back in reserve. After that they had been taken out to refit and were now going in again for the second time. I think I must have said to him that I was expecting to go to Amiens,

for he asked me to get him some delicatessen and send them to him if I
could not come myself.

My trip to Amiens, however, did not come off. Perhaps it was the
burial party that prevented me from going. Then on July 14th a second
attack was launched to the east of Albert and a few square miles of
territory and several villages were gained. I decided to set off with my
faithful Dartnell, see what I could of the battlefield and take a few tins
of *pâté* that I had by me to Ralph. After staring for so long at the line
of German trenches that stretched like an iron frontier from Switzerland to the sea, I had a strong desire to see what was on the other side.

At this point I must break off for a moment to speak as a historian
of my sources. Up to now I have almost always had some letter or
scrap of writing or even full literary description on which to base my
recollections, which naturally after the passage of so many years vary
greatly in clearness and intensity. Also I have always had exact dates.
For this month, however, I have nothing to rely on but a long hurried
letter to my father which runs together two separate trips to the battle
zone. Some of the scenes and places mentioned in it I can remember
vividly, while others have totally gone. Obviously a sightseeing expedition like this into the back regions of a battle is much harder to
recall than events in which one was personally engaged.

After passing through Albert, gaunt and shattered from the shelling
it had received, we left our cycles with a sentry and continued on foot.
As we crossed the old front line we seemed to be leaving a windswept
yet solid shore for a treacherous, chaotic region recently abandoned by
the tide. The further we went the more desperate and confused the
landscape became—shattered woods and villages, shattered trenches,
abandoned equipment and then unburied bodies. But it was also
thickly populated: there was a continuous heavy traffic of mule-
drawn limbers and wagons choking the roads and tracks and all
round us batteries of guns were firing from the open without any
attempt at camouflage and soldiers were camping by companies and
battalions round their stacked rifles in great open bivouacs. The whole
country swarmed with khaki figures, some on carrying parties, others
cooking or brewing tea in black dixies, others lying on the ground or
sitting up to clean their rifles or rewind their putties. Others again were
foraging for firewood or souvenirs or squatting to relieve themselves.
After a little we came to a large wood which the map told me was
Mametz Wood. Its trees were torn and shattered, its leaves had turned
brown and there was a shell-hole every three yards. This was a place
where something almost unheard of in this war had taken place—

fierce hand-to-hand fighting in the open with bombs and bayonets. What seemed extraordinary was that all the dead bodies there lay just as they had fallen in their original places as though they were being kept as an exhibit for a war museum. Germans in their field-grey uniforms, British in their khaki lying side by side, their faces and their hands a pale waxy green, the colour of a rare marble. Heads covered with flat mushroom helmets next to heads in domed steel helmets that came down behind the ears. Some of these figures still sat with their backs against a tree and two of them—this had to be seen to be believed—stood locked together by their bayonets which had pierced one another's bodies and sustained in that position by the tree trunk against which they had fallen. I felt I was visiting a room in Madame Tussaud's Chamber of Horrors, for I could not imagine any of those bodies having ever been alive. Yet the effect in its morbid way was beautiful.

On beyond, in the direction of Bazentin le Grand, the fighting had also been very heavy. Both sides had dug themselves in with entrenching tools and round one hastily scraped-up gun emplacement, which commanded a drive through the trees, the khaki bodies lay in heaps. We kept on across the battlefield—corpses of men, dead horses and mules, rifles, hand-grenades, gas-masks, those gimcrack spiked helmets worn by the Boche on parade, water-bottles, scattered like the debris on a beach after a winter storm—till we came to Trônes Wood which, though greatly battered, had kept its green leaves. Here we were close to the front line and machine-gun bullets began to whistle over us, so, as I could not get any news of Ralph's battalion, we turned back. After this my memory becomes hazy. All I remember is that we ran into heavy shelling, had to skirt a shattered village that was being 'strafed' and finally got back to Albert. Here I made the inquiries that I ought to have made at the beginning and learned that the 6th Warwicks were at Ovillers on the extreme left of our new salient. But it seemed too late to go there now, so we turned for home, putting off our visit to Ralph to another day.

If this expedition took place, as it must have done, between the 16th of July and the 19th, then my visit to Ralph must be dated to between the 20th and the 23rd. We stopped for a moment in Albert to watch two battalions coming out of the line. How familiar this sight was becoming! One fine morning one would see them marching up from the back villages, the men singing and their uniforms neat and clean. A week later one would run into them coming back, haggard and filthy, shambling, limping and shuffling along and half, or perhaps less than half, their previous strength. A few days of a Somme battle were sufficient to effect this change.

We left the town by the main Bapaume road, passed through what was left of La Boisselle and turned off towards Ovillers. Everything here was in a terrible state, the ground torn up by shells and littered with dead bodies, some of which had been lying around for three weeks. The stench was quite unbearable. In the first attack on July 1st it had been impossible to rescue the wounded and one could see how they had crowded into shell-holes, drawn their waterproof sheets over them and died like that. Some of them—they were north-country troops—had taken out their Bibles.

I found Partridge commanding a company. The further end of the trench he was occupying was held by the Germans. What was needed, he said, was to bomb up it so as to reach a machine-gun that was holding up our advance, but his men were tired and not out for taking risks. He himself seemed to be completely in his element: he described the part he had taken in the battle for Ovillers, speaking in his usual half-jocular, half-ironic tone, and then went on to talk of the present situation. Meanwhile his batman had set out lunch, which consisted of a tin of Hungarian goulash washed down with a bottle of German champagne, followed by a German cigar. While he smoked it he began to talk in a more serious and gloomy manner.

As usual, he said, the staff was execrable. It took hours to get messages back to Brigade H.Q. and the orders they received from them were usually impossible to carry out because they came too late. A thing that had happened again and again was that our troops pushed their way up a trench and took a strongpoint without loss and were then told to retire in order to consolidate. Two hours later, there having been no change in the meantime, they would be ordered to retake the strongpoint, which was now full of Germans, by a frontal attack. This might be impossible, but it had to be tried and perhaps fifty men would be killed in the attempt.

The letter to my father on which I have been drawing now breaks, in a way that amazes me today, into a eulogy of battle. Although, I wrote, everything one could see was horrible, I could not help liking it. Partridge, when he was out in rest, always longed to get back and had even said that he wished the war would go on for ever. In fact, it was only kept going by the presence on either side of a few men like him, for the majority had no heart in it and would down arms on the first opportunity. The really demoralizing thing was the stench of dead bodies, which never left one.

Considering this again today, I feel sure that Ralph thought as I did that war was horrible and looked forward to its end. But the young love to test themselves and a battle is a great challenge. Anyone who feels himself rising superior to that challenge experiences a sense of power and elation and he had risen so far above it that he must at times have felt that war was his true vocation. For this reason I envied him for being in the thick of things while I was still an *embusqué*, yet I could not help wondering how well I would show up under such circumstances. I knew that I could take shell-fire, for I was doing it all the time, but there was a small voice inside me that persisted in asking how I should stand charging a machine-gun or bombing with my weak arms down a trench or dealing with a German bayonet. I might have a certain brittle sort of courage, but I did not feel in myself the solid stuff of a good soldier.

A few days after my return from seeing Ralph the VIIIth Corps, or what was left of it, got its marching orders. We were to set off for the Ypres Salient. An easy six days' trek on our cycles took us to Vox Vrie Farm near Poperinghe where, for lack of anything better to do, we began to train for the break-through that would certainly come in the spring. For wasn't the German manpower melting away in the heat of our great Somme offensive? A writer called Hilaire Belloc, who up till now had thought of this war in terms of Napoleon's campaigns, was publishing every week in *Land and Water* an article that proved statistically that the Germans were almost at the end of their resources. We were winning the war by attrition. I tried to think that he was right, but couldn't quite manage to because I had seen so many of our own dead.

CHAPTER XIV

Ypres, Passchendaele and the Marne

I spent the next six weeks with my battalion at Vox Vrie Farm. Our colonel was a tall, bleak-looking man, impressive on the parade ground, whose chief interest in life lay in his two dogs. I found him pleasant and easy to get on with, but as a soldier he was unsure of himself and afraid of responsibility. None of my brother officers attracted me especially so I spent most of my evenings at Skindle's Club in Poperinghe, reading for the second time Gibbon's *Decline and Fall*. On Sundays and free afternoons I would explore the country on my cycle, especially the windmill-crowned Mont de Cats, but now that Ralph was no longer there to encourage me I took little interest in girls. I had been told that I was to be put in charge of an O.P. in the Ypres salient and was waiting for that.

Meanwhile I went on leave and found my parents established in a new house. Miserden Park had been bought by one of the Willses of tobacco fame and since my father did not care to live 'under the thumb of a man who stank of money' and Mr Wills wanted our house for his estate agent, we moved a mile along the hilltop to a farm-house in the small village of Edgeworth. It had been sold to my father by the squire, a confirmed bachelor who, like his elder brother, recently deceased, was famous both for his fear of women and for his dislike of entertaining. Except on the three days of the annual pheasant shoot, no one was ever invited to a meal in his house. But during the past year or two Mr Alfred James had formed a close friendship with my father. He was the first friend of his own age my father had ever been known to have and since Mr James was not given to friends either, it surprised everyone.

Our new house was modern and, in spite of its sober Cotswold materials, ugly because its proportions were bad. But it was compact and dry—two things that Miserden House had not been and which my father with his love of neatness greatly appreciated. What *I* liked about it was its situation, for the valley fell steeply away from the edge of the garden to the stream, which meandered along through its ribbon of water-meadow far below. The slopes were hidden by beeches, the abode of screech-owls and nightjars, and the whole district was so thickly wooded that one could walk for miles in almost any direction without coming out of the trees.

In the first days of October 1916 I moved into my new O.P. on the east bank of the Ypres Canal. If one thinks of the Salient as a flattened semicircle with its centre at Ypres, then the Canal followed the line of its base. Three miles to the north of the city the German trenches came down to it and followed it to the sea. This sector was held by the Belgians and my O.P. stood rather less than a mile from where they began.

The Ypres Canal was at this time a decidedly unprepossessing place. Broader than most English canals and shut in on either side by raised embankments, it had taken on the baleful aspect of the front region and grew more and more sinister and tainted as it approached the point where it became the boundary between the two lines. With the destruction of the locks, much of its water had run out, leaving only a few feet of black oily liquid resting on a bed of black and even oilier mud. Broken branches and nameless objects of twisted metal rose out of its surface and the rats had perforated its banks in many places with their tunnels. The more daring of these crept about by day, but after dark they swarmed, so that if one turned one's torch onto a garbage can one would see twenty or thirty fat wriggling creatures scrambling obscenely over it. To supply the front line a number of light bridges, made of duckboards, had been put up and each of these had its special character. The two most northerly (numbers 6 and 7 if I remember right) were little used because they were under view of the Germans by day and by night swept by machine-gun fire, whereas the more southerly were frequently shelled, especially after dark when the mule transport came up the road and trench reliefs were carried out. Number 4 Bridge, which adjoined my O.P., was one of these.

But if the Ypres Canal was no longer a thoroughfare for barges, it had become a street for people. Both its banks had been excavated to form a line of dugouts, built of black circular steel and covered over with bricks and earth, which made them proof against everything but a direct hit by a 5.9. Here were lodged the Battalion H.Q. and Quartermaster's Stores of the troops in the line, the Advanced Dressing Station and the Signals. I occupied one of these dugouts on the west bank, immediately opposite my O.P., and my twelve men were lodged in a large one next door. I had a bed, two tables, a chest of drawers and a shelf for books, while my cooking was done on a Primus stove in the porch.

This snug but sombre little cave was to be my home during the next six months. Here I lived in a deliberately Spartan style, eating nothing but a biscuit for lunch and for supper a Maggi soup tablet dissolved in a stew of vegetables and sometimes a little meat. In those days I did not smoke and drank only on special occasions, but I allowed myself several brews a day of the best Mocha coffee and plenty of Lapsang Souchong tea. I kept two stray cats and, as I rarely had a visitor, came to feel rather like one of the anchorites of the desert.

My principal duty was to observe what the Germans were doing. The view from our O.P. showed a brown, featureless plain, riddled with shell-craters, all of which were filled with water, and ending about a mile away in a low rise known as the Pilckem Ridge. Just below the summit of this stood High Command Redoubt, the principal position on the German front line. We would scan it for signs of fresh digging, but rarely saw any, while on many days the weather was so thick that we did not even man our post. I used therefore to take our smaller telescope round to other points of the line and try what I could see from them. In this way I got to know our trench system pretty well and as much as could be seen of the Germans'.

My other duty was to report at first hand both on our raids and on the enemy ones. This did not make me popular with the battalion and company commanders, who distrusted anyone who was connected with the Staff, but they could not prevent me from being in the front trenches to watch our men going over and coming back. The German raids were a different matter. The moment their artillery barrage began I would be out of bed and down the communication trench with one of my men who had been told off before to be ready. As soon as it ceased we would go through, and that was always an uncanny experience. The shattered trenches, the reek of powder, the black darkness fitfully lit up by a flare, the knowledge that one was approaching the site of the just committed crime, on the very steps of the possibly not yet departed raiders, were decidedly unnerving. Once, knocking against something with my foot, I turned on my torch and saw a man's head completely severed from his body. Then, when one came to the front line, there would be the groans of the wounded or shell-shocked and the shattered looks of the men who had survived. No one who has not lived through one of these barrages can form any conception of what they were like. The whole earth, even if one is in a dugout, appears to rock and shudder. The air is filled by a persistent rushing sound, broken by the crash of explosions, while if it is daylight one can see the shells passing like long ghostly pencils overhead and if it is dark one is dazzled by the light flashes. The mind cannot think, the arms and legs tremble automatically and the tough man is the one who recovers quickest. In these trench raids the weight of shells fired per twenty yards would be as much as in the preliminary bombardment of a great battle, and I have been told by men who were at Alamein and in the Normandy landings that the shelling there did not compare with that of the First World War.

In these German raids my relations with the infantry were especially delicate. At such nerve-racking moments the company officers did not want an outsider around. And the report I would send in would, as everyone knew, be valueless because it would merely duplicate that of the battalion commander. It was only if I were reporting on the progress of a battle that I could be of any use at all. Yet if there had been one or two able and intelligent staff officers who lived with the troops during battles and whose only duty was to observe and comment on what happened, it is possible that the infiltration tactics, which in 1918 nearly won the war for the Germans, might have been adopted by us much earlier. What no one on our side took in was that, thanks to the power of the machine-gun, a small unit could hold its own with both flanks exposed. The generals of the First World War not only lacked imagination but were out of touch with battle conditions. These defects could not make up for their administrative skill in handling large bodies of men and in mounting attacks.

The Ypres Salient was a melancholy place in which to spend the winter months. East of the Canal the country was far more blasted and eroded by the war than the Somme had been. Not a trace of a house remained and the trees, when they still existed, were reduced to stumps. The ground was pock-marked with shell-craters and after crossing Bridge 4 one had to keep to the communication trenches, which were built up with sandbags. For this was the sector where the gas attack had been launched and it had been fought over again and again.

To the west of the Canal, however, it was very different. Here the trees, though torn and dishevelled, continued to put out leaves, and the farms, though knocked to pieces, still existed. No one lived here for the soil was waterlogged. All the ditches and ponds were full to the brim and even the shell-holes had developed an aquatic vegetation like the pools in sea rocks. In some places the thistles and aromatic plants had grown to extravagant heights, while the grass that covered the fields was long and tangled by the rain so that one tripped over it as one walked. Little sodden woods and copses swelled the angles of the hedges and round every shattered farm there was a moat filled with black water and occupied by a pair of moorhens. There were plenty of partridges too in spite of the spent bullets that soughed past overhead. Seeing this, I had brought out my gun from England with the idea of shooting some for the pot, but after bringing down a brace or two and winging others, I gave it up. There was enough killing and maiming at Ypres already.

Since my work did not take up all my time I was left with several hours a day for reading. I had with me a number of travel books on Central Asia and also a collection of Tolstoy's later stories and religious tracts. When I first read these last they produced a strong effect on me. I saw the war as wicked and senseless and wondered whether I ought not to declare myself a pacifist and submit to a court martial. Then, as I knew I had not got it in me to do that, it occurred to me that I might desert and escape across the Pyrenees to Spain and the free life on the roads that I longed for. But this mood did not last for long: almost against my will I was acquiring a sense of responsibility. The demon of the war could not be ignored nor could my pride in being ready to take anything that came to me. In a more than usually objective letter that I wrote Hope in January I reproached him for his defeatism. There was nothing, I said, to show that we were either winning or losing. The generalship might be bad, but hadn't that been true of most of our wars? Meanwhile I could not see that there was anything to be done but hold on and hope that the end would come some day, for no peace would prove lasting that did not follow from the complete defeat of the German army. Then, answering a question of his, I said that the worst thing about the war was not the fighting, which was soon over, but the boredom which went on and on. Yet even this was preferable to the hatred and hysteria that were worked up at home by the women, the old men and the newspapers.

Yet perhaps I was exaggerating the boredom. I found my work interesting. I no longer felt so envious of the infantry, for I was as much swallowed up in the war as they were. If my life was more comfortable, I was a permanent resident at the front, whereas they were relieved every fortnight. However, there was a sense of envy all the same. I had recently been gazetted a captain, not through any merit of my own but by the mere effect of casualties in the 5th Gloucesters, though, as my battalion commander seemed unaware of it, I was careful not to inform him lest he feel obliged to withdraw me from my O.P. and give me a cyclist company back among the hop-fields of Poperinghe. But I should have liked to command an infantry company in the line. The mess in the tiny dugout with its charcoal brazier, the bottle of whisky on the table, the red faces warmed by candlelight, the inspections and working parties and wiring parties and stand-to's at dusk and dawn made up a routine that had the power to absorb one utterly. I longed to lose myself in the little group, bound together by their duties and their mutual obligations and by their ever-present awareness of danger, and slough off my sick and feeble individuality in a sense of responsibility for others. And when I consulted my cult hero, Rimbaud, I saw that he had ended by feeling the same.

In the last days of March I was told that I was to move into another and better O.P. a couple of miles away, but before going there I was to have two days' special leave at St Omer. A staff car came to fetch me and I remember my delight at seeing women and children and cows and farmyard animals as well as houses that had not been shelled. The only animals at Ypres, apart from my two cats, were mules and rats, and I had not driven in a car since the war began. On arriving at St Omer I put up at the Hôtel de France and after dinner exchanged a few flirtatious words and a kiss with a young waitress. An hour later I was lying in bed reading Sven Hedin when she opened the door and turned off the light. Then, fully dressed, she jumped into bed beside me. The sequel was peculiar. By the way she threshed about I realized that she was a virgin and had not the least idea of what going to bed with a man entailed. Unable to convince her that she might at least remove her shoes, I gave up, turned over on my side and went to sleep. Next morning she woke early, gave me a hurried kiss and left the room, no doubt delighted that she had at last discovered what was meant by sleeping with a man. I was pleased too, for the encounter had left a faintly pleasant taste behind it, as though a wild animal had condescended to sit on my lap, and none of the usual disillusion. The last time I had been to bed with a girl—with a peasant at Merris, three days after I had landed in France—I had been left wondering why I had done it.

My new O.P. was in a disused brick-field known as La Brique, just to the north of the city: I had three fairly good dugouts and a wide view over almost the whole of the Salient, but the German lines were more than a mile away. Two thin elm trees stood out on the top of the hill, so we drove horseshoes into the trunk of one of them and, as the leaves came out, thickened them with green camouflage. Then we installed our best telescope some thirty feet above the ground.

This front was suddenly becoming important and with it, in its tiny way, my O.P. I was now supplied with full intelligence bulletins and the latest air photographs and encouraged to make myself an authority on the whole northern half of the Salient. Generals and staff officers would call at my dugout—among them was the Army Commander, Gough—and sometimes they would require me to take them to some point in the line. Since the times and places of German shelling could usually be predicted, I was able to conduct them by the safest route.

As the summer drew on I learned that our big attack of the year was going to be launched in my sector. The Germans appeared to know it too. Most of the traffic that supplied the Salient had to pass through Ypres and so morning, evening and night the heavy shells would fall on it, scattering clouds of whitish dust from the great mound of the Cathedral and Cloth Hall that rose like a ruined Babylonian temple above the heaps of rubble which were all that remained of houses and streets. I had watched this beautiful city crumble slowly away through the past two years and now nothing but bricks and stones were left.

One morning in late June a distressing thing happened. I was sitting just outside the door of my dugout waiting for breakfast when a few whizz-bangs began to fall near. As one of them seemed to be coming rather close, I tipped back my chair to get better protection. At that moment my batman (a temporary one, for Dartnell was on leave) was approaching with my coffee. He was not more than three yards away from me when a shell hit him and burst. I was blown back down the steps, but not hurt. We picked up what was left of him, put him on a stretcher and carried him to the cemetery by the Canal bank. A grave was waiting, the padre was there, so the service was recited at once and the earth shovelled in. A cross with his name and regimental number stamped on an aluminium ribbon was put up to mark the spot. Then I walked back to my dugout and found another breakfast waiting.

A man whom I did not know very well had been killed within a few feet of me. That was something that had happened to me several times before. One learned to shut one's mind to such things for, if one didn't, one would not be able to carry on. But the rapidity of this proceeding shocked me. While a second breakfast was being made for me this man, still warm, had been buried and prayed for and had a cross put over him. That brought the inhumanity of war home.

The great advance was to begin at dawn on 31 July 1917. I was to go over with the second wave and send back reports on how it went by runner. The weather was fine, the ground dry and, as tanks were to be used, I was, like everyone else, full of optimism. Then came a pleasant surprise. Ralph's battalion was to attack on my sector and one morning he arrived at my O.P. to look at the ground. Since I had last seen him he had had the terrible experience of being buried alive by a shell and dug out when almost dead by the loyal persistence of his batman. Then he had been back in England, had been awarded a well-deserved Military Cross, and here he was out again. He was very pleased to learn that I was at last to go over the top and it was settled that I would pay him a visit.

On the morning of the 29th I was standing outside my dugout when a heavy shell burst some distance away. Then I heard a piece of metal flying slowly towards me: it hit me and knocked me down. I got up and saw that my sleeve and the side of my coat were torn and oozing with blood. The wound seemed quite light so I tied it up and walked down to the Advanced Dressing Station on the Canal bank to have it dressed. The R.A.M.C. major looked at it and bound it up and then told me that he was sending me back at once to the Base Hospital. At first I could not believe my ears: all I had was a cut on my arm and another on my side and I felt perfectly well able to carry on. So I expostulated, pointing out that my work was important, that Corps H.Q. relied on getting my reports of the battle and that there was no other officer to take my place, but he refused to change his mind. It was a deep disappointment to me because I had worked out carefully what I meant to do and no one likes to have his plans upset.

At the First Field Hospital a Canadian surgeon operated on me immediately. I should soon be well again, but in the tent next door I could hear the groans of those who had severe stomach wounds. Nothing could be done for them, so they had been left to die. I could not sleep for thinking of them. Then twenty-four hours later I was in a military hospital at Camberwell. After a week or so I was able to go out and enjoy the experience of having girls get up to offer me their seat on a bus. I was a wounded hero and yet I did not know a soul in London except my great-aunt. In the Soho restaurants I saw girls with bobbed hair who I knew must be artists, but though I longed to speak to them, I could not.

Ralph wrote to me from the line, where he was holding a post in the mud. 'The rain', he wrote, 'has made a glutinous mass of everything—great muscular tanks stand on their haunches and essay vainly to move round, while the perfectly good *Morituri* entone *mañana*, disheartened with just keeping their heads above water at the shallow end of the camp.' Then at the end of August he was wounded and sent back to England with a bar to his Military Cross. I went to see him in hospital and when he had recovered he left with his regiment for Italy and saw little more of the war.

In October I was released from hospital and posted to the Herts Yeomanry at Sevenoaks: their horses had been taken from them and replaced by cycles and none of them had yet been out to France. A week or so after my joining them they were sent to Colchester for intensive training before going abroad. As I had no desire at all to accompany them and sit about at the Base with the Army Service Corps and the Cavalry, I wrote to my old C.O. asking if he would apply for me to be sent back to my O.P.

Meanwhile I had reached a little oasis in the dreary desert of the war and the next six weeks provided an explosion of happiness. Taking a boat from Salcott, I went down the narrow estuary with the tide, landed at West Mersea and returned by moonlight. It was a repetition of a trip I had made with three of my men soon after I had joined the Divisional Cyclists and it led to a long 'hallucinated' prose poem something in the manner of Rimbaud's *Bateau Ivre*. A fortnight later I spent my leave on a five days' walking tour in the Lakes. The passes were covered with snow, a low sun shone palely in the sky and the mountain air was crisp and sharp. I was deep in Wordsworth at the time and after I got back I wrote a long poem called *Ecstasy* in Words-worthian blank verse.

Hope had returned from Greece and was working in the Foreign Office. He came down to see me, bringing a bottle of mescaline which I took without any effect. One could always tell whom he had been mixing with from the style and subjects of his conversation and now I found him full of gossip about political intrigues and little interested in Eastern travel or in the ascetic mode of life we had worked out on the roads and in which I still believed. But he was ready to talk about poetry, in which he had a good eye for the significant passage or line. Among other poets whom I remember we discussed was T. S. Eliot. I had been greatly impressed by the poems of his that had appeared in 1915 in the *Catholic Anthology* and now *Prufrock* had come out in book form. Hope knew Eliot, 'a curious, rather deliberately *posé* American', and admired his work, but thought that he had been too much in-fluenced by Jules Laforgue. His verse, he said, was not nearly so poign-ant as that of Laforgue, which was after all made up from poignancy. He struck him as being more sophisticated and less sincere, though still perhaps the most interesting of the younger poets. As for Pound, he could not make up his mind. There was so much fluff and nonsense about him, but *Cathay* was very beautiful.

I remember that while I agreed with Hope over Pound I thought Eliot's *Prufrock* had a strength and condensation as well as a vividness of imagery that the lighter and more fluid verse of Laforgue lacked.

Another contemporary whom I admired, but Hope did not, was James Joyce. I had not thought much of his *Portrait of the Artist*, but when *Ulysses* began to appear in the *Little Review* I was full of enthusiasm for its vividness. D. H. Lawrence, on the other hand, I did not take to at all. *The White Peacock* had seemed to me a very feeble affair and it was ten years or more before I read anything else by him. Outside the Middleton Murry set no one that I knew spoke of him, and they seemed to me squalid.

Christmas came and I learned that I was to be sent back to my unit in France. That was what I wanted and I at once wrote a letter to Hope expressing my delight. All through the war I fluctuated between three attitudes towards it. In one I would recall in rapturous detail the life I had led on the roads in Provence and Italy and wish at any cost to survive in order to return to it. This intense longing, which was almost like that of a lover for his wife or mistress, fills pages of my letters to Hope. But then there was the Demon, the spirit of the front line and of the battle, that drew me like so many other men of my age towards it. It seemed to offer the only *real* life to be had at that time and it was a mark of escapism and of denial of the will to live to try to avoid it. My hatred of the poisonous war atmosphere in England, whipped up daily by the Northcliffe press, and of the smug safety-first of the Base camps increased my wish to be totally committed. And to this must be added pride: among the crowd of *embusqués* I felt proud of being a front-line soldier and I would have felt prouder still if I had been in the infantry. Lastly there was the moral attitude. If I usually thought of the war as a volcanic eruption for which no one was responsible, there were other times when I thought of it as a thing brought about and kept going by human intentions. And then it horrified me. In June, when I was living in comparative safety and much absorbed in my work, I had written to Hope:

'Any talk of which side is in the right is altogether beside the question while this slaughter is going on. At times it makes an impression upon me so dreadful that I cannot express it. One wonders how all the people who countenance this under some ludicrous pretext or another can have hearts so petrified. Also I wonder how people can possibly delude themselves that they are following the teaching of Christ.'

But I was never able to reconcile these three modes of feeling to one another, though my conduct showed that, when not influenced by emotion, I believed that the only practicable course for the Allies was to fight on till they won and that I myself could only preserve my integrity if I shirked nothing.

In January 1918 I left Colchester for Tonbridge to await the order to cross to France. Here I was attached to another Yeomanry battalion and messed with a crowd of rich, self-satisfied men who after three and a half years of war had still not seen a shot fired or a shell explode. Till I was much older I was subject to violent fits of disgust and anger against people who seemed to express too blatantly the bourgeois attitude to life, and so now in a letter to Hope I exploded with rage against these 'unspeakably disgusting, hog-like officers who seemed to think of nothing but eating and drinking all day'. Among them there was 'a pot-bellied Academy artist' who shared a room with me and especially excited my indignation. One of his sayings was, 'I get as much genuine *aesthetic* pleasure from a good dinner with liqueurs and coffee and a clean shirt front, a cigar after it, as from any picture in the National Gallery. The masses should be encouraged to feel this and to encourage the artist who feels it even more strongly than they do.' And I ended my letter: 'Oh for floods, invasions, fire, water, sword for these animals! I would cheerfully give my life too that we might all be exterminated.'

A few weeks later I was back with my battalion at Poperinghe. Here I learned that the men who had served with me at the O.P. had suffered heavy casualties during the first days of our attack: those that survived were all wearing medals. My C.O. told me that he had recommended me for a Military Cross and that the VIIIth Corps Staff had supported his recommendation so that he had been surprised not to see my name in the Birthday honours. But I didn't care. All I wanted was to get back to an observation post. A few days after I had been wounded my observers' unit had been withdrawn for lack of a suitable officer to command it, but now that I was back the Staff were anxious to set up another in Passchendaele. Although my C.O. had at last discovered that I was a captain, he agreed to put off giving me the company I was entitled to and to let me go back to my old job.

The five months' battle that was to have broken through the German defences and sent them scurrying back to Antwerp had carried us less than six miles forward over a dreary expanse of mud to what had once been the village of Passchendaele. This place with the beautiful name crowned a low ridge which provided cover from view till one was almost in the front line. My O.P. was a tiny ramshackle affair put up on the site of a demolished house, but our living-quarters lay nearly three miles back in a large white concrete 'pillbox' known as Kansas House and built by the Germans. It was panelled with wood and completely waterproof and shell-proof, but it had sunk a good deal in the mud and one had to stoop low to enter it. Here I settled down in the middle of March with my dozen men.

The country round was as strange to look at as anything I had ever seen. All about us stretched a broad, slightly undulating plain composed of brown sodden earth and of shell-craters filled to the brim with water. These craters touched and intersected one another so frequently that it sometimes seemed as if more space was occupied by the round pools than by the enclosing mud. The valleys were completely flooded and not only was there no sign of houses or trees, except for an occasional stump, but there was no grass or vegetation. The only objects that stood out of this morass were the white German pillboxes, massive and rounded as elephants, and now and then in the back regions a half-buried tank. In the fine misty weather this barren scene was beautiful.

It goes without saying that there were no support or communication trenches. The way up to the front line, which was itself comparatively dry, consisted of four-mile-long footways made of duckboards and raised on piles above the mud. If one fell off, one would sink to one's waist or deeper, which made them unpleasant places on which to be caught by shell-fire. The villages marked on the map had completely vanished. I went to look for St Julien, near which Taylor had been killed, but could not find a single stone belonging to it.

Our concrete pillbox was slowly sinking too. After three weeks its doorway became so low that we had to crawl into it. Fearing that we might be trapped if it settled deeper during the night, I moved my men back to our old dugouts at La Brique where we camped down as best we could, since both of them had been damaged by shells. Meanwhile the great German break-through in front of Amiens had been followed by another even more dangerous break-through round Armentières and Messines, so to shorten our line we gave up all we had gained and more in the battle of Passchendaele and took up a position just in front of Ypres. The VIIIth Corps handed over its divisions to another corps and I went back with my observers to Cassel, twenty miles in the rear.

How was it, every soldier asked, that while we had been attacking for more than two years on the largest scale, at enormous cost, without obtaining any significant results, the Germans had in a few days smashed through our front in two places? It became obvious to even the most simple that our generalship was at fault and the morale of the troops, whose quality had in any case been greatly impaired by poor drafts, fell to a low point. Hadn't the Staff above brigade rank always been disliked by the infantry, except in Plumer's Army? Now their instinctive distrust of these haughty brass-hats whom they never saw except when they were resting in reserve and who treated them like dirt seemed to be justified. However, I myself had no time in which to brood over these matters, for I was thrown at once into the middle of things. Although the VIIIth Corps H.Q. were no longer holding a sector of the line, they expected to be given one if the situation in front of Hazebrouck Junction deteriorated any further. They therefore sent me with a small patrol to keep in touch with the fluid front round Bailleul and report back to them.

During the second half of April then I was moving round on my cycle with three men between Mount Kemmel, Meteren, Merris and the Mont de Cats. It was a country that I had first got to know three years before and had later explored with greater thoroughness during the weeks I had spent at Poperinghe: a country that I loved for its leafy exuberance and lushness, for its old brick farm-houses, its dome-shaped elms and its tangled lanes, and I hated to see it ravaged by the war. Just now the spring was at its highest point: daisies and cowslips grew thick in the young grass: the dandelions were opening wide their yellow suns: chervil and stitchwort, campion and ragged robin were pushing up in the shade of the hedges and there was a feeling of growth and promise in the air. All this was contradicted by the presence of the war. Even before we got close to it, its marks were there, for as we rode down the great paved, tree-shaded road that leads from Cassel to Bailleul we saw the ditches on one side littered with dead horses, abandoned there by the French Cavalry Division that had been rushed up from the south to fill the gap in our line. They had fallen out from exhaustion because they had been pressed so hard and I could not help reflecting that if the British Cavalry had been sent for they would have arrived without the loss of a horse—but too late.

It was strange after nearly four years of trench warfare to see fighting taking place in the open country just as was laid down in *Infantry Training*—men lying behind hedges or advancing by sections in the open, others semaphoring, field-guns cantering along and then un-limbering and firing from the most unlikely places. French uniforms alternated with British ones, but when I first arrived there was little shelling because the Germans had not brought up their artillery. Instead one heard the sharp rat-tat-tat of machine-guns and the crack of rifle fire. No one seemed to know where the front line was and without intending it I got mixed up in a German attack near St Janscappel. Later I followed and saw the aftermath of a French one.

Unfortunately my memory of these events is very hazy. I recall a nasty moment during the German attack and some pitiful battlefield scenes after the French one, but the picture is too disjointed for me to be able to piece it together into a narrative. Two of the three men with me were killed by a shell, but I had forgotten even this till I found it recorded in a pocket diary and in a letter. One of those killed was Burroughs, whose face I remember well because he had been in my platoon since Essex days and later with me at our O.P.s. The survivor was Williams, a man I was much attached to and whom I usually took with me when I went round the trenches. Like my batman, Dartnell, who had now left me to join the Veterinary Corps, he had been with me in the 5th Gloucesters and I am glad to say that he lived to return with a medal on his chest to his native Winchcombe. Dartnell got through too and after the war became the leading vet in Cheltenham. While I was living in comparative poverty in Spain my father would meet him splendidly mounted in the hunting field.

But I will quote from a letter I wrote to Hope on 3 May 1918, the day after my return to Corps H.Q. at Cassel:

'I have been more or less in the line for a short time. It made a change. I hatched down in a cart outside a farm: all the country was very beautiful and flowery. Then I reconnoitred the fronts. Two of my men were killed by a shell—one of them I had known for more than three years.

'When I shut my eyes I can see the piles of bodies waiting to be buried: blue uniforms of French soldiers on the bright green grass, drenched, absolutely drenched with blood, so brilliant and red—then the faces of the corpses like the finest marble.

'Now I am out again living in comfort and all by myself with nothing to do and no apparent chance of going into the line again. I should like to be in the infantry, to be dirty and covered with sweat and perhaps to be wounded, killed and stained with blood. . . . I want to be revenged on myself and on those embusqués who sit and grow fat on the profits of this war and who preach, on various excuses and under various beautiful headings, the happiness of the present state of things and the necessity for its lasting as long as possible.

'And how some women love this war, the glamour, the prestige, and those who have lost their husbands require that others should lose theirs also; if not, their sense of justice, their faith in the Bon Dieu receives a shock. And so on and so on.

'You will gather that I am mortally sick of the war. Indeed I am, and I can think of nothing else. The political situation, always the political situation—God, that one should have to give such things a single thought! And the spring moves on like a procession, there is such a sweetness over all the fields, new birds arrive and begin to sing and one of the few springs of my own short life is wasting away. And I feel in me a strength to live and to love all this and to be part of it. O cottage in Spain and the life on the roads and books and liberty! It is not possible that such happiness can come to pass. Men are somehow never so happy.'

Then, in a postscript written a day or two later, I returned to the same subject:

'Is there really a fatality against our happiness? Shall I and that word never meet? Is that terribly precious thing, so entirely my own, so irreplaceable—my life, to be suddenly destroyed without cause or reason? . . . Feeling like this, one might expect me to take the safest job, but these safe jobs are horrible to me because I feel I perish on them so fast that my bodily survival will mean nothing. Like a glacier moving down to the plains where nothing is left but a few stones. And in the contact with the war itself I do find something. The blood and the bodies, the grass and birds and flowers, and the continual expectation of death, which sometimes I think of as though it were a relief—all this is more or less life-bringing.'

One may perhaps see a vein of masochism in these feelings. In December 1915, when speaking of my wish to be more deeply involved in the war, I had written, 'Does not everyone feel this—the desire to be consumed, to learn to be genuine at any cost?' Before the war my dull, sheltered childhood and my too romantic disposition had made me think that the medicine I needed was Reality. This had taken the form of poverty, hunger, doss-houses, deserts and mountains. I imagined I could only obtain and hold on to my vision by such means. I could only burn up the impurities in my nature and become a real and authentic person if I sought them. Now, in the middle of the war, a life in the infantry offered me much the same opportunities.

On my return to my battalion a couple of days after this I was given the command of a company. A week later we entrained for a completely new area far to the south—Châlons-sur-Marne in the Champagne. Forty miles or so to the north of it lay the Chemin des Dames, where three British divisions were sandwiched between French ones and the VIIIth Corps was to be reconstituted and given this sector to hold. It had also been decided that henceforth our Cyclist Battalion was to be used as infantry, and, since we were attached to the French, we settled down to learn how to fire French machine-guns. As I have no instinct for mechanical things there were few privates in my company who did not prove more proficient than I did.

But it was nice to be in a warm vine-growing country again where the crickets sang all night and the frogs kept up a continual croaking. I slept out in a field and was reminded of my days with a donkey and cart in Provence.

Then suddenly the news came through of another German offensive. They had attacked on the Chemin des Dames on May 27th and within three days had advanced thirty miles to the Marne. Our value as mounted infantry was at once apparent. On the 30th we set off and reached Vandières, a little short of Dormans, the same afternoon while the Germans entered Verneuil, three miles in front of us, next morning. Our left flank was the River Marne, on which they would have to broaden their grip if they were to get any further, so we expected an attack at any moment.

The villagers were streaming out with their carts as we came in and that evening a French division moved into the empty place on our right. My company sector was on the left, next to the river, so I traced out the posts we were to hold and the men dug themselves in with their entrenching tools. That night and the following day passed quietly and at dawn I sent out a patrol consisting of a lance-corporal and four men to crawl through the long grass and watch a farm-house that stood halfway between the two lines and which I knew to be occupied by the enemy. After keeping it under observation for a little they saw the sentry leave his rifle and go inside. Following quickly, they surprised seven Germans eating at a table and brought them back. They belonged to a *corps d'élite*, the Prussian Guard—a valuable piece of information—and the French Divisional Staff were very pleased.

Our only orders were to hold our positions and my C.O. seemed satisfied with that, but I thought that this was the psychological moment for a small offensive effort. A mile and a half down the river-bank there stood a substantial building which, in the absence of a large-scale map, we called the White Mill. It was occupied by the Germans and I suggested to my C.O. that we should make a surprise raid on it after dark and even perhaps try to hold it. He agreed at once and sent me off to get permission from the French. They seemed delighted to discover that we were so full of aggressive spirit and promised artillery support though, as they had hardly any guns, I wanted this chiefly for the sake of the noise and distraction and asked them to direct their fire not at the mill, but at the village beyond. The company on the right was to help by letting off their machine-guns. It seemed important that the raid should take place that night before the Germans got settled in, so there was little time in which to make the preparations. I took some of my N.C.O.s out through the long grass to look at the ground and then I was called away to a staff conference. Since I was the only officer in the battalion who spoke French, my services were continually being required as an interpreter. Then, just before we were due to start, a French staff officer turned up to see what we were up to. He produced a large-scale map and to my horror I saw that the White Mill stood closer than I had thought to the village of Verneuil, which, because of its key position on the German left flank, was bound to be held in force. The mill had probably been organized as a strong-point and from some of the details shown I saw that we had not reconnoitred it sufficiently. The French officer made no comment—what could he care if we had heavy losses?—so I went off to find my C.O. and ask him if he would cancel his orders for the attack. But he had not returned from a consultation with the VIIIth Corps Staff and there were my men drawn up, ready to leave. This put me in a terrible quandary—should I on my own initiative wash out the whole operation or should I go through with it? I was responsible for the lives of my men, and yet we were at a critical moment of the war and this seemed an occasion when a vigorous action might produce an effect far in excess of its immediate results. Besides I had my orders. Unable to come to any decision, I moved off at the head of my little column along the thick belt of poplar trees that followed the river.

After covering a short distance we halted and I explained the general plan to the men. I told them that while the first two parties, led by N.C.O.s, would steal up through the long grass and bushes and rush the two entrances to the mill, I would follow immediately behind with the supports and deal with all resistance inside the premises. As I said this I heard a voice at the back of the column mutter, 'I thought an officer was supposed to lead', and it touched me to the quick. I knew that theoretically, as the commander of the operation, I ought to be with the supports, but this might be one of those occasions when for the sake of morale I should lead from the front. However, I said nothing and we began to move on along the road that followed the river-bank to the point where we should separate to take up our assault positions. I was now in a greater agony of doubt and foreboding than ever, convinced in myself that everything would turn out badly yet lacking the moral courage to cancel the operation because I knew that, if done now at the last moment and without excuse, it would show the whole company that I had cold feet. Then another question—if the mill was indeed so strongly held, was not that a reason for leading one of the two small assaulting parties myself? I had a feeling deep down inside me, a feeling I would not acknowledge even to myself, that I didn't want to, yet I would do it if I were sure it was right. Why couldn't someone give me an order?

All this time we were moving on with scouts out in front. Far above me I could see the poplars shaking their leaves in the moonlit sky and I wished I could be up there with them, an anonymous leaf among the millions of anonymous leaves, rather than down here on the earth with my terrible problems. Then I looked at my watch. We were nearly an hour late and it was past the time for the artillery to begin firing. But not a gun could be heard to break the silence and the occasional stutter of a machine-gun on our right gave us much less sound cover than we needed. Suddenly I saw my excuse. Since the French had let us down I would cancel the whole affair and take my men back. I halted the column, called up my sergeants and told them we could not make the attack without artillery support. 'Those bloody French,' I said, feeling the need of a scapegoat and knowing my men would respond to it. Then we turned back and, while the poplar leaves danced joyfully above us and glittered in the moonlight, marched home.

On getting in I found the C.O. sitting up in a state of nervous anticipation and explained to him why we had returned. He completely exonerated me—indeed he seemed much relieved—but I could not exonerate myself. Either the whole idea had been a folly from the start, in which case I was greatly to blame, or else I had wriggled out of it at the last moment because I had cold feet. That terrible phrase, 'I thought an officer was supposed to lead', went on echoing in my mind: none of my men, I felt sure, had ever before dreamed of doubting my readiness to lead them and yet this time I felt that there might be some justification for one of them having done so because, while I could take almost any amount of shelling, I instinctively shied away from the idea of personal combat. I therefore felt shaken in my confidence in myself and the patrols that I began to take out every night—for patrolling is not usually one of the duties of a company commander—were intended to wipe away the disgrace I felt I had incurred.

On the following day the French took over part of our battalion front and my company was withdrawn from the line and put into support just behind it at Vandières. We were given some trenches to dig, but were also told that we were to be used for patrolling the front and carrying out any raids that might be feasible. An opportunity for one of these offered itself at once. On our left there was an interval of nearly two miles between the lines, but on the right they were only a few hundred yards apart. Here the French held the edge of a wood that ran along the flat crest of a hill while the Germans occupied the small hamlet of Trotte that lay just in front of it. One of our companies had held this wood for three days and on their last night a patrol they had sent out had stumbled on a gap in the German lines, a little to the right of the last farm-house. I went to look at the ground and decided to take out a small patrol that night and go through.

There were four of us—a lance-corporal, two privates and myself. The moon, though well past its full, was still bright and we had to cross a flat stubble field on which any dark object stood out plainly, passing within less than two hundred yards of a German machine-gun post. Moving very slowly therefore, our bodies pressed flat against the earth, we approached the haystack on the slightly sunken lane that we were aiming at and found it unoccupied. Another few yards and we were in an orchard and could stand upright. Soon we were right behind Trotte, on the further slope of the hill, and could see the broad valley below us and hear the sound of heavy motor traffic. We were in no danger, for if we had seen other figures approaching us, we would have sheered away and they would have taken us to be Germans.

A deep exhilaration came over me at the thought that, after all these years of trench warfare, I was actually walking about in complete freedom behind the enemy lines. That was something I had often dreamed of doing. At the same time a distant memory of my childhood rose suddenly and with great vividness in my mind. I remembered how at the age of four I had crept down under the bedclothes as I lay beside my nurse and put my hand on her sexual parts because I wanted to know what they were like. That had been an act of discovery, a stealthy breach of a stringent prohibition, and so was this. In the lightness with which I trod the grass, in the delight with which I looked on the valley lit by the thin moon, I was having my reward.

At first I did not know what to do with our new-found liberty. We might throw our bombs at the transport men unloading at the bottom of the hill, and then get away. The absurd idea even came to me that we might seize the first lorry in the column and drive it back across the lines. That anyhow would be a spectacular action. But before we had gone very far towards the main road I had a better idea. The hamlet of Trotte overlooked the whole of this valley and if we could seize it and hold it we should make it much more difficult for the Germans to mount a fresh attack. This was a place a hundred times more worth seizing than the White Mill and with any luck it could be taken by surprise from behind with few casualties. We turned back therefore to reconnoitre it more carefully.

In the shade of the big barns we crept up till we were within twenty yards of the German posts. I located two quite close to one another, each manned by three or four men, but we had no time left for investigating the further group of farm buildings. We went back therefore by the way we had come, planning to return and pinpoint them on the following night. This time, I resolved, every detail was going to be worked out beforehand.

The next night came and I took with me a platoon sergeant and two men. We got across safely. I showed the sergeant where the first German posts were and after that we moved on to the other end of the hamlet. Making use of the deep shadows and of the carts that were standing about in the yard we located a third post and also, in a building that stood back a little and was guarded by a sentry, what must have been a company headquarters. It did not look as if we would have more than forty or fifty men to deal with in this village and most of these would be resting within doors, because the Germans relied for defending the place on their machine-guns.

But there was one other point that I wanted to look into and to do this it would be necessary to get to the road that formed the German front line and crawl a few yards along it. We had just reached our destination and had turned to come back when a German emerged from a building and began to walk slowly down the road towards us. At first I thought that he would turn off to the Company H.Q., but he came straight on. We were crouching one behind the other in the shadow of a wall and in a moment he would see us. Then when he was six yards away he did. I covered him with my revolver and said *Hände hoch*, but he paid no attention. Slowly and deliberately he unslung his rifle from his shoulder and raised it to aim at me. I saw his blue saucer eyes just under his helmet, saw a Lombardy poplar behind him waving its tip against the sky, and I did not want to pull the trigger.

This man from another world looked so innocent and mild that I did not seem to have it in me to do that. But then he would kill me. Just now that did not seem to matter, for my life was riveted to that poplar tree that was swaying so gently its tip against the sky, its silver-pointed tip that was made up of leaves that glistened as they turned, that was made up of separate leaves and yet was all one tree, one tree that was one of a species of tree that belonged to all trees and those trees members of all plants and those plants of all life that came together and were made One for ever in the blue moonlight—out of which One I might become a single leaf on a single glittering tree in one moment, my last moment, in which my life poured into it, because I had given myself to it in the last moment of what was yet me. Through my trance I heard someone behind me call, 'Shoot, sir, shoot.' But it was the German who shot and I felt a blow in the side and fell over saying 'I'm hit.' Two of my men leaped forward and either shot or bayoneted him—for I did not see, or do not remember seeing—while the third took hold of me. But I was not hit: the bullet had passed between my arms and my tunic, tearing the cloth, and so we all began to run out across the field towards the French lines in the wood. About fifty yards on there lay a dead cow and we threw ourselves down behind it just as a machine-gun began to open fire. As we did so a dozen rats leaped out of its belly and scurried away over our backs. There we lay for a long time, pressed into the earth with the bullets, each time the gun traversed, passing just over us, almost shaving us, their notes suddenly altering when they slished through the carcass of the cow, until at length, the fire having ceased, we thought it safe to wriggle slowly off on our bellies. Then there was the fear of being shot by the French as we came in. It was daybreak before we got back to Vandières.

The prospects for the capture of Trotte were no longer so good because the Germans had been alerted. But at least, I supposed, they would have no reason for thinking that we had penetrated behind their lines. One must expect them to keep a better look-out at the point where their man had been killed, but would they put a new post by the haystack on the other side? That remained to be seen. Aware that my men might think I had been too 'windy' to shoot—although it hadn't been that—ashamed of my cry of 'I'm hit' when I hadn't been hit, I meant to lead the first party across the lines again as well as the assault on the principal post. Since I was afraid of a trap I took only two men with me, but my single subaltern (another was on leave) was to follow at a short distance with seven or eight men and behind them

a sergeant with another party. Two platoons would wait at the edge
of the wood and cross rapidly when the firing began.

We set off in single file at a crawl, each of us within reach of the
ankle of the man in front of him. After doing the first hundred yards
like this, we began to go more slowly, creeping on our bellies over the
sharp, prickly stubble on which everything under that clear summer
sky seemed to show up so distinctly. Suddenly in front of me I thought
I heard the chink of metal and the N.C.O. behind me grasped my leg
to show that he had heard it too. After that we began to go more
slowly still, moving only when a shell passed overhead because that
hid the sound of rustling our bodies made. We were so close now, not
more than forty yards away, that I felt almost sure that no one could
be there behind the bank, because if there had been we should have
heard them. Then all at once a head looked over the top and ducked
down again and I thought I could see the domed crown of a German
helmet just appearing over the bank. They were waiting for us, and
on the slightly downward slope of the ground which fell towards
Trotte we must have been fully visible to them, though only as a
vague, darkish blot. No signal to the men behind me was needed.
Very slowly, by inches at a time, we started to edge back, our tunics
catching in the stubble as we did so. Each time a shell passed we gave
ourselves a shove, but our progress was so slow that it was a couple of
hours before we reached the wood. There I found that my subaltern
had gone home, taking all the men with him, and when I reached
Vandières I learned that he had given the C.O. a detailed account of
how we had been either captured or killed, inventing to justify his
story the sound of bombs and rifle fire. He was a man who had just
come out from England and was new to the war, but there was not
one of my N.C.O.s who would have behaved in that way.

I had now suffered one failure after another and, though this last
had not been my fault, I felt deeply disappointed. The French had
sent us word that they wanted a prisoner for identification, so I decided to take out a patrol again that night. I chose a place on high
ground to one side of Trotte, where there was a broad space between
the two lines, because I reckoned that the Germans would be sure to
send out a patrol here themselves and this would give us a chance to
find it and intercept it. Meanwhile the sky had clouded over and just
as we set off it began to drizzle. We had been moving for some time
across dry pasture land, intersected by wire fences, with only the
vaguest idea of where the German front posts lay, when we saw some
men walking in file on the skyline. In every fighting patrol the aim

must be to catch the other party on their feet while you are lying down and then to throw your Mills bombs and close. We manœuvred therefore to intercept these men, but lost them. However, after a little we seemed to come in touch with them again. We were all certain that we heard voices and the chink of metal and several times one of the long wire fences would be struck as though by someone passing through it. We made a circle therefore to cut these men off from their base and then lay down to wait and listen. But by now the wind had got up and though we could hear noises on every side of us we could not be sure whether they came from the Germans or not. It was all very baffling.

Meanwhile my men, lying out in the fine rain, were becoming more and more impatient. They wanted either to close at once with a German patrol or to go home, whereas I was quite ready to go on prowling round till dawn in the hopes of catching one going back to its lines. But their feelings had to be considered and I saw that I could not keep them out all night. We set off therefore in a new direction and kept going for some time till, hearing noises quite close to us, we lay down. Yes, there were low voices coming from just in front of us and heads moving against the dull skyline. We crawled forward a little and then waited, hoping they would get up and give us our opportunity, but nothing happened. Were they an illusion of the wind and night, or were they Germans? I wasn't certain. Too tired to think clearly, only aware of my men's impatience and of the need for some decisive action, I got up and walked towards them, calling out *Hände hoch* and expecting at any moment to be shot. But there was no shot and when I reached the place I saw that they were dwarf thorn bushes, shaped like heads, with one or two plants of ragweed swaying in between. In deep gloom and disappointment we went home.

It seemed that I would have to go out the next night too. The French so badly wanted a prisoner, alive or dead, that they actually suggested places which we might raid to get them. One was an isolated post to the left of Trotte and the other was still further to the right, on the edge of Sabot Wood. My company was given the first and A Company the second, and I went up with two N.C.O.s to have a look at the ground, but found it impossible to reconnoitre properly.

I was now beginning to feel very tired, for I had been out on patrol for four nights in succession and had been far too busy to lie down by day. Not only had I my company to run and the night's patrol to prepare, but I was continually being called off to interpret for the French. Ever since we had taken over this sector I had been living keyed up to a high pitch of nervous excitement and now the reaction was beginning to set in. But I had no confidence in my one subaltern and knew that if I entrusted the business to a sergeant and it went badly I should feel to blame.

Just as we were getting ready to start the Germans began dropping a few whizz-bangs in Vandières. I was standing in the yard of my Company H.Q. when one burst on the road outside and there was a cry. Going out, I almost fell over a man who was lying there. Someone produced a torch and I saw that the whole of the lower half of his face had been shot away, leaving a red, palpitating hole between his cheekbones and his neck. But he was still alive, for his eyes were moving about in a serious, inquiring manner as if he did not understand how a thing like this could have happened. Thinking that he might perhaps be conscious, I sent a man to try and get him some morphia, after which we lifted him onto a stretcher and carried him into the orderly room. Here the light was better and I could see that he was very young, perhaps no more than nineteen. We covered him with a blanket and he lay there, his eyes travelling slowly to and fro with such a wondering, penetrating expression in them that it was hard to believe that he was not aware of everything that was going on around him. But now it was time to start. As I trudged up the road with my men I kept seeing those eyes and they gave me a bad feeling inside.

We got to the wood on the summit of the hill and passed through it to the further edge. Here a ditch had been deepened a little to form the front trench and it was full of *poilus* sitting about in easy attitudes. The casualness of the French troops both on the march and in the line always pleased me because it showed a familiarity with war, whereas our army seemed to have been trained chiefly for parades. A sergeant came up to me and told me rather sharply that he had strict orders not to let any patrol go out. On my asking to speak to an officer he replied that his captain was away but would be back soon. So we squatted down to wait and then from the grey open country beyond a machine-gun began to fire from close range. The bullets swished by overhead, bringing down the small twigs and leaves, and I realized that it was firing from the German post that we had orders to raid. As I sat there in the moist, warm trench with the dark trees clustering thickly around, listening to that infernal rat-tat-tat, rat-tat-tat, repeated again and again, a very unpleasant feeling came over me. I had never had quite that feeling in the pit of my stomach before.

We sat there for some time, listening to the ear-shattering stutter that came from such a short distance away, and then the captain arrived. I explained to him that my orders to raid this post had been issued by his own Divisional Staff, but he replied that he had been told nothing about it and would not permit any patrol to leave his lines that night because he had a working party waiting to go out and did not want any trouble. I asked him to sign a paper to that effect and with unspeakable relief took my men straight back. Then I went to bed and slept till late in the following afternoon because my C.O., prompted by my considerate company sergeant-major (I always found him up when I came back from patrol), had given orders that I should not be woken.

When I did wake I learned that the man who had had his face shot away was dead and that the raid on Sabot Wood had ended badly. Caldwell, a young lieutenant just out from England and whom I had taken a great fancy to, had been killed while trying to rush a machine-gun and two or three of his men had died with him. No prisoners had been taken. My C.O. went on to say that we were not sending out any patrols that night and that next morning we were being relieved by the French. We had been in the line for eleven days and during that time I had only had two nights' sleep.

Back at Damery, six miles behind, I went over the record of my first experience of commanding a company in the line. I had failed at everything I had tried to do. I had gone out on one patrol after another like an over-eager boy scout, but had not shown myself so very anxious to close with the Germans. No doubt too much had been left to my initiative, for in war the hard and disagreeable things must be enforced by precise and definite orders, yet it was clear that, though I enjoyed taking moderate risks, I lacked that capacity for headstrong aggressive action that, I imagined, lives somewhere at the bottom of every good soldier. So, after spending more than two years in or close to the front line, I had not yet faced the ultimate experience of war and did not know how I should stand up to it if I had to. I have stressed these feelings of doubt and uncertainty about how I should behave in certain situations not so much to throw light upon myself, but because they are the feelings that every front-line soldier carries about with him from the beginning of a war to its end and one cannot understand what is going on inside him unless one remembers it.

Yet one good thing had come out of my twelve days in the line and that was that I was on closer terms than before with my company. I felt that my N.C.O.s liked and trusted me in spite of my having so few of the true soldierly qualities, and certainly I liked and trusted them.

And so a new ideal opened out before me—that of the good company officer who puts the welfare of his men before everything else. This seemed to me a Christian ideal and more in accord with the teaching of the Gospels than the negative one of pacifism. Also it gave me a warm human contact with other men which, after my long isolation in O.P.s, I badly needed. All that was required, I thought, was to forget politics and look on the war as a plague that afflicted humanity, and then one would be content to play the best part one could find in it.

We left Châlons by train on June 15th and on the same morning the Germans attacked again, crossing the Marne on pontoon bridges and overrunning our old positions at Vandières. But we never knew it. After detraining at Abbeville we settled into a village on the clear-watered Somme, far from the war. Its gardens were full of pinks and roses and one could take a boat out on the meres and lie back under the tall, leafy poplar trees, listening to the call of the water birds.

A day or two after our arrival I learned that I had been cited in the orders of the French 120th Division and then that I had been awarded the Croix de Guerre. This seemed logical. I had done a great deal of interpreting for the French and had heard a staff officer say of me to General Mordacq, 'Cet officier est très intelligent. Il parle Français.' I did not have to suppose that I was being rewarded for military reasons.

The terrible Spanish flu that was decimating the army had now struck us and my men were falling down like ninepins on parade and having to be carried off on stretchers. In the middle of this I was sent on a Lewis-gun course to Paris Plage and on my second day there I developed it too. I was just beginning to recover when I had a letter from my C.O. telling me that he had recommended me for a Military Cross. I wrote to him at once to say that I would much rather not have it because, since everyone knew that the patrols I had led had accomplished nothing, my position in my company would be stronger without it. I meant every word of this. I had always disapproved of the old army custom of giving medals to officers who commanded units that had done well, because it created a feeling of injustice. I believed that they should be the last persons to get them and then only for feats of outstanding personal gallantry. In any case the whole currency of awards in these latter days of the war had been debased and I knew that by normal standards I had done nothing whatever to deserve one. But my letter to my C.O. produced no effect, for a few days later I got a telegram to say that I had been awarded the medal. My first reaction to this was one of shame—how could I return to my company wearing that little blue-and-white stripe? The fantastic account printed in the

Gazette of my supposed exploits behind the German lines only made it seem more unmerited. But flattery has a way of seeping through in the end and when I got back to England I found that I was quite pleased to walk about with my two medals on my chest and rather cynically gratified by the pleasure they gave my parents. Now perhaps they would stop treating me as a semi-delinquent child.

The flu of 1918 was a serious complaint and it was three weeks before I was well enough to be moved. Then I was sent to another hospital, at Croxteth Hall outside Liverpool. Here the half-trained nurses were in a state of permanent erotic excitement and on the first evening of my arrival the dark-haired little pixie who attended to my ward was pressing in her offers to give me a bath. My modesty refused to permit this and I was glad when, after another three weeks, I was sent to a convalescent home at Moffat across the Scottish border where the emotional atmosphere was cooler. Here I spent a further three weeks, taking long walks over the moors and up the Yarrow valley, but still in a state of post-flu depression.

As usual I was greatly divided as to what I wanted to do. The more rational part of me insisted that I must find a safe job in order that I might survive the war and so I played with the idea of getting a commission in the temporary police force that was being raised to patrol the Persian-Baluchi frontier. I also made some effort to get a three months' job in the Foreign Office. But my battalion was now again in the line and suffering heavy casualties in the advance from Amiens. Knowing that, I could no more escape the pull of the war than a racing driver can escape the lure of the track. My place was with my company, even though I had not yet been passed fit by the Medical Board.

On August 18th I expressed these feelings in a letter to Hope:

'The Infantry means almost everything that I most dislike and it represents, to my emotions at least, death. But at any rate one is in the full flood: all that there is of life in this generation is there—at the war or else in prison. I feel sure that to be in shelter—with all those little literary types—is to be in a backwater. To be in Spain, free—ah, that would be different!—but, as you said before, this war is no interlude, it is a large part of one's life, and I begin to starve on hopes.'

After this there followed an attack on the people of Moffat:

'The men look like butlers who have gone out for the day in their masters' shooting clothes. . . . The women are of several sorts: some are of that elderly class which imitates china knickknacks, others are like ants, earwigs and certain species of beetles—one would like to inquire their Latin names. . . . All of them beyond the human.'

In September I went on leave to Edgeworth and Ralph Partridge, back from Italy and a major, came to stay with me. His Italian campaign, or so he said, had provided little fighting but instead a succession of lovely girls and now he was at the Senior Officers' School at Aldershot and going out every night to dances. He had also, he wrote in his next letter, met a friend of Hope's—'a Miss Carrington, a painting damsel and a great Bolshevik who would like me to strike a blow for the Cause'. She lived in a house at Pangbourne with a certain Lytton Strachey 'who is of a surety meet mirth for Olympus'. These were the people with whom he was to spend the next thirteen years of his life —until their death in 1932.

After Ralph had left I had an experience of a very different kind which I described in a letter to Hope. It concerned one of those revelations of what the world really is, if only one had the spiritual force to grasp it.

'I had sat up nearly the whole night reading *Macbeth*. The following day was a Sunday and I got up early and went with my mother to Communion Service. I had the words of *Macbeth* ringing in my ears and lines of Rimbaud, Shelley and Coleridge. . . . The weather was like that of another world—the sky so blue and kind, the clouds, white and rosy, sailing past. Everywhere the robins were singing. I was so gay, my heart so full I could hardly control myself. In the church it was cold and still: green branches rubbed against windows of clear glass. Then, when the priest said *Lift up your hearts* and the response came *We lift them up unto the Lord*, I saw, felt, understood something that was new to me.

'I cannot easily explain it, but what I felt was the holiness of life, the presence of the innumerable worlds. How under the sea the fishes swam among the weeds and the snails and worms fed there: how the birds filled all the bushes, all the trees: how everywhere the animals roamed, free, happy, virginal, beneficent: how the crayfish crowded the little streams and the moles and worms lived underground: how the beautiful leaves and grasses were covered with uncountable insects. And the other worlds, the million other worlds that lay beyond ours. And the men and women too, beautiful, kind and pure in heart— really, if one could only see it.

'*Lift up your hearts*. Response—*We lift them up*. I so over-flowed with a feeling of all this that was going on around me that it was an effort not to break into dance and singing. And this feeling lasted all day.'

I have given this example of one of the so-called 'mystical' experiences that I used to have because I find it recorded in a letter and not, as was usually the case, worked up into a bad prose poem. They continued to occur at irregular intervals till I was past thirty, when they merged into other feelings more closely connected with my life. On the other hand the outbursts of disgust and hatred that would come over me at the sight of some excessive display of bourgeois life or sentiments ended when I left for Spain after the war.

From my parents' house I went to Canterbury where I was attached to another Yeomanry regiment. To get away from this I made a vague attempt to join the force that was being sent to Archangel. There I would at least see the Arctic. But as October drew on and the war visibly approached its end I gave up these attempts to reach some front or other and even considered faking my symptoms at the medical board in order to avoid being sent back to France. I felt that, after surviving for so long, it would be just my luck to be killed on the last day of the fighting.

Soon news of the peace negotiations began to appear in the papers, but the war had gone on for so long and been fanned by such Hate-the-Huns propaganda that the civil population did not seem in any hurry to see it end.

'Down here,' I wrote, 'people are taking the news very calmly, just as though they had been told that the frost had killed some of the cabbages or that the white hen had laid an egg. "Oh, we can't make peace with the *Germans*," they say. "What, peace with them? Never." '

Then on November 11th the armistice came and I danced in the High Street with a policeman.

*

The war was now over and the future I had so long looked forward to began to peer over the horizon. But I could not rouse myself to any proper degree of elation. Although, unlike most young soldiers, I had awaiting me a mode of life in which I really believed, I felt listless and lacking in enthusiasm. Only those who have served a term in the Army know how deadening its effect can be and how completely it destroys the roots that connect one with civil life. And war, however deeply it is hated, is a stimulant like alcohol and leaves a lethargy behind it when its powers of arousing excitement are removed.

Even before the news of the armistice broke, I found myself at loggerheads with my father. He had written to me to say that there was an opening in the Indian Army that was 'too good to be neglected'.

I should apply for it at once unless I was prepared to put my name in again for the Indian Police, which on the strength of my war service might be prepared to waive an examination. The thought of my going off to the other ends of the earth obviously filled him with enthusiasm. I replied that I had saved up enough money to fend for myself and had no intention of entering the Government service. I should first spend a year or two abroad in reading and study and after that I should see what I wanted to do. Unfortunately in a fit of frankness, I added that even if I had gone into the Indian Police in 1914 I should only have remained in it long enough to save a few hundred pounds. This shocked him and he replied that, since I had not been open with him, he had no other course but to break off all communication with me. Although at that time it had scarcely been possible for me to be open with him, I felt that he had scored a point.

Actually, though I had not in the least given up my plans for Eastern travel, I wanted to postpone them for a little. For one thing those parts of the world that most drew me were still very unsettled and then I felt a great need to study and generally, in my own way, educate myself. I had decided therefore to find a cottage in the south of Spain, which I thought would be the cheapest country to live in and also one of the most congenial because it had escaped the war fever. There I should settle down in peaceful, peasant surroundings to read the couple of thousand books I had already begun to collect.

My financial situation, however, was not nearly so rosy as I had painted it to my father. Since Hope's return from the East we had, on my suggestion, shared a common purse just as we had done in Provence. This meant that, as he had no income of his own worth mentioning, I was supporting him until he was called up into the Army, and even after he returned from Greece, when he was employed by the Foreign Office, had to provide substantial sums because —these mishaps were peculiar to Hope—his salary was not being paid in. Besides this, in spite of my strong misgivings, he had invested what remained of our joint savings in Italian War Loan, which at once with the inflation sank to nothing. All I should have left to keep me in Spain would be my war bonus of £250, less the rather large sums which I was spending on books. It took me hard experience to learn that Hope was the opposite of King Midas and that every gilt-edged security he touched turned instantaneously to dross.

Soon after the armistice I was sent to Ireland to await demobilization. I spent Christmas with my parents at my uncle's house in County

Down and there had some sort of reconciliation with my father. His detestation of my Uncle Ogilvie made him a little better disposed towards me, though my mother did not succeed in soothing my resentment at his sharpness of manner when she explained that his job of guarding the railways had affected his nerves. This was true and, considering his deafness and his dislike of having his life upset, quite understandable, but I felt that in pressing this my mother was taking my own experiences in the war too much for granted as well as failing to grasp the true cause of his annoyance. In those days 'I am proud to have given a son to my country' was a very current phrase and I guessed that one of the reasons for my father's irritability was that he had not been given the opportunity for pronouncing it. Although it would be putting it too strongly to say that he disliked me, it is certain that my disappearance from the world would have taken a load off his shoulders. He was a man who longed to get rid of everything and everyone that inconvenienced him—the cows and chickens, the house, the cook, my mother, her family. His daydream was the clean sheet—a life lived all to himself without impediments or commitments, for then something new, say a young woman, might turn up and start a fresh chapter.

I now returned to the Curragh, where I found regimental life harder to bear than ever. My colonel was an old dugout with a sadistic temperament who never missed an opportunity for saying that he would like to shoot or hang all Germans, Irishmen and conscientious objectors. His jealousy of my war service and his suspicion of my Irish name made him dislike me and, though I kept very quiet, he did everything he could to snub and humiliate me in public. Quite apart from this, I was in a particular hurry to be demobilized because it was clear that an Irish rebellion was about to break out and, had that happened, I should have felt obliged to resign my commission. Then there would have been a court martial and I should have lost my precious war bonus.

The Peace Conference had now begun. The Allies were demanding that Germany pay the entire cost of the war. This was what the four-year-long hate campaign of an unscrupulous press had led to. 'Could anything more shameful be imagined?' I wrote to Hope. 'It is like the Mithraic ceremony of eating the bull. We have eaten Germany in a solemn and public manner—and become Germans.' At the election that March I voted Labour. Then at last on April 14th I got my demobilization papers and after a short walking tour through Connemara and Achill returned to Edgeworth.

Hope had been offered by Roger Fry the editorship of the *Burlington Magazine* and had accepted it. He not only wanted to remain in London, but had no money with which to settle abroad. He had rented a dusty workshop in a mews off Maple Street and furnished it with his usual taste. It had two exits, one into the mews and the other into Fitzroy Street, which was convenient when he was dunned for debts. It also had some picturesque features: that summer a circus menagerie took up its residence in the stables and when one got up in the morning one would see a camel's head chewing the cud and staring satirically in through the window.

I spent part of the summer here with Hope and he would take me, as he had done during the war, to see his literary and artistic friends. On these occasions I was always very silent: apart from the fact that I felt dedicated to some remote purpose, not easily to be explained, his presence had an inhibiting effect on me because he talked so fluently and in such a clear and impersonal style. I had to approach people in a more halting and exploratory manner and that irritated him. He was in a very euphoric state at this time, with two women in love with him and a rosy future opening out paved with success and money, so, as I did not approve of this but regarded it as a fall from virtue and austerity, we were rather on one another's nerves. I was too diffident to follow up my acquaintance with any of the people he introduced me to so that almost the only one of whom I have kept any recollection is Osbert Sitwell, who charmed me by his wit and delightful conversation.

However I did accept an invitation to stay with Augustus John and his wife in Dorset. They lived in a substantial stone villa, surrounded by ten acres of heath and pinewood, off the Parkstone Road near Bournemouth. The house, though it contained only four rooms, was surmounted by a Gothic battlement that did its best to give it a manorial aspect and outside it there was drawn up a row of gipsy caravans in which were lodged the eight children and the various visitors, some of whom stayed for months on end because their hosts were too polite to hint that they had overspent their welcome. There was a boat on the lake and a good many ponies, but the days when the children had run naked through the woods, shooting their arrows at anyone they saw approaching up the drive, were over. They now went to a day school and behaved much like other schoolchildren, and they were all of them extremely good-looking. Among them, though not at home at this time, was Caspar, who had astonished and even shocked his father by preferring the disciplined life of a naval cadet to the easy freedom of a bohemian upbringing. Today he is not only an admiral, but First Sea Lord.

The person who dominated this patriarchal establishment was naturally Augustus, though in those days no one called him by his first name. He was an imposing and to me at least formidable figure: silent and moody, unpredictable in his actions, but thawing in the evenings under the influence of drink and congenial company. Then, as his irritability and melancholy melted, his natural good humour and tolerance came out. He had a fine vein of wit and could sing ballads and old pub songs with feeling.

Although John had generally been a regular worker, spending most of the day in his studio, he was not painting much when I came down this time. Every morning therefore he would harness his dog-cart and we would set off at a sharp trot in the direction of the nearest country pub. Here we would have brandy and soda and throw a few darts (it was he who made darts the fashion), after which we would get into the dog-cart again and move on to another pub. These expeditions alarmed me a little, for I did not know how to talk to him. Silent people have always disconcerted me and then the weight of his personality oppressed me and made me unsure of myself. He was a man who could not sit in a room without charging it with his presence, even though he never said a word.

However, his wife Dorelia was as easy to be with as he was difficult. She was not only a very beautiful woman, as lovely in figure as in face, but her beauty seemed to have given her whole being a sort of harmony. She talked little and rarely said anything that one could single out as witty or striking, but one was always aware of a sympathetic presence. With an air of complete ease and leisure, without hurrying or raising her voice, her long pre-Raphaelite robes trailing behind her as she moved, she ran this lively house, cooked for this large family and their visitors, yet always appeared to have time on her hands. Her sister Edie, who looked after the children but lacked this faculty for effortless action, seemed in comparison bustling and vociferous.

Dorelia was a shy woman and she had made of her shyness a shield for her inner life. Though easygoing and tolerant, she was always a little detached from other people. She was stoical too and disliked any sort of fuss, only grumbling mildly when too many visitors arrived unannounced for week-ends. To escape from them she would take refuge in the walled garden, where she did most of the weeding and planting herself. But I remember her best as she sat at the head of the long dining-table, resting her large, expressive eyes with their clear whites on the children and visitors and bringing an order and beauty into the scene that helped to soften the almost too dominant impression made by her husband.

I saw in Augustus and Dorelia two of that rare sort of people, suggestive of ancient or primitive times, whose point lay rather in what they were than in what they said or did. I felt that they would have been more at home drinking wine under an olive tree or sitting in a smoky mountain cave than planted in this tepid English scene. But at least they were bohemians and kept up with style and lavish hospitality the old tradition of artistic life that had come down from William Morris and Rossetti. This I thought was important because I believed that the proper antithesis to bourgeois values lay in bohemian or anarchist ones and not in those of the Socialists. For the paradox of Socialism seemed to be that it could only obtain the economic justice it aimed at by treating men as ciphers for bureaucratic manipulation and thus imprisoning them more firmly than ever in dead conventions.

Reynolds Ball had just returned from spending a few months with the Friends in Russia and I went to pass a week-end with him at an inn outside Oxford. He was full of a burbling, incoherent enthusiasm for the Bolsheviks, but did not convert me to any liking for them. However, it was wonderful to have him back again, for he was a good and lovable man, the nearest thing to a saint I have ever known. A few months later he died of cholera in Poland, giving his life in a strange country for unknown men and women as he had always been ready to do.

Ralph Partridge had returned to Trinity College, Oxford, where my brother, though seven years his junior, was now an undergraduate. He was supposed to be reading for law, but spent as much time as he could with Carrington—she was always known by her surname—at the mill house which she and Lytton Strachey had rented near Pangbourne. I went to see him there and met for the first time the blue-eyed, honey-mouthed girl he had fallen in love with and who for seven years was to be the leading person in my life. But I did not take to her then because I had heard that she had made fun of Hope to whom I was very loyal.

I spent most of this summer with my parents at Edgeworth and here I have a stupid and pointless episode to relate. Just before the war broke out a niece of Mrs MacMeekan, our neighbour, came to live with her She was a half-Italian, half-German girl, the daughter of an official in the Egyptian civil service, and her name was Anna Maria von Dummreicher. She was regarded as being very pretty, for she had a well-shaped body crowned by a pussy-cat face, and when the war broke out she threw herself into it with enthusiasm, becoming a land-girl, working for a baker, dressing in a boy's shirt and breeches and enjoying this rough life very much. Till now I had only known young ladies: she was the first modern girl to cross my view.

I used to meet her when I was on leave and one evening, while seeing her home across the valley after dinner, I kissed her and we lay down under the trees and made love. It was not her first sexual experience, for there had been a man in Cairo, but she fell in love with me while I, every time I saw her, liked her less. I found her sentimental in the heavy German way and regretted that I had ever got mixed up with her, yet having gone so far and living so close it was difficult to draw back. Partly for want of something better to do, I used to steal out of the house at midnight and meet her in the woods. She would arrive wearing a waterproof and nothing underneath and then, throwing it off, dance in an Oriental fashion for my benefit. At length, to see if she could make me jealous, she started an affair with a young Belgian who, after my departure for Spain, put her in the way of having a child. When this could no longer be concealed she was sent back to her father in Berlin. Here she took to drugs and, a few years later, killed herself.

I ought to feel remorse for my part in this depressing story and yet I never have. I had come to dislike the girl because I felt that she was trying to get hold of me and I was determined to keep my life free from entanglements. My affair with her was really a consequence of the deadness and lack of deeper feelings which the war had left behind it. This took more time than one would have supposed to clear up. When on 25 September 1919 I sailed for Spain, it was not with the exhilaration of a man embarking on a new and long-desired mode of life, but in low spirits and with considerable anxiety about the state of my banking account. A hundred and eighty pounds is not a large sum on which to educate oneself, and I saw little hope of getting any more.

*

I have now told the story of my life down to the age of twenty-five —childhood, prep school, then a violent adolescent revolt caused by my dislike of my public school and by my need for escaping from the ultra-conventional world in which I had been brought up. This was followed by a time of testing and consolidation of character in the war which, since I was lucky enough to survive it, brings to an end the first period of my life. Then I went to Spain. Here I was to find a house in a remote mountain village in Andalusia and spend, with brief intervals in England, five happy and industrious years. In *South from Granada* I have described this village and its customs and traditions as well as the neighbouring country and towns. A second volume of this autobiography will give a more personal account of this time, of my subsequent life in London and of my long struggle to train myself as a writer.

Index